Feminists and Psychological Practice

Gender and Psychology

Series editor: Sue Wilkinson

This international series provides a forum for the growing body of distinctively psychological research focused on gender issues. While work on the psychology of women, particularly that adopting a feminist perspective, will be central, the series will also reflect other emergent trends in the field of gender. It will encourage contributions which are critical of the mainstream of androcentric or 'gender-neutral' psychology and also innovative in their suggested alternatives.

The books will explore topics where gender is central, such as social and sexual relationships, employment, health and illness, and the development of gender identity. Issues of theory and methodology raised by the study of gender in psychology will also be addressed.

The objective is to present research on gender in the context of its broader implications for psychology. These implications include the need to develop theories and methods appropriate to studying the experience of women as well as men, and working towards a psychology which reflects the experiences and concerns of both sexes.

The series will appeal to students of psychology, women's studies and gender studies and to professionals concerned with gender issues in their practice, as well as to the general reader with an interest in gender and psychology.

Sue Wilkinson is principal lecturer and head of the psychology section at Coventry Polytechnic.

Also in this series

Subjectivity and Method in Psychology
Wendy Hollway

Feminists
and
Psychological
Practice

edited by
Erica Burman

SAGE Publications
London · Newbury Park · New Delhi

Introduction, Afterword, editorial matter and arrangement
© Erica Burman 1990
Chapter 1 © Carolyn Kagan and Sue Lewis 1990
Chapter 2 Part I © Sue Sharpe 1990
Chapter 2 Part II © Jane Jefferson 1990
Chapter 3 © Jane Ussher 1990
Chapter 4 © Meg Coulson and Kum-Kum Bhavnani 1990
Chapter 5 © Corinne Squire 1990
Chapter 6 © Ann Phoenix 1990
Chapter 7 © Maye Taylor 1990
Chapter 8 © Celia Kitzinger 1990
Chapter 9 Part I © Sue Wilkinson 1990
Chapter 9 Part II © Jan Burns 1990
Chapter 10 © Erica Burman 1990
Chapter 11 © Christine Adcock and Karen Newbigging 1990

First published 1990

SAGE Publications Ltd
28 Banner Street
London EC1Y 8QE

SAGE Publications India Pvt Ltd
32, M-Block Market
Greater Kailash – I
New Delhi 110 048

SAGE Publications Inc
2111 West Hillcrest Drive
Newbury Park, California 91320

British Library Cataloguing in Publication data

Feminists and psychological practice. — (Gender and psychology)
  1. Psychology related to feminism 2. Feminism related to racism
  I. Burman, Erica II. Series
  150

  ISBN 0-8039-8232-1
  ISBN 0-8039-8233-X Pbk

Library of Congress catalog card number 89-63112

Typeset by AKM Associates (UK) Ltd, Southall, London
Printed in Great Britain by
Dotesios Printers Ltd, Trowbridge, Wiltshire

Contents

Acknowledgments   vii

Notes on the contributors   ix

Introduction   1

PART ONE: CHOOSING PSYCHOLOGY?

1 'Where's your sense of humour?' Swimming against
   the tide in higher education
   Carolyn Kagan and Sue Lewis   18

2 Moving out of psychology: two accounts
   Sue Sharpe and Jane Jefferson   33

3 Choosing psychology *or* Not throwing the baby out
   with the bathwater
   Jane Ussher   47

4 Making a difference – questioning women's studies
   Meg Coulson and Kum-Kum Bhavnani   62

PART TWO: CHANGING DEFINITIONS OF
PSYCHOLOGICAL KNOWLEDGE

5 Feminism as antipsychology: learning and teaching
   in feminist psychology
   Corinne Squire   76

6 Social research in the context of feminist psychology
   Ann Phoenix   89

7 Fantasy or reality? The problem with psychoanalytic
   interpretation in psychotherapy with women
   Maye Taylor   104

8 Resisting the discipline
   Celia Kitzinger   119

PART THREE: STRUGGLES AND CHANGE

9   Women organizing within psychology: two accounts
    Sue Wilkinson and Jan Burns   140

10 Steps towards silence: women in educational psychology
    Anonymous   163

11 Women in the shadows: women, feminism and
    clinical psychology
    Christine Adcock and Karen Newbigging   172

Afterword   189

Index   195

Acknowledgments

There are specific, and specifically different, academic and feminist discourses around who and how to thank. I will try to be brief. My thanks go to: the contributors for writing this book and putting up with my editorial harassment; Sue Wilkinson, Sue Jones and Nicola Harris for their advice and comments; Jo Campling who confirmed my belief that such a book was both possible and important; my mother, Berenice Burman, for her support; Liz Bondi and Poddy Peerman for their comments as feminists (differently) positioned outside psychology; my friends for their interest and help; and the women students I teach, especially successive cohorts of women taking the psychology of women third-year option who constantly remind me of the purpose of this book. The book is dedicated to women in psychology.

The enthusiasm, commitment and excitement which has gone into this book derives from the belief of all of us who have written that what is said here will contribute to the political activity of feminists inside and outside psychology. The rest is up to you.

Erica Burman

Notes on the contributors

Christine Adcock, Community Support Team, North Manchester Health Authority, studied psychology at North East London Polytechnic, Oxford and Birmingham University, where she qualified as a clinical psychologist. She then worked as a Health Education Officer for people with learning disabilities or with mental health problems. For the last five years she has worked with a team of Health Service employees working for people with severe learning difficulties in north Manchester.

Kum-Kum Bhavnani and **Meg Coulson** have both been teaching women's studies and arguing with each other and with others about the political challenges involved.

Erica Burman, Department of Psychology and Speech Pathology, Manchester Polytechnic, teaches developmental and educational psychology on various undergraduate and professional courses, including a Psychology of Women course. She has been politically active as a Jewish feminist for some years, and is currently interested in working on issues of feminism, discourse and subjectivity.

Jan Burns, Regional Secure Unit, Wakefield Health Authority, read psychology as an undergraduate at Manchester University, and then went on to do a PhD in the Department of Applied Psychology in Cardiff. Her research concerned the evaluation of community-based services for people with learning difficulties, and meant that she worked a lot with women who were employed as 'carers'. While finishing her PhD she taught psychology part-time at the Polytechnic of Wales and has recently finished training as a clinical psychologist at Leeds University.

Jane Jefferson is currently researching for a PhD in the social impact of genetic screening at the Department of Science and Technology Policy at the University of Manchester.

Carolyn Kagan has taught applied social psychology, counselling and the psychology of women at a northern polytechnic since 1976. During this time she spent a year in Australia, had two daughters, wrote two books and qualified as a social worker. In 1987 she reduced her teaching and took a half-time research post with the North West Mental Handicap Development Team.

Celia Kitzinger, Department of Psychology, Polytechnic of East London, was, until recently, Research Fellow (sic) in the School of Education, University of Leicester, researching young people's experience of and response to unfairness in school. Her earlier research included work on concepts of human rights, and constructions of lesbianism. She is the author of *The Social Construction of Lesbianism* (Sage, 1987), as well as numerous articles and book chapters (both 'scholarly' and 'popular') on lesbianism, feminism, Q methodology and moral education. She is author (with Sheila Kitzinger) of *Talking with Children about Things that Matter* (Pandora, 1989) and *Feminist Morality* (forthcoming), and is on the editorial board of the Inquiries in Social Construction series published by Sage.

Sue Lewis lectures in a polytechnic psychology department. Her teaching interests include personality, counselling and organizational psychology, particularly women and work. She is co-author of *Career Couples: Contemporary Lifestyles and How to Manage Them* (Unwin Hyman, 1989) and is currently editing a book on cross-national perspectives on dual-earner families, to be published by Sage.

Karen Newbigging read psychology at the University of Dundee and subsequently did the Lancashire in-service training course in clinical psychology. Since then she has worked in the National Health Service as a clinical psychologist for seven years and for the last three in inner-city Manchester as part of a community mental health team. She currently works in Burnley.

Ann Phoenix is a researcher at the Thomas Coram Research Unit, Institute of Education, University of London. She has a background in developmental psychology.

Sue Sharpe works as a freelance writer and occasional computing assistant in the Department of Academic Psychiatry, Middlesex Hospital Medical School.

Corinne Squire's research concentrates on the relationship between theories of subjectivity and psychoanalytic and feminist theories. She has also worked on film theory and women's writing. She has taught psychology and women's studies to polytechnic, extramural and university students, and has worked on a community video project. She taught at South Bank Polytechnic and has recently finished a book on feminism in psychology. She is currently doing research at the Centre for the Study of Women and Society in New York.

Maye Taylor is an experienced feminist psychotherapist working with several women in long-term therapy, and supervising other women in their own work as therapists. She makes a substantial contribution to the two-year training programme in dynamic psychotherapy at the Uffculme Clinic in Birmingham. She is in post at Manchester Polytechnic's Department of Psychology on a half-time basis, lecturing in clinical psychology and also including an option on the Psychology of Women. She also tutors the Open University's Gender in Education part of their MA. From time to time she also acts as management consultant and trainer to organizations seeking to implement equal opportunities programmes.

Jane Ussher is a clinical psychologist, presently working as a lecturer in the Department of Psychology at Sussex University. She was involved in the formation of the Women in Psychology organization, acting as Honorary Secretary from 1986–8, and the BPS Psychology of Women Section, acting as Honorary Secretary from 1988–90.

Sue Wilkinson is Head of the Psychology Section, Department of Social Science and Policy Studies, Coventry Polytechnic. Her main research interests are in the area of gender atypical women; the experience of women in higher education; life stress in the elderly; and the analysis of feminist work in psychology. She has published an edited volume, *Feminist Social Psychology: Developing Theory and Practice* (Open University Press, 1986) and is series editor for the Sage Gender and Psychology series. She was a member of the steering group to form the British Psychological Society's Psychology of Women Section and is the current (1989) Chair of the Section committee.

Anonymous contribution The authors of Chapter 10 are educational psychologists who have worked in LEAs for ten years or more. They have also been involved in activities inside and outside the educational system on equal opportunities issues. They would like to acknowledge all the other women educational psychologists who have given their support.

Introduction

The function of an editorial introduction is to locate a book in its context and demonstrate both its relevance and its coherence. However, in accordance with the feminist commitment to make visible the processes involved in producing an academic artefact, I will also describe why and how this book came about. What the account will illustrate is the importance and urgency of the issues this volume addresses. In particular it shows the difficulty of bringing into a public academic arena precisely that which the structure of the arena has sought to suppress. These issues are the marginalization of gender (as well as 'race', class and sexuality): in both the theoretical frameworks offered by psychology, and in the experience of women who are or have been involved with psychology – whether in teaching, research or 'professional' capacities.

The book addresses what feminists do in psychology, what these experiences demonstrate about the functioning of psychology, the issues that women are faced with in their work, and in some cases why they may no longer regard themselves as 'doing psychology'. The term 'practice' functions to highlight the *productive* nature of psychology. Psychology as a reflexive discipline, created by people about people, is founded on a bedrock of 'explanation' shot through with ideological assumptions, most of which form part of the taken for granted currency of modern western culture. Hence psychology can be said to construct its own object of enquiry, reflecting and perpetuating particular social interests. The emphasis on psychology as a social practice thus serves to draw attention to the material conditions that constitute institutional psychology (or psychologies) and its (their) effects.

This book, then, traces a trajectory of feminist intervention within and in relation to psychology. It is structured around three themes; Part One explores the extent to which feminists are positioned inside or outside orthodox psychology, and the corresponding implications of these positions; Part Two examines the changing definitions of psychological knowledge produced by feminist practice; Part Three is organized around current debates, dilemmas and strategies for resistance. A more detailed and systematic summary of each chapter precedes each section of the book – so you should look there for more formal brief outlines. At the end of the book I identify key areas for further development, debate and action.

In the rest of this introduction I will outline the institutional context in which the issues addressed within this volume take place and then indicate the particular political functions that have come to define and structure psychological practice. In contrast to this, the final section argues that the position of feminists working in psychology can be seen necessarily to involve challenges to the discipline's dominant practices. Applying the issue of reflexivity to the production of this book I finish by describing and indicating some implications of the difficulties and dilemmas encountered when producing a book of this kind.

Institutional context

The initial impetus for this book was both startlingly simple and obvious. I had been working on a temporary contract in a polytechnic psychology department, and as the year drew to a close and I began to have a little time for reflection, the gnawing doubts about what I was doing, why I was doing it (and why I still had not finished my PhD) resurfaced. There were so many 'good', valid reasons I could find to justify my ambivalent involvement in psychology, yet here I was, after years of conflict and acute feelings of political compromise, with an academic job – somewhat to my surprise. The time lapses skated over in my CV testify to political activities I am proud to have been involved with but which are not considered legitimate, academic psychology. Moreover, in talking with other women I have found out (in feminist consciousness-raising fashion) that my headaches about teaching, research and staff relationships, engagement with academic practices, political commitments, competing with pressures for public acknowledgement and job security, all these are general problems. A little reflection made clear that these problems are not only common to the experience of feminists in psychology, but they also provide a key route to understanding what psychology is and what it does.

The discussions and stories that recur every time feminists working in psychology happen to meet, the issues we talk about between or after sessions at conferences, the horror stories we exchange privately with friends, these are precisely the issues that need to be raised publicly. The experiences of women, of feminists in psychology, should not be confined to the domain of private support (although this of course is often a necessary step). The stories we have to tell, our perspectives, strategies and practices, provide a vital commentary on and challenge to the existing operation of psychology (and may well extend much further).

There is now a developing feminist critique of academic psychology which interrogates both the selection of research areas and its methods of investigation (Wilkinson, 1986). As the contributions in this volume make clear, the broad rubric of 'equal opportunities' has made some impact in clinical and educational psychology, although specifically feminist concerns have had little hearing. The conviction that prompts this book, then, is that we must not only scrutinize the outcome of what we do, but also address the processes and effects of processes as they arise and resonate across the whole spectrum of psychology. With this understanding of our own positions we will be better equipped to intervene in and change the practices in which we are involved. The issues encountered by this project are both specific and general: specific to psychology, to the British context; general to higher education and to western psychology.

In many ways the audience this book addresses is not yet formally constituted; we write here to create the space in which the experiences, insights and positions of women in psychology can come to be talked about and acted upon. In some ways this creates tensions in constructing and addressing the positions from which this book might be read, so it is worth identifying who you, the reader, might be.

This book is published in a series which explicitly addresses psychology and psychologists. This is where its main point of intervention lies. But it also adds to and extends the developing literature on the experience and history of feminist initiatives in further and higher education and in the 'helping professions'. It is helpful for feminists in parallel disciplines or professions to know how our struggles compare, and to amplify the debates within and around women's studies. While it adds to the general sociology of psychological knowledge and practice that enables us to contextualize current positions both culturally and historically, this book appears at a time of crucial political transition – the ramifications of which are being felt far and wide. In particular, the issues of 'professionalization' and working within the system to change it pose major dilemmas in the current climate of the 'restructuring' of education, social services and local government. The outcome of these changes is that the space for critical commentary and intervention is dwindling dramatically. It is significant that it is at this time that the British Psychological Society, as the central organization of psychologists in Britain, is instituting the procedure of 'chartering' psychologists and has produced a major public document which defines and directs the *Future of the Psychological Sciences* (BPS, 1988). The implications of these developments are taken up at the end of the book. The final incipient but developing audience for whom this book is written is also potentially the largest; the undergraduates. The issues raised in this volume are of personal and professional interest to the women who are embarking on a 'career' in psychology. In particular this book addresses undergraduates taking (the growing number of) Psychology of Women-type courses, where we should learn to analyse our own position within as well as outside the discipline. Which is where we begin.

Women's entry into the institution usually starts at degree level. It is often observed that the majority of undergraduates taking psychology degrees are women (in my department something like 90 per cent last year). Around half of all postgraduates are women, but only a tiny fraction of teaching staff are women, and these are rarely in positions of seniority (Kagan, 1989). Here we have a pattern of women's visibility and employment that broadly reflects women's positions in higher education and 'the professions' generally. There are of course features that are specific to each discipline that structure particular issues for women. So it may be the image of psychology as a 'soft science' that attracted so many women in the first place; and it is precisely this image that current funding strategists are anxious to dispel – hence the widespread transfer from BAs to BScs in psychology. While this shift in title may not be reflected in the actual content of material taught, nevertheless as the contributions in this book argue, the current ethos (one might almost say the current ideology) of psychology is that of science, and an irrevelant, outmoded model of science at that. Much has been written about the history and development of psychology as structured by the effort to demarcate its rightful territory and to avoid any contaminating association both with sociology (Parker, 1989) and with psychoanalysis (Urwin, 1986). The drive to prove the scientificity of psychology is especially active at the moment given current government priorities in secondary and higher education. These have been translated in real terms into the creation of academic 'centres of excellence' with the closure of less favoured or more troublesome departments and, imminently, demands that academic institutions become profit-making businesses.

In many respects psychology shares this political context with higher education in Britain generally. But the elaboration of these issues within psychology poses particular problems for women, problems that are not peculiar to the British context but are inherent to the structure of western psychology. The areas which the discipline has tried to sanitize or exclude from its domain are those which look at the socially constructed determinants of behaviour and explore the experience and explanation for contradiction and ambivalence – precisely those issues to which (without necessarily being essentialist about this!) women are drawn. As in Essed's (1988) analysis of the structure of racism, it is its very ordinariness and taken for granted nature that confers an insidious inevitability on women's subordinate position. In this volume, Carolyn Kagan and Sue Lewis's contribution testifies to the subtle and often inadvertent (as well as more blatant) forms of devaluation and differential treatment to which women teaching in psychology departments are subject. Corinne Squire's chapter explores how a feminist understanding of psychology necessarily transforms both the content and relations of teaching and Celia Kitzinger documents the ideological deployment of the rhetoric of science to demarcate and exclude feminist and lesbian feminist research on the grounds that it reflects a 'political' or partisan position.

This gives us one set of clues about why women may be voting with their feet, if indeed they are enfranchised, and leaving psychology, or at least leaving academic psychology, after their first degree to work in arenas where more congenial frameworks of explanation are available and acceptable. This sets up a variety of positions for women psychologists. In this book Jane Jefferson describes how she moved from a teaching post to take up a PhD place in a different discipline which has a more explicit political perspective and sociological framework. Although many women are forced to adopt personal strategies of this sort, at a more collective level of action it is tempting for women academics, particularly feminists who feel marginalized and isolated within psychology, to make efforts to broaden their scope and move into (or set up) women's studies-type courses. However, as Meg Coulson and Kum-Kum Bhavnani point out in their chapter, the development of women's studies and the consequent promotion of (some) women into senior positions is not without its problems. On the other hand the personal costs of working outside the remit of orthodox academia to engage in relevant research set up on feminist terms are clearly articulated by Sue Sharpe. Moreover, as the contributions on these areas point out, if we compare staff teaching psychology with educational and clinical psychologists, we find that many more women are 'professional' psychologists.

Normalizing and pathologizing

Even outside 'academic' psychology we find progressives and feminists hampered by concepts and frameworks that have come to define the scope of psychology. The domain of the psychological is experience and behaviour, that is *individual* experience and behaviour. The age-old tensions between mind and body, between the individual and society, between nature and culture, are inscribed in the structure of psychology. We waver uneasily between the particular and the general, more often slipping into the terminology of the 'pathological' and the 'normal'. And here we hit the bottom line, where we see the direct ramifications of psychology's effort to partake of the respectability of science. In particular, psychology has vied with medicine for its institutional status and social power (Rose, 1985). But while medicine operates with at least some foundation for a notion of normal functioning or health, based on adequate functioning of an organ or body, *psychology*'s concepts of mental health and normality, though cast in the syntax of science, are based on social definitions or (at best derived from statistical regularities whose force blurs the distinction between description and prescription. The consequences of this for psychology's support and for representation of a particular ideology of families (as white, two heterosexually partnered, and married) are elaborated by Ann Phoenix in her account of the theoretical challenge presented by her research with young black mothers.

Hence the legacy of psychology as a discipline founded with the purpose of sorting out and classifying individuals according to social and administrative categories is clearly visible today. Progressive clinical psychologists working in mental handicap are forced to operate within the human rights framework of normalization theory. As Christine Adcock and Karen Newbigging graphically illustrate, this confronts them daily with dilemmas that grotesquely play out the inadequate or reactionary interests and practice of psychology in contemporary society: do we encourage a woman with a learning disability to take on gender-typical roles, behaviour and dress and thus render her vulnerable to sexual abuse? The sexuality whose garb we thrust upon her is *hetero*sexuality; and when she acts on this we typically respond by controlling and denying it through compulsory sterilization, and artificially regulate her menstrual cycle to control awkward moods and emotions. It is psychology which has successfully marketed such processes as 'socialization' and 'normalization', which have inscribed within them particular assumptions about what society is like and what it means to be normal; normalization theory in this example accepts and perpetuates a model of society where gender is the fundamental social category, where men dominate women, and heterosexuality is privileged (see Riley, 1983, for a critique of developmental psychology and Rose, 1985, for educational and clinical-type roles).

These are the issues which Celia Kitzinger takes up in her analysis of the significance of the place accorded to 'science' in psychology, and the challenges to both theory and practice presented by a radical feminist critique. Her account of the structuring of psychology so as to delegitimize progressive political projects illustrates a key feature of the curtailed structural positions permitted to feminists and feminist issues within psychology: any dissent from the prevailing or dominant ideological position is defined as either outside 'proper' psychology, or else is theorized only in pathologizing terms.

Psychology has successfully proved itself to be indispensable to the functioning of industrial society, fitting people to jobs, fitting environments for maximum efficiency and even translating those areas taken up as potentially progressive, such as interpersonal skills, assertiveness training, into 'management' skills. The ways in which certain aspects of 'gender research' have become incorporated into mainstream psychology illustrate some of the dilemmas and compromises involved in struggling for recognition and working within the system. The now widely acclaimed notion of 'androgyny' originally developed to liberate men and women from the crippling straitjacket of rigidly demarcated sex roles, has itself been turned into an instrument for capitalism (so that the 'androgynous' person is enabled to sack an employee with sensitivity; Bem cited in Billig, 1982). The history of the struggle to create the recently formed Psychology of Women section of the BPS illustrates the promises and costs of the project to find a place for women within the mainstream professional association. Jan Burns and Sue Wilkinson's accounts of these developments show that the different institutional responses to the organization of women in psychology in various countries demonstrate significant features about the particular political status and position of psychology.

Reflexivity

It should be clear by now that this is not an 'academic' book in the ordinary sense of the word. Presented in a broadly familiar format, produced by a well-known academic publisher, it clearly cannot but be an academic product. But this book is about the experience of women who are involved in the practice of psychology, the issues that we face, the perspectives we bring to bear. This is a book *about* psychology rather than an instance of it – though it is impossible to draw absolute distinctions due to the inherent reflexivity of the nature of our object (or perhaps more appropriately our 'subject') of study. Rather than speculate about feminist theory or methodologies in psychology, the point of departure for this book is to provide a forum for feminist comment and critique on the practice of what it is we do when we 'do psychology'.

Taking this remit bridges two of the great gulfs that have structured the social sciences and psychology in particular, namely the theory–experience split and the academic–practitioner (or theory–application) divide. The separation of the realm of 'pure' theory from 'hands-on' practical work in psychology reflects the general structural (and gendered) division between mental and manual labour, and its realization in psychology is both an artificially maintained and tense relationship. The retreat to theory is often a defence used to avoid taking responsibility for the implications of psychological research. The history of psychology testifies to how seemingly objective and detached research is structured by social and political agendas, not to mention how psychology has always benefited from war and other such 'natural' disasters (Wexler, 1983).

It is of course no accident that it is through women's accounts that we see the breakdown of these oppositions which are so central to the maintenance of the cultural hegemony of academia. The feminist prioritization of experience necessarily throws into question accepted academic rules and practices, while feminist perspectives inform our own understanding of women's positions (Stanley and Wise, 1983). Taking seriously the feminist project to make ourselves visible within our work means that an adequate account of women's relation to psychology must include not only the products of our work (be it as teachers, researchers or service providers) but also an analysis of the (sexual-)political processes involved in their production and practice. So, for example, the predominance of women, traditionally positioned as carers and domestic labourers, in 'caring professional' roles such as clinical and educational psychologists (although not in positions of seniority) rather than research or teaching, reveals much about the ethos and structure of academia (and is commented upon by most contributors in this book as they document how the dilemmas have touched their own lives). While these issues arise in many academic disciplines, one feature that crosses both psychology and feminism, though usually in quite opposed ways, is the inherent reflexivity of the psychological enterprise which (for feminists) raises questions of power relations between expert and client, teacher and student, student and supervisor, researcher and researched and within management structures (Culley and Portuges, 1985). A feminist analysis of psychology highlights the complex matrix of theory, theorized and theorizer, and in a society structured around the individual with mass demand for popular psychologies, positions us all as *subjects* of psychology and subjects us to its practices (see Henriques et al., 1984).

The enquiry here is reflexive in an additional sense; contributions not only interrogate psychology but also reflect insights gained from this domain back on to feminism. Several chapters in this book highlight issues that challenge and extend feminist thinking. Exploring the diverse ways feminists are to be positioned in psychology, this book considers the implications and dilemmas for feminist practice. Should we be working inside the British Psychological Society to make it and psychology more woman-friendly? Or are the concessions involved too compromising? Is feminism compatible with working in psychology? What role and contribution do feminist psychologists have in relation to the feminist community? Should we act to challenge and demystify uncritical adoption of dubious psychological concepts that are coming to inform feminist accounts? Are women who set up women's studies courses reproducing inequalities and hierarchies within feminism? Does highlighting gender issues in clinical practice obscure other important structural power relations? And what can psychology offer to a progressive, feminist practice?

Taking reflexivity as the starting point for a feminist enquiry also has effects to which the production of this book can testify. Many of the contributors to this volume have commented how useful the process of writing their chapters was for them. For some women it presented an opportunity to set down on paper ideas they had been thinking and talking about for some time but had not fully articulated. For others it offered a springboard for discussion with colleagues and personal exploration of similarities and differences between their views and positions. In one case the act of writing so empowered the authors that they were able to take a stronger stand in their workplace and actually start to change some of the oppressive practices that their chapter describes. From these beginnings the feminist intervention in psychology gathers force.

Many voices

Beyond the usual disclaimers about time and space there are a number of priorities that have guided my selection of contributions that should be stated clearly. First, I wanted a range of involvements in psychology to be covered in this volume, not only women who were teaching or writing psychology but also women who, in the BPS's terms do 'practise' psychology, in the narrower sense, and although only clinical and educational psychology are addressed here I would like to think that subsequent books will address other arenas in which feminist psychologists work. In particular the positions of women involved in occupational psychology call for exploration and the many areas where psychologists are employed (without professional titles but as psychologists) as in personnel work and advertising.

Second, the accounts which appear in this book are selected on the basis of women I knew or knew of, rather than 'stars' (though using this term is to displace rather than identify the problem). I did not want to publish the accounts of women who are particularly well known: although some of the contributors have published quite extensively before (though interestingly not necessarily for a psychological audience), most have not. One of the recurring issues for feminists in relation to academia is that of publishing: the pressure to be in print, to measure your reputation by column inches or quantity of papers. As Celia Kitzinger's contribution graphically illustrates, competing publicly for institutional approval (or at least notoriety) presupposes some commitment or at least collusion with the prevailing rules of the discipline. Many women have been much too ambivalent to take this step. For myself, this will be my first publication that solidly (but not solely) addresses a psychological audience – and I feel comfortable about this because its appearance challenges and intervenes in dominant meanings. I say more about this at the end of the book.

Third, just as the women who publish in psychology are a (self-) selected few who precisely by virtue of this selection may be the exception rather than the rule, so no account of feminists' relationships with psychology could be complete without comments from women who have left the discipline. For every feminist who is working in psychology there must be dozens who have left, whether by drifting away from doctoral research into more pressing political pursuits, or taking their skills and commitments to arenas where they could be more usefully and easily practised. Even with this knowledge it was surprisingly difficult to persuade women not only that they had interesting and relevant things to say, but also that it was worthwhile for them to say it. It is surely illuminating that for a number of the women I contacted the investment involved in digging over their memories and articulating in print their reasons and their feelings was too much to overcome the psychological distance they had built between themselves and their previous involvement with psychology. Two women who write in this book have both moved out of psychology to do their research – in Jane Jefferson's case to another discipline, in Sue Sharpe's case outside any explicitly formulated disciplinary framework. The women who no longer have any tangible involvement with academic and psychological practices, whose perspectives would also be most valuable, do not appear.

Difficulties

A text is constituted not only by what it is, but also by what it is not. There are a number of other significant absences in this book. Perhaps the most striking of these is the absence of accredited authorship accompanying one chapter. Far from reflecting a radical critique of the ownership of ideas, these women write anonymously because they do not feel able to give public expression to their views with impunity. The women concerned consider that they have already suffered discrimination by virtue of voicing dissent and highlighting sexism in their workplaces, and so although committed to radical critique and practice cannot admit to this in such a public forum. It is a sad reflection on the state of psychology that debate can only be introduced under such circumstances, and is testimony to the backwardness of British psychology in relation to other countries. Jan Burns and Sue Wilkinson describe this in more detail.

I am also acutely aware of other significant omissions. It would have been particularly illuminating to have included an undergraduate account which could highlight with the clear sight of the relative novice what is involved in learning the rules of the discipline and becoming culturally competent members. Another useful contribution could have been to apply perspectives from discourse analysis and feminist methodology to analyse the resistance exhibited by men when they are put in the subordinate positions of student or respondent or 'client' (O'Brian and McKee, 1982; Walkerdine, 1981). Although these accounts usefully inform the occupational experience of women psychologists, they also serve to draw attention to the power dynamics structuring these relationships which this disjunction between gender and professional status brings to the fore.

There are further difficulties that arise from the style of presentation adopted in this book. Producing writing based on experiential accounts dismantles the traditional defence of intellectualization and poses difficulties of vulnerability and misinterpretation for the authors. So, for example, a chapter which was commissioned to discuss research and supervisory relationships had to be abandoned because the author came to the conclusion that whatever she wrote would be interpreted as personal criticism rather than an exploration of the general issues raised by her own experience.

There are also of course many differences present within this volume. Feminism is not an orthodoxy, and there are clear tensions and even contradictions between the chapters in this book. My purpose here is neither to excuse nor erase these differences, but to draw attention to and comment on them.

The first of these is the relative emphasis placed on theory and on experience. Although all chapters are based on the author's (or authors') experiences, she (or they) write with varying degrees of personalization. Some women write in what are clearly general terms about the implications of issues raised from their own experience, whereas others have made a conscious effort to speak only for themselves. Hence some women present more theoretical analyses based on their own experience whereas others draw on concrete examples to illustrate their points. Where these involve descriptions of women with whom contributors work as service providers, as in the chapters by Maye Taylor and by Christine Adcock and Karen Newbigging, the authors adopt a variety of techniques to try to avoid objectifying them. For Maye Taylor this means giving examples of situations rather than individual 'cases', while Christine and Karen use both vignettes and accounts of specific relationships to illustrate the contradictory positions individually oriented clinical practice sets up.

These differences are reflected also in the variety of forms of presentation; some women use conventional academic formats including the citation of supporting and relevant literature, whereas other accounts primarily focus on the author's own perspective alone. It is frequently a difficult experience for women schooled in the academic discourse of 'objectivity' to learn to own the statements they previously had to put in others' mouths to gain credibility and acceptability.

Following from this, there are different levels of address. While Jane Jefferson and Sue Sharpe's accounts may 'speak to' undergraduates' experiences and those of women who have recently been involved with psychology (and thought better of maintaining the involvement), Carolyn Kagan and Sue Lewis document the issues raised by their experiences as women teaching women students. At another level, Meg Coulson and Kum-Kum Bhavnani's chapter presents a more theoretical and wider-ranging interrogation of the general situation of feminists in higher education, in which psychology participates in particular ways. Both Corinne Squire and Celia Kitzinger comment on how the understanding of the relevance and usefulness of psychology gained from within psychology contrasts with the perception of feminists outside, providing a practical illustration of the role they affirm for feminist psychologists of demystifying psychology. Hence the positions from which women write vary enormously as do the questions about psychology that their practice raises. It is the commitment to feminist interrogation of psychology, and a shared understanding that women's particular positioning exists relative to the rest of psychology that unifies the book.

There are also a number of political differences between the accounts. Jan Burns for example clearly envisages the development of a disciplinary area of 'the psychology of women' as, given certain conditions, progressive and possible, whereas Celia Kitzinger sees it as necessarily contradictory and compromising to work within the boundaries of psychology. Meg Coulson and Kum-Kum Bhavnani mount a general challenge to the notion that women's greater promotion and progression within academic power structures necessarily serves the interests of all women, while Sue Wilkinson and Jane Ussher acknowledge the difficulties but maintain the value of claiming a space for women within psychology's academic and bureaucratic structure. Differences of this kind reflect broader debates about separatism and the dilemmas of working inside or outside a disciplinary framework that are part of any fruitful feminist enquiry. Some of these issues are taken up both within the main text and in the editorial endnote that concludes this book. But you, the reader, will supply a further framework of commentary and enquiry for yourself.

References

Billig, M. (1982) *Ideology and Social Psychology*, Oxford: Blackwell.

British Psychological Society (1988) *The Future of the Psychological Sciences: Horizons and Opportunities for British Psychology*. Report prepared for the Scientific Affairs Board by the working party on the Future of the Psychological Sciences, Leicester: BPS.

Culley, M. and Portuges, C. (eds) (1985) *Gendered Subjects: The Dynamics of Feminist Teaching*. Boston; Routledge and Kegan Paul.

Essed, P. (1988) Understanding verbal accounts of racism: politics and heuristics of reality constructions. *Text Special Issue: Discourse, Racism and Ideology 8* (1/2), 5–40.

Henriques, J., Hollway, W., Urwin, C., Venn, C. and Walkerdine, V. (1984) *Changing the Subject: Psychology, Subjectivity and Social Regulation*, London; Methuen.

Kagan, C. (1989) Transforming psychological practice. Paper given at the Psychology of Women Section symposium, annual conference of the British Psychological Society, St Andrews, April.

O'Brian, M. and McKee, L. (1982) Interviewing men: 'taking gender seriously'. Paper presented to the BSA annual conference on 'Gender and Society', Manchester University.

Parker, I. (1989) *The Crisis in Modern Social Psychology and How to End It*. London: Routledge.

Riley, D. (1983) *War in the Nursery: Theories of Mother and Child*. London: Virago.

Rose, N. (1985) *The Psychological Complex: Psychology, Politics and Society 1876–1939*. Oxford: Polity.

Stanley, L. and Wise, S. (1983) *Breaking Out: Feminist Consciousness and Feminist Research*. London: Routledge and Kegan Paul.

Urwin, C. (1986) Developmental psychology and psychoanalysis: splitting the difference. In M. Richards and P. Light (eds), *Children of Social Worlds*. Oxford: Polity/ Blackwell.

Walkerdine, V. (1981) Sex, power and pedagogy. *Screen Education* 28, 14–23. Reprinted in M. Arnot and G. Weiner (eds) (1987) *Gender and the Politics of Schooling*. London: Hutchinson.

Wexler, P. (1983) *Critical Social Psychology*. London: Routledge and Kegan Paul.

Wilkinson, S. (ed.) (1986) *Feminist Social Psychology*. Milton Keynes: Open University Press.

PART ONE

CHOOSING PSYCHOLOGY?

This part of the book explores the variety of positions in which feminist psychologists find themselves.

Testifying to the common but rarely articulated occupational experience of women, Carolyn Kagan and Sue Lewis highlight the subtle but systematic devaluation and marginalization of their work and interests in psychology. This devaluation takes the everyday form of occasional comments betraying expectations that having children will necessarily reduce their involvement in work and their developments at work; of reduced promotion opportunities because their teaching and research interests are not defined as central to the concerns of the department; of having continually to counter the casual but blatant sexist comments made by male staff about women students; and of being defined as lacking in confidence because they choose not to take on the administrative commitments that pave the way for advancement. They also describe how their developing feminist consciousness in turn became reflected in the work they do.

Several issues emerge from this account: first, the authors point out that the presence of women staff has consequences not only for the mutual support and for the ethos of a department, but also determines the choices available to the (predominantly female) student population, particularly in relation to research and project supervision. Second, the undermining nature of these daily experiences is in turn reflected in the presence of women staff. The examples discussed here, some of which are both long-standing and recurrent, testify to the frustration of the seemingly ineffectual battle against the intransigence of institutions. This underlines the pervasiveness of the 'drifts' described in the following chapters. Significantly, the authors report that of the six women who were in their department ten years ago, all but one have either gone half-time or have moved out of psychology completely, whereas the male staff have stayed on. Finally, they indicate how, in a paradoxical way, the difficulties they have encountered have worked to their advantage. Released from the pressures of competition within the mainstream hierarchy, out of the limelight, they have been able to develop their own areas of teaching, research and consultancy with 'relative autonomy'.

These difficulties, compromises and struggles for women in academic psychology have forced many women to leave, either to work in more practical ways in professional psychological roles (although as later contributions show, these too are not without their problems), or to do women-centred work outside psychology. The next chapter presents two different accounts of how feminists have found they had to move out of the domain claimed as psychological in order to do work in the areas and with the methods they see as central to feminist research. Sue Sharpe locates her dawning awareness of the limitations of traditional psychological approaches in the political context of her training. The strategy she was forced to adopt to conduct and present her research in ways that do not patronize or objectify her informants and reduce them to numbers was to give up the security and salary that accrue from institutional support and work freelance. While this has in many respects proved challenging and successful, enabling her to develop collaborative research relationships and present her work in an accessible and accountable form, she acknowledges that the space for independent research is rapidly dwindling and that the personal costs in terms of insecure and inadequate funding are likely to prove too great.

In her account, Jane Jefferson describes the progressive choices she took which led her into and out of psychology as she pursued her interest in the role of science and its impact on women's lives. She was lured into abandoning her initial facility and fascination with physics by psychology's promise of finding ways to understand and investigate how individuals, groups, settings and society function, together with a critical analysis of its role within this. As with Sue Sharpe, at each stage her choices involved costs, and losses of career opportunities – it is significant that a course on women's studies could only be taken in her degree programme at the expense of forgoing future eligibility for a 'professional' psychology training. Having found better research training and more 'relevant' work outside psychology, she recently returned to the institution to apply some of her experience in community work and women's health issues through teaching social psychology. For reasons that are common to young feminist teachers, the experience was not a happy one. Undermined by the sexist culture of higher education where consultative teaching is seen as ceding control and therefore wrong, and embarrassed by the poverty and banality of prevailing trends and explanations in social psychology, she has gladly moved on to do more congenial work elsewhere.

Although the accounts offered here are presented as personal histories they do much to throw light on why women's presence in psychology is so transient. Women leave psychology not because they fail, nor because they are no longer interested in issues central to the domain of the psychological. They leave because they do not want to participate in a practice that ignores or even exploits women's experiences, occupationally and theoretically, or at least seems to discourage any alternative.

It is this challenge of changing the discipline to make it address the very issues that drew her in, rather than leaving it in disillusionment like so many women, that is taken up by Jane Ussher in the next chapter. Reflecting on her own experiences as an undergraduate, a research student and a trainee in clinical psychology, she argues that participation by feminists within the mainstream structures is essential to challenge the masculine and patriarchal practice of psychology – at the level of theory, organization and clinical practice. Feminist presence within psychology ensures that alternative approaches cannot be dismissed as belonging elsewhere, and offers new hope to successive generations of undergraduates. She affirms the importance of creating a feminist community within psychology without romanticizing or underestimating the issues raised for women working within existing structures, and creating new ones. For Jane Ussher, leaving psychology to the rats, pigeons and men is to deny its progressive and empowering potential – in her words, throwing the baby out with the bathwater – thus robbing feminism of a useful tool for change.

In a fitting close to this section on 'Choosing Psychology?', Meg Coulson and Kum-Kum Bhavnani take up the wider question of what happens when women do become part of the system, or attempt to use it for our own (feminist) purposes. While this emerges as a continuing theme throughout this book, a particularly useful feature of this account is that it locates the debates and developments in psychology in the wider context of the changing relationship between feminism, feminists and academia, raising key issues for feminist psychologists committed to progressive political practice. Subverting the dilemma set up in the previous chapter, they ask: are we throwing out our feminist politics when we join the mainstream structures of academic institutions? Their investigation of this question in relation to women's studies is particularly relevant for feminist psychologists, many of whom, because of the difficulties they experience (as documented here) as well as commitment to women's education, find the prospect of setting up and teaching on women's studies courses very attractive.

Setting their enquiry within the international context of the current state and achievements of feminism, then, Meg Coulson and Kum-Kum Bhavnani take a critical look at the development of women's studies in terms of the political dilemmas it brings for the women staff involved. They point out how through its participation with patriarchal academia, women's studies can reproduce the same patterns of elitism and inequality, for example in relation to black people and education. They caution against interpreting the promotion of women to senior academic positions as necessarily progressive and identify key areas of compromise for women who take up management positions in academic institutions. They contend that we need to distinguish between two projects that coincide within the general women's studies rubric: promoting women students and developing a women-centred area of knowledge. While the first is concerned to facilitate greater accessibility to education for women students, the other aims to change the educational system in which it is located. They highlight the tension between these projects, but conclude that both factors need to be recognized and understood for the construction of progressive practice.

1

'Where's your sense of humour?'
Swimming against the tide
in higher education

Carolyn Kagan and Sue Lewis

Most students of psychology are women. However, academic psychology in Britain is dominated by men. They outnumber women in nearly all academic psychology departments at the present time. The gap is even greater in relation to senior positions. During the last decade we have taught and researched psychology in a department which is no exception. In October 1977 there were five women and eight men teaching psychology in our department.[1] In June 1988 there were two full-time and two half-time women and eleven full-time and two half-time men. Two more women were appointed in December 1988 to replace two men who had retired. The senior psychology staff are – and always have been – men.

We think about, teach and practise psychologies that are very different now from those that we practised when we began our teaching careers. We, and our personal lives, are also different, and these changes cannot be separated from the psychologies we practise.

What has changed for us?

Sue: When I took up my post I was (and still am) married and the youngest of my three children was one year old. My first child was born before there was any legal entitlement to maternity leave, so I took an extended break from full-time employment. When I returned to my career, it was without any understanding of how domestic and work life must change to accommodate the needs of working mothers. I became aware of these issues only gradually. This process, together with an emerging feminist consciousness, influenced my choice of research topic when I registered as a part-time PhD student some years later.

My major teaching responsibilities when I first joined the department were in the field of personality theory to undergraduates and others, as well as traditional introductory psychology courses on non-psychology degrees. I still teach in these areas, but have changed the slant to reflect applications of psychology and include feminist critiques of mainstream psychology wherever possible. I have also broadened my teaching interests to include counselling, stress and the psychology of women. All these areas are of personal significance to me, as are the topics I choose to research and supervise. Having completed my doctorate, I am now attempting to pursue the applications of my research in terms of easing the burden, on women in particular, of combining career and parenthood.

Carolyn: When I began, I was single, living alone, and had recently 'dropped out' of my doctoral research at Oxford. Prior to that I had achieved, academically, and had forsaken a career in social work to pursue academic research. I had come into psychology after working with disturbed adolescents and had witnessed the practice of psychology *on* people and not *with* or *for* them. My interest in psychology was in its use for empowering vulnerable and disadvantaged people. I had remained totally untouched by the emerging Women's Movement. In my first year of teaching I taught experimental social psychology to undergraduates from a number of different degree courses, via lectures and seminars. Gradually these courses came to include critiques of mainstream psychology in terms of its failure to encompass matters of social inequality.

Now, I live with a partner and my two daughters. I completed my doctorate, taking the full seven years. I have trained as a social worker and work half-time with health and social services to people with mental handicaps. I teach applications of social psychology, interpersonal communication, the psychology of women and counselling to (mostly women) students on vocational courses, using a number of participative and experiential methods. In both my jobs I try to demystify psychological knowledge and make it accessible for people to use to the advantage of vulnerable people. My actual and supervised research projects use feminist, mostly qualitative, methods.

In this chapter we will show some of the ways in which our personal lives, our experiences as women working in academic psychology and our practice of psychology have been interlinked over the years. We will include dialogues, based on conversations which have taken place at various times. Some of these examples comprise several incidents or are condensed over time, and we have chosen them because they accurately reflect our experiences. While it is probably inevitable that we highlight some of the difficulties and obstacles to change, we will also describe some of our positive gains.

Private lives – work lives

Our private and work lives cannot be separated, but the interface between the two has changed over the years, both with changing domestic circumstances and changing priorities.

Traditionally, research on work and family has tended to be segregated. One has been the concern of organizational and industrial psychologists, the other studied by developmental and social psychologists. More recently, research on women and work has led psychologists to acknowledge the interdependence between these two areas of people's lives (Gutek et al., 1981). This development mirrors our own experiences. In the 1970s we were concerned that our domestic lives should be seen to be outside and independent from our working lives. In attempting to emulate the male patterns of work we were defensive about the question of our ability as women to cope with domestic commitments and careers, and we were reluctant to ask for concessions.

> *Male colleague*: We hear you don't really want a full-time job because of the lack of flexibility that will give you in terms of your family?
> *Union rep*: I cannot allow that question.
> *Woman staff*: [*wanting to be seen to be co-operative*] I've been teaching eighteen hours a week part time as it is. A full-time job still requires eighteen contact hours.

> On starting work:
> *Male colleague*: How are you going to cope with such a young baby and getting into a new job?
> *Woman staff*: I don't really think my domestic arrangements are relevant to how I manage this job. By the way, how do *you* manage with your two children?

> Middle of summer holidays:
> *Porter*: What are you doing here in the middle of the summer?
> *Woman staff*: Oh, I'm admissions tutor.
> *Porter*: But your baby is only a few weeks old.
> *Woman staff*: Oh yes, but I'm admissions tutor. She's very good. If I bring her in with me I can get two hours work done in a day.
> *Porter*: Couldn't someone else have done admissions?
> *Woman staff*: I suppose so. I never thought of asking and certainly no one offered. I don't want to be treated differently just because I've got a baby. I'm not going to let anyone say that I don't pull my weight just because I've got a baby.

Assumptions about our private lives and the ways they may affect our work lives have been everything from annoying to potentially discriminating.

> *Male colleague*: Congratulations on being awarded a research assistant on the strength of your proposal. I am sorry to say it has been decided not to allocate the post to you as you will be on maternity leave when the appointment is to be made. The post has been advertised in another department.

Woman staff: I haven't applied for maternity leave.

Male colleague: But everyone knows you will.

Woman staff: Who's to say I'll be on maternity leave? Last time I took five weeks maternity leave. Five weeks would mean I'd be back long before the person was in post.

Male colleague: But you *may* be on leave. Maternity leave is treated as any other kind of leave of absence – just as if you were in America, say. Then you would not be able to supervise a research assistant. Don't worry, you will be the first in line for the next research assistant in two years time.

Woman staff: If I take maternity leave, I will not be in America. I live two miles from work. I'm sure your action contravenes the Sex Discrimination Act, as men cannot ever be in the same position as they cannot be on maternity leave. Thus this type of decision can only relate to women, and would certainly disadvantage them in terms of their professional experience and development.

Male colleague: [*some weeks later*] I have taken legal advice . . . you have been reallocated a research assistant.

No allowances have been made because we have families, and no formal or informal offers of reorganizing responsibilities or timetables have been forthcoming. It is not only women who have had families. However, all the men with families have had wives who stopped working for varying lengths of time when their children were born. Thus the experience of working and having a family is very different for men and women staff. If a woman student or staff member makes a special appeal for consideration of domestic responsibilities, she is generally treated with sympathy. The issue is, though, that she has to ask for special treatment; domestic responsibilities are not taken into account as a matter of course. Over the years we have both become much clearer about our priorities in demarcating private and work lives, and more assertive in making our preferences known. We no longer feel that we must do as much and as well as all our colleagues, although the pressures to do so are still there.

Male colleague: We've got the chance to contribute to the new Masters' scheme. Your work would make a good module.

Woman staff: I'm sure it would, and it's nice of you to ask me to be involved. However, I do not want to take on any extra work because I want to spend more time with my children.

Male colleague: What about putting on some short courses? You have always been interested in that.

Woman staff: I'm still interested, but unless you can provide some clerical help and money for cover for my teaching, I do not have the time to do anything just now. I do not want to take on any extra work because I want to send more time with my family.

We now acknowledge the importance of our personal and domestic struggles, particularly those associated with motherhood and health, for our working lives, and we emphasize rather than minimize the difficulties. This has had an impact on our teaching, research and writing. Our personal experience adds a further dimension to an important body of literature which we teach on a wide range of courses. Finally, as psychology is reflexive, not only does our personal experience impact on our teaching and research, but this in turn has helped us make sense of our own lives.

Career opportunities and professional development

Judi Marshall points out that although the surface structure of organizations has become more accepting of women since the 1970s, the deep structure of valued characteristics and modes of behaviour is still largely patterned by 'male values' (Marshall, 1987). This well describes the situation in higher education, as elsewhere. Women are judged by such 'male values', but a double standard applies in that women must outshine their male colleagues in order to achieve recognition.

Within our department, there are a number of routes to professional advancement. Strengths in teaching, research, publications and administration all contribute to promotions. In practice, however, the one single criterion that all those (men) who have been promoted seem to share is leading a major course. Thus the criteria for advancement are established in accordance with male patterns of behaviour. Women who wish to develop in ways which deviate from this established male route are perceived as lacking in ambition or confidence. Hence, a myth which operates in our department is that women are provided with opportunities but decline to take them.

> *(New) woman staff*: It's very noticeable that none of the senior positions here is held by women.
> *Male colleague*: Yes, it's true. But it might interest you to know that women in the department have been offered opportunities for course leadership and turned them down.

It is interesting to examine the nature of these so-called opportunities. Here is an 'opportunity' that was offered to one of us as a last resort. Despite the rational objections raised, her refusal to take the opportunity is received in the context of her lack of confidence in herself. None of the other members of the department who had been invited to take the course leadership and refused were told they lacked confidence in themselves.

> *Woman staff*: I've just received your very formal letter instructing me to take on that course leadership. I was amazed. You never discussed it with me. I know you have offered it to every other member of staff and they have refused.

Male colleague: Let me explain my position. The pool of people available to do this job next year is very small. There really isn't anyone else to do it.

Woman staff: That's very flattering. And I suppose you thought I'd be an easy person to order around?

Male colleague: That's not it at all. I've discussed it with the senior staff in the department and we think you could do it.

Woman staff: Yes. I know I'm capable of doing it, but like everyone else in the department, I don't want to. I'm quite happy to take on any other administrative task and thereby free someone else to do it.

Male colleague: I'll try to find someone else. [*As she is leaving*] I've obviously got more confidence in you than you have in yourself.

Our achievements in other fields go largely unrecognized. Instead, they are used to urge us to take on unpopular tasks. Our own perceptions of our strengths are denied and any refusal to do what is being urged is seen as our lack of self-confidence, rather than as a positive choice.

Sometimes we have been offered 'opportunities' to take personal responsibility for male colleagues' actions. In this example, refusal to do so opened the way for the particular applied psychology course to be dropped in favour of a further development in straight academic psychology. The decisions were not made rationally. They were left to the woman to take over if she wanted to (and thereby accept the blame for losing the course when she did not want to).

Male colleague: There's been a lot of trouble and conflict over the development of the course while you have been away. If you want the course to run you will have to take over the course leadership and see it through the validation. Remember, it's the only vocational course in the department.

Woman staff: But wait a minute! Two years ago I was leading this course development and it was taken away from me by someone at a senior level who said it was totally inappropriate for me to be leading it. He made a senior male colleague responsible for it.

Male colleague: But that is because you were so junior.

Woman staff: But I'm still junior, so that can't be quite right. From what I hear there's no chance the course will get through because of how it's been handled and because of the interdepartmental conflicts. It seems to me that I'll be carrying the can for these male colleagues who have been arguing throughout the year. I'll be very happy to teach and support the course if a senior person leads it.

Male colleague: Ah, but there's a problem. In the department, another course development has been proposed by some male colleagues which has greater overall support. If you don't take on the leadership of the course, it will just go to the other department.

Woman staff: So I'm in a no win situation. If I had been leading the course throughout, of course I'd be happy to continue. However, I am not prepared to take it over at this stage.

Male colleague: If that's what you want . . .

By not recognizing our perceptions of the opportunities being 'offered', and by not recognizing the kinds of activities we do well or the kinds of psychologies we are interested in, some male colleagues have continually marginalized our work, our contributions, and belittled our worth. Not only is this wearisome and demoralizing, but it may also have curtailed our career progressions.

Every departmental promotion panel that has been convened during the decade has been made up entirely of men, and although the proceedings of promotion panels are confidential, it is highly likely that (senior) male colleagues will continue to use criteria for promotions that women will not fit. Barbara Gutek maintains that the predominance of one sex in any particular job leads to 'sex-role spillover' (Gutek, 1985). This means that the whole occupation is viewed as an extension of the stereotypes attributed to the majority group. Managers are therefore expected to conform to masculine stereotypes, whether they are men or women. Hence male promotion panels may not consciously be looking for another man to swell the senior ranks, but they will be looking for someone who thinks and acts like a man. These processes make it virtually impossible for the department and the institution to fulfil their claims to be equal opportunities employers. Whilst such claims are widely perceived to be the truth, they are potentially damaging to women's self-esteem (McAuley, 1987), and hence there is always the danger that attitudes to women may become self-fulfilling. Of course there are also men who have not been promoted during the period of our employment, but it would be a mistake to draw parallels between the experiences of men and women.

Marginalization of our work

Our interests in the applications of psychology, with emphases on interpersonal relations and subjectivity, reveal characteristics and skills that are usually linked to feminine traits. This can be contrasted with objective and scientific endeavours in which men are thought to excel. Clearly these are stereotypes. Nevertheless, Rosabeth Kanter presents ample evidence showing that activities labelled as stereotypically feminine are under valued in organizations as well as in the wider society (Kanter, 1977). She points out that where masculine values are regarded as the norm, women's skills are regarded as less important. Dale Spender uses a similar line of argument about the dominance of male values to explain why women are, and have been for centuries, 'invisible' in education, generally (Spender, 1982).

Over the years there has been a constant tension in the department between applied and theoretical psychology. Although most people do see the two as being closely linked, there continues to be a view that devalues the teaching of psychology in terms of its applications. Applied psychology in the genre of empiricist, experimental psychology is acceptable; the application of psychological issues and controversies to professional and personal experience, less so. Most of our teaching falls into the latter camp, and much of it is done for vocational courses in other departments. This 'service work' is seen by several colleagues as low-level work, inessential to the department.

It is not only our servicing work that has been criticized. We are confronted with the fact that we do not teach and research 'rigorous' psychology. Much of our work is seen as marginal to the real business of psychology.

> *Woman staff*: So, are we agreed that it is important to include interpersonal skills work in the new degree?
>
> *Male colleague*: Yes, yes. You can do all your touchy/feely stuff if that'll keep you happy.
>
> *Woman staff*: Who will teach it?
>
> *Male colleague*: It doesn't matter – anyone can do it. Just find someone who says they'd be willing to do it.

Because our work is seen as relatively unimportant, decisions about changes to courses can get made without our involvement.

> *Woman staff*: I have just seen the new syllabus you have put forward to replace the one we have been teaching together for the last few years. I see that I'm no longer involved in the course and that none of the issues about women are included.
>
> *Male colleague*: No. It's a completely new course. It's firmly based on cognitive psychology. I didn't think you'd want to teach that sort of thing.
>
> *Woman staff*: I think that students who are taking this option ought to know something about the social context – especially those aspects that are relevant to women's experiences. After all, most of our students are women.
>
> *Male colleague*: But my dear, what we're planning to teach is what most people would recognize as rigorous psychology.
>
> *Woman staff*: Well, it's a shame because nearly all the students chose to write their assignments on the parts of the course I taught, if you remember.
>
> *Male colleague*: Yes! I remember hours of double-marking all that feminist claptrap!

We are frequently disparaged for attempts to include feminist analyses in our teaching and sometimes the criticisms become quite personalized. Thus it seems at times that we work in a hostile environment where every day we struggle for recognition and acceptance. This reflects the position of women who challenge patriarchical ideologies in other fields (Rosser, 1988).

Atmosphere at work

Sexual division of power within the department is reproduced regularly in conversations with male colleagues, promoting a climate in which women are tolerated or patronized and in which their problems are ignored.

> *Woman staff*: I have just submitted my PhD.
> *Male colleague*: Oh, good. I knew you could do it.
> *Woman staff*: I'm a bit worried about the viva – my pregnancy's making me very sick at all sorts of times during the day. Do you think they'll mind if I munch my way through rich tea biscuits?
> *Male colleague*: Who's examining you?
> *Woman staff*: 'X' and 'Y'.
> *Male colleague*: That should be a doddle.

Part of working in an academic environment is an acceptance of the rules of academe. As men have held the senior positions over the years, these are rules set by men. Within the academic culture, gaining a doctorate, publishing papers in academic journals and speaking at conferences are valued activities. We have played these games, but we see our other work, which includes writing books on applications of psychology and producing reports for community groups, public sector bodies and industry as being of equal – if not greater – value.

> *Woman staff*: Did you hear I spent the summer on the public enquiry?
> *Male colleague*: I never could see why they asked you to sit on that.
> *Woman staff*: [*flippantly*] Oh, I don't think they knew what they were getting!

The put-downs we have received regarding our academic achievements are only part of the attitudinal context in which we work. We also have patronizing attitudes expressed towards us in public places, such as meetings or committees. This sort of disparagement highlights, again, the unequal power relationships we are caught up in.

> At a meeting:
> *Male colleague*: You've changed your hairstyle, haven't you? It suits you.
> *Woman staff*: Thank you.
> *Male colleague*: [*to male colleague*] Now, let's get down to the serious business.

> During a meeting:
> *Woman staff 1*: . . . so that's the issue and I think we should make a decision about it.
> *Male colleague 1*: [*to male colleague*] What a waste of time that all was. How anyone can make something so potentially interesting sound so boring is beyond me.
> *Male colleague 2*: Any other business?

> Later . . .

Woman staff 1: Where did I go wrong at the meeting? Why did I make such a mess of that point?

Woman staff 2: Well, it wasn't your fault, was it? All those men deliberately yawning and shuffling about would put anyone off.

Woman staff 1: Yes, I noticed that. It really did distract me and made me feel dreadful. And then when X walked out in the middle, it made me feel really nervous.

Woman staff 2: They do the same to me.

Explicit sexist attitudes towards students are sometimes expressed. These conversations have taken place at various times during the decade.

Woman staff: Are you ready to interview another prospective student yet?

Male colleague: Yes. What have you got there? I don't want just anyone – give me another of those pretty little girls. I like talking to them.

Woman staff: I'm not sure which student hasn't handed in her essays yet.

Male colleague: You must know. Brown hair. So ugly you wouldn't even want to mug her.

Woman staff: Oh, come on! Out of order. I really don't think comments like that should be made.

Male colleague: Your trouble is you can't take a joke. Where's your sense of humour?

Woman staff: Have you got the rest of the application forms there?

Male colleague: You don't need to see them. All we need to know is if they've got long blonde hair and big boobs.

What is significant here is that some male colleagues make these comments freely in our presence and, indeed, are untouched by our remonstrations over the years. It is rare for a male colleague to call anyone to task for overt sexism, although we find ourselves continually doing so.

As we take on our roles of 'moral guardians' somewhat wearily, some colleagues deliberately goad us and we obligingly rise to their bait. Others still do not understand why such comments are offensive, and we are charged with the famed feminist humourlessness. We are not suggesting that all male colleagues are deliberately sexist, but rather that the male-dominated culture permits this type of behaviour and allows it to go unchallenged, or challenges to go unheeded, on too many occasions.

With the lack of awareness that abounds, we have often found the department an unpleasant one to work in. For this we do not blame individual people but rather look to structural factors to explain it.

Presence of women staff

Rosabeth Kanter (1977) maintains that the relative position of women and men in organizations can be explained in terms of the structure of opportunities, the structure of power, the actual numbers and proportional distribution of men and women. All of these are interrelated.

We have already touched on the structure of power and opportunities in our department. The number and distribution of women and men are also important factors perpetuating the dominant masculine culture. With very few women, and none at a senior level among the psychology staff, men, with their particular perspectives on the practice of academic psychology, make most of the decisions. We have shown how this affects us directly in terms of the (lack of) recognition we get for our work. Two-thirds of the students are women and they, too, are sometimes forced to make compromises in their studies because of the shortage of women staff.

> *Students*: You had a notice on the board about projects. Anyone who might want you to supervise them was to come and see you.
> *Woman staff*: Oh, yes. I'm afraid I have already said I would supervise six people. We have a policy of no more than six people to any one member of staff.
> *Student 1*: Yes, I'd heard that. It's just that I want to work on some aspect of women's psychology, and I want to use women as my subjects. I wouldn't feel comfortable talking to a man about it.
> *Student 2*: And I want to use feminist research methods. I wouldn't feel comfortable with a man either.
> *Woman staff*: Have you tried any of the other women?
> *Students*: They have all got six people already. The equivalent of three women staff only accounts for eighteen students out of all those on the three degree programmes!

Recent decisions to restrict the numbers of students any member of staff may supervise have meant that some students change the nature of their final year research project: they compromise, not according to their interests and competencies, but according to the sex of their supervisor. We are not suggesting that women staff should have an inequitable number of students to supervise, but rather point out another consequence of the availability of so few women staff.

We wonder the extent to which students make sense of the psychology they receive from the mouths of men, in relation to their own personal experiences. (We actually have a very good idea of the struggles some students have in making sense of psychology in relation to their own lives, because they tell us!) For the majority of our students, who are women, there remain relatively few role models of women academics, especially in senior positions.

Solidarity and solutions

There is no doubt that it has been difficult and often unpleasant working as women in academic psychology. However, the very same structural forces that have created the demands on us – particularly the shortage of women and the attitudes of male colleagues – have contributed to positive experiences too. We have become friends and our relationships have never been characterized by conflict and threat. This contrasts quite vividly with the patterns of relationships among male colleagues.

> *Male colleague*: I am really cross with the decision to approve Mr X's time off.
> *Woman staff 1*: Mr Y wasn't so pleased about that, either. You should have heard him go on after it was announced.
> *Woman staff 2*: Oh, but he would have been annoyed for very different reasons.
> *Male colleague*: Yes, something to do with his early childhood. The only time I find Freudian analysis useful is when I try to make sense of Mr Y.
> *Woman staff 2*: I can't keep up with you lot. One minute you're the best of buddies and the next you have fallen out and are stabbing each other in the back.
> *Woman staff 1*: Yes, only the other day Mr Z said he didn't mind which admin. task he did next year, as long as it didn't involve working with Mr Y. Not so long ago you were right behind him, now you don't miss an opportunity to get at him.

The literature about relationships between women at work has focused on the complexities of vertical relationships (O'Leary, 1988). There is relatively little about horizontal relationships, although from our experience, they are more interesting. We have derived a great deal of support from each other, both professionally and personally. Indeed, some of our colleagues have found our friendship difficult to fathom and, it seems at times, threatening.

> *Male colleague*: You girls have been huddled together over coffee and over lunch for two days on the run. What are you plotting?
> *Woman staff*: Just because you spend your lunchtimes talking about work and hatching your devious plans, doesn't mean we do the same. All we talk about is women's magazines, children, sex and men!

At a time when all staff could have had their own offices, we specifically requested to share a room. This was quite deliberate as we had become very much aware of how potentially isolating academic work is. By sharing a room we could give each other much-needed support and encouragement as well as generate collaborative work. Consequently we have mounted some short courses which involve team teaching (no longer possible in our ordinary work) and have developed joint consultancies. Together, we have made sense of our experiences at work and this has contributed to the emergence of our feminist consciousness. We laugh a great deal and, far from losing our sense of humour, are able to make very good use of it.

Strange as it may seem, we have gained, too, in being marginalized, and 'invisible' within the department. By and large we have been able to develop what we like in an ad hoc way without being saddled with the 'key positions' within the department. Almost unnoticed we have been carving out areas of expertise which give us interests outside the department and allow us to get our work into perspective. We are not alone in this.

Of the five women who were in the department in 1977, one has retired to the Outer Hebrides; one has left psychology to become a student counsellor; another has transformed her job to half-time in order to conduct research (although she had to change to half-time initially at her own expense in order to secure the funding for the research); another has changed to half-time in order to work with services for vulnerable people; and one remains teaching psychology full-time while writing about and researching stress on women at work!

One of the earlier developments to arise out of the close relationships between women in the department was a course in the psychology of women. There is now an established base for the teaching of psychology of women both in and outside the department, but its history illustrates many of the themes we have raised above and it makes a good case study of the realities of practising academic psychology as feminists.

Woman staff: We have a proposal for a new option called 'Psychology of Women'. This reflects growing interest and psychological research in this area. You may be interested to know that the American Psychological Society has a Division for the Psychology of Women.

Male colleague: I really don't think we can put on a Psychology of Women course without one on the Psychology of Men . . .

Women staff: Isn't that the rest of psychology?

Male colleague: We can't be seen to be biased. What if the course were called Psychology of Sex Differences?

Woman staff: OK.

Male colleague: Then you will have to change the content of your syllabus to include men. For example, where you have 'mental health of women' you must have, instead, 'mental health of women and men'.

Woman staff: So what will go in the Abnormal Psychology course?

Male colleague: If this is a course on Psychology of Sex Differences, there must be a man teaching it. If it is only to be you two women teaching on it, it will be biased.

Woman staff: But lots of the courses we teach are taught only be men – after all, you do outnumber us by two to one!

Male colleague 2: Ah, but they aren't about the psychology of sex differences.

Six years later:

Woman staff: The two of us have been teaching the Psychology of Sex Differences course for several years. No men teach on it now. As you know, our interest has always been in the Psychology of Women, and because that has been the students' interest too, that is what we have been teaching. We would like to change the title of the course to Psychology of Women.

All: OK.

Two years later:

Male colleague: I have some concerns about the Psychology of Women exam paper. Almost every question has the word 'oppression' in it. This course has worried me from the start and this confirms my suspicion that it is politically biased. There is plenty of other material on sex differences in the brain and so on that does not feature on this paper.

Woman staff: That is because we are not teaching the psychology of sex differences. We are teaching the psychology of women and the course reflects published research on women's psychology.

Male colleague: Well, I would like it to go down on record that I and others are not happy with this course.

Woman staff: Students like it!

Need we say more?

Conclusion

We have discussed some of our perceptions of working in academic psychology over a decade during which we changed profoundly in our contact with, understanding of and experience in feminism. The structural forces of attitudes to women, number of women in academic psychology and dearth of women in senior positions in the department have led to our feeling frustrated, annoyed, powerless and devalued. Despite this, we have had the space to develop solidarity with each other and to transform our work, without the millstone of departmental responsibility that seems so heavy to our male colleagues.

The constant battling against received psychological wisdom and social attitudes reflected by our colleagues has been both wearisome and stimulating. It gives us a sense of purpose and of commonality which is lacking elsewhere in the department. We are aware that many of the issues we have raised in our account concern male colleagues – this is inevitable given the context in which we are working. We should make it clear that we like and have good working relationships with the very same male colleagues. We are also aware that other people in the department may also have changed the ways they practise psychology and may have experienced similar incidents: we do not wish to minimize this, but our understanding is only of our own situations. One thing we can say, to end positively, is that now, some good number of years after entering psychology, we are beginning to realize some of the interests we started out with and to be able to practise psychology in the ways we have always wanted to. We are also learning to reclaim our personal lives by managing our work lives better than we did. The intervening years have been tiring and turbulent. They have also been very funny.

Note

1   Throughout our discussion, 'department' refers to the group of permanent psychologists who are responsible for teaching the psychology degrees and other courses associated with them. There are other psychologists in the institution, some of whom are women. There are also several women teaching part-time in the department on temporary contracts.

References

Gutek, B.A., (1985) *Sex and the Workplace: Impact of Sexual Behavior and Harassment on Women, Men and Organizations*. San Francisco: Jossey Bass.

Gutek, B.A., Nakamura, O.Y. and Nieva, V.F. (1981) The interdependence of work and family roles. *Journal of Occupational Behavior* 2 (1), 1–17.

Kanter, R.M. (1977) *Men and Women of the Corporation*. New York: Basic Books.

McAuley, J. (1987) Women academics: A case study in inequality. In A. Spencer and D. Podmore (eds), *In a Man's World: Essays on Women in Male Dominated Professions*. London: Tavistock.

Marshall, J. (1987) Issues of identity for women managers. In D. Clutterbuck and M. Devine (eds), *Businesswoman: Present and Future*. London: Macmillan.

O'Leary, V.E. (1988) Women's relationships with women in the workplace. In B.A. Gutek, A.H. Stromberg and L. Larwood (eds), *Women and Work: An Annual Review*. Volume 3. Beverly Hills, CA: Sage.

Rosser, S. (1988) *Feminism within the Science and Health Care Professions: Overcoming Resistance*. New York: Pergamon.

Spender, D. (1982) *Invisible Women: The Schooling Scandal*. London: Writers and Readers.

2
Moving out of psychology:
two accounts

I

Sue Sharpe

This account is of necessity a personal one. However, it may reflect certain conflicts and contradictions felt by many women who have passed through the educational system and the academic world on a similar kind of route to mine, seeking to study or work within psychology. While the general nature of these experiences may be familiar, the actual course of events was very specific, and culminated in taking me out of this academic area.

There must be many women within higher education who are trying to make some sense of what they are studying or teaching and who want to pursue it in their own way, but find that this is not as easy as it should be for a multiplicity of reasons – from personal to political. That women are still discriminated against in higher education is not in question, and within the field of sciences the odds are even more heavily stacked against them. For those of us interested in research, the dominance of male personnel and ideology in these subjects puts the emphasis on traditional scientific method, the practice of which requires the collection of quantitative data to test a hypothesis. Psychology aspires to be a science although it has often been looked down on by the 'pure' sciences, and my attempts to follow a more flexible and feminist pathway within it have proved crucial in my life.

For me psychology was a belated choice. At school in the 1960s, I seemed destined for a job or career in science. At the last minute I recoiled from higher education in this field because it felt too abstract. It didn't seem to connect with people, an aspect that has always attracted me, just as it has also attracted many other girls and women to pursue certain areas of work often designated as 'women's work'. As a compromise I got a job with the Medical Research Council, working in a biochemistry laboratory as a junior technical officer. It had seemed to me an area of science which eventually had some connection to people's lives, even if centrifuging hundreds of samples of the genetic material of rabbits seemed a bit removed at times.

Although some men were employed at the technical level it was mainly women who did the laboratory work, under the supervision of the independent researchers (with PhDs) who were predominantly men. It was a familiar picture and what soon became apparent was that it didn't lead anywhere unless you took a degree. You would be forever working on someone else's research and never on your own. Meanwhile I had become fired with enthusiasm for psychology through reading popular psychology paperbacks and at the last minute applied for university to get out of this situation.

Thus I took a combined studies degree at Leicester University, specializing in psychology, with sociology and philosophy as my joint second subjects. There at that time (and maybe still today) the orientation was traditional and behavioural, with much emphasis on experimental psychology. There was a high proportion of women taking psychology, both as a combined subject and as a single degree subject, but only one woman lecturer. We were given the statutory lectures in physiological, developmental, experimental and 'abnormal' psychology. I learned about the habits of fruit flies and rats, and experimented with various visual illusions and memory tests on other students. The practical exam each year required a team of local pre-pubertal grammar school boys to be recruited for our experiments, lured by the promise of chocolate bars. I'm not sure what I had expected from psychology, but I found a lot of it very dry and little related to my concern with people as living social beings. It was also a very lecture-based course, with relatively few seminars or tutorials. Social psychology, which like Jane Jefferson I found the most interesting, unfortunately only occupied a small fraction of the course. In my final year I cast desperately around for something to do next. I was accepted for a job with a market research company, but had also applied for an MSc in social psychology at the London School of Economics. Once again I was attracted to what seemed to me at the time had most to do with ordinary people's lives. Social psychology appeared to me to offer this potential by exploring people's experiences and behaviour in a social context, not removed as in the laboratory situation.

LSE was buzzing with political activity at this time (1968–69), which understandably made it rather difficult to concentrate fully on the course. My tutor was eventually sacked for his involvement, but as I had hardly met him this had little effect on my performance. At that time everything was being questioned, including psychology, and the ideas of people like R.D. Laing and David Cooper were being avidly taken up and discussed, and there had been the radical Dialectics of Liberation conference at the Roundhouse in London. But although the Women's Movement in Britain was already germinating, feminism was hardly on the agenda. In psychology it did not feature at all, and for me the only aspect related to gender that I can recall being discussed was sex differences in aggression. As there was no theoretical framework within which to question gender development, we simply didn't do so. I'm glad to say that in many places this has changed enormously through the sustained efforts of feminist lecturers.

Although I demonstrated with everyone else against the Vietnam War at this time, and for student rights, I was not very politically conscious and had barely thought about feminism. At the same time I was also finding it hard to identify with the prospect of being an academic, couldn't get into high-level discussions on psychological theories and had so far not enjoyed my experiences of teaching. Judging by the aspirations of other people on my course, it seemed that if you didn't go into teaching or take another course there was not much else to do. Unlike today, there was no overriding urgency to enter a career structure. So at the end of the MSc year I drifted into helping with the data preparation of PhD material collected by a lecturer within the social psychology department. A few months later I was still doing it, but had moved on to a more permanent basis as research assistant, and was learning about data analysis. This was to prove very helpful as it taught me how to use the computer, a skill that has stood me in more practical stead than much of my knowledge of psychology.

At the end of a year I was encouraged to register for a PhD myself. This focused around the vocational aspirations and expectations of English, West Indian and Asian children at secondary school. My supervisor's approach was almost motherly and I would go round to her family home for supper and my tutorial. But despite this, little progress was being made and I could not get into any theoretical framework that seemed relevant. Then she went on sabbatical and my supervision was handed over to the professor, also a woman and one who possessed a very imposing personality. With less than a year's grant left, she streamlined my supervision. Including both boys and girls, and sex and race differences, had always felt problematic, so in the context of my increasing involvement with the Women's Liberation Movement, she suggested I threw out the boys and concentrate on exploring the nature and perception of the 'feminine role' in teenage girls. As I had assumed the necessity of including both sexes for some kind of comparative study firmly rooted in a theoretical foundation, this relatively simple solution was a most welcome surprise. My interest and motivation soared and I changed my research materials accordingly.

There was no question of doing a qualitative study, as the essential thing was to collect data, and in fact I did not question this at all at the time. While I was going into schools to administer questionnaires, I could see that the open-ended questions intended to generate background information were yielding things that I very much wanted to follow up. I selected out a smaller number of girls to interview in more depth. This had not been part of the approved research plan. I was not sure at this time exactly what I would be doing with the material apart from perhaps illustrating the PhD with a few quotes.

For my PhD, the most scientific and valid part of research was considered to be, of course, all the questionnaire material, and I too had been convinced by such an empirical approach. This was what constituted the basis of a thesis in social psychology, unless you got some special dispensation. There was safety in numbers (the earlier project I had worked on had a cast of over a thousand!), and with easier access to computing facilities, a whole range of statistical and therefore 'scientific' analyses could be easily carried out. I duly coded all my material up and put it on cards ready for the computer.

When my grant ran out I got a part-time job doing computer analysis for a longitudinal educational research project investigating IQ. It was a project that held little personal interest for me but it paid the rent and left me time to work on my own data. As time progressed, I accumulated ever-increasing piles of computer output which seemed to have little relationship to the real lives of the girls who had filled in my questionnaires, and those I had talked to in more depth. I was trying to make global generalizations about them by factor analysing attitude scales or motivation measures. Some analyses showed me trends that were useful, if depressing, such as the indication that traditional attitudes and expectations were still strong. But I definitely felt pressured to do some oversophisticated analysis on data that probably did not warrant it, and to reduce people's experience to a series of statistical significances. I know others, such as Jan Burns in her chapter, have had similar doubts.

Since that time (1972–73), ethnographic research has found increasing favour, especially with the development of a feminist research perspective that has emphasized the validity of qualitative methods. More recently however, there has been a move back towards empiricism and large-scale data collection, reflecting the general political move towards conservatism. It seemed then as if psychology (social psychology in my case) was still trying to prove itself as a scientific discipline. I was awash in a sea of numbers, the actual statistical analysis of which I was probably more technically competent at doing than my supervisor (who had returned from sabbatical), from which I could not see any meaningful escape.

Luckily for me, I communicated my discontent to a friend who put me in contact with a publisher interested in feminist ideas. He asked if

I'd be willing to write a popular-style book based on my research. Overjoyed to be given this opportunity and challenge, I turned my thesis material into a book about the development of sex roles, *Just like a Girl* (Penguin, 1976) doing it in a way I hoped could be read and understood by girls themselves. This was not easy at first, my editor patiently sent back my drafts asking me to use shorter sentences, plainer language, and get rid of the inevitable 'third person' I had learned to hide behind. What eventually emerged was not any different in meaning but a lot easier to understand. I do not underestimate the need for academic and theoretical books, but I also feel strongly that social research should be written up in a way that is comprehensible to many people, and especially those on whom it is based. The characteristics of academic style tend to be long-winded and long-worded, and I was too when I started my book. After I had finished it I was urged to complete my PhD, but at that time I felt I had done what I wanted with my research and I would get stale doing more, and I could not bear to return to such an esoteric style. In the social sciences, in which I include social psychology, research should not only be intelligible to its participants, but also relevant and accountable.

Since this time, I have concentrated on doing my own research and writing it up in books that I hope are accessible to many people. I have not done this in conjunction with any institution, and this has to some extent been my choice. In contrast to my previous experiences as a research assistant, I have preferred the freedom of deciding on and organizing my own work, and not being answerable to anyone following a certain sort of approach or analysis. I made a few grant applications in the late 1970s to bodies such as SSRC (as it was then) and the EOC for my research on working mothers. Being a feminist was and still is very important to me, but it is also a biased position in some people's view, and I felt obliged to make my research proposals sound more formal, theoretically based, and socially neutral. This meant compromising the feminism inherent in my approach so as not to be penalized for apparent political bias. They still refused to fund me because I was working as an individual and not attached to any institution, and were not very happy about the qualitative nature of my research proposals.

In retrospect, I might have been able to succeed through applying via some of my tenured friends, but without a job myself, this would still have probably involved them acting as principal researchers theoretically supervising my research. Anyone without an academic job and wishing to do their own research is relatively powerless. In polytechnics or universities, academics doing research often try to combine it with a full-time teaching job and employ research assistants to do the fieldwork and analysis while they supervise and do the ultimate writing up. These research assistants themselves have little autonomy and work with the insecurity of yearly renewable grants subject to the decisions of the appropriate funding body. Specially designated research units are a possibility that may offer some autonomy to the established researcher, but I felt too impatient to apply and work up to such a position, and usually they too are bound by funding approval. In the academic world, research is highly valued, gives prestige and brings in crucial funds. In status, salary, and other conditions, however, those carrying out the research do not generally fare so well.

By rejecting this path I have enjoyed a privileged 'freedom', but its appeal is diminishing because there is so little money to be earned from books of this nature, however satisfying they are to write. The initial advance vanishes within months while the book takes at least a year to research and often more to write. This means doing part-time or freelance work to survive while researching and writing, and in the earlier days I also spent some time on social security. In the seventies it was easier, there was more part-time research and teaching around, and I was financially cushioned through living in a communal house in which rents were kept low. The Conservative eighties are totally different; priorities have changed, research is tight and economic cuts are rife. My 'freedom' has turned into a hand-to-mouth existence that is becoming more and more untenable.

The sort of psychology that I originally specialized in – social psychology – left me with the main choice of teaching or research. There was, I suppose, some possibility of work in commercial areas such as market research and industry, but I was not attracted to these. I took on bits of teaching because I felt I ought to and there was often some available, mainly short courses or filling in a term here and there at polytechnics when someone took a sabbatical. I was always overanxious, overprepared and didn't enjoy performing, and also felt certain contradictions about some of the areas I had to teach. It was with great relief that I eventually admitted this and made a personal decision not to do it any more. This left research, which I enjoyed, but I was afraid that a psychology department would not be very sympathetic to my qualitative methods, not seeing them as 'acceptable' psychology. Working independently, I seem to have ended up somewhere between sociology and journalism in my explorations of women's lives as in *Falling for Love* (Virago, 1987) (about teenage mothers): although in *Double Identity* (Penguin, 1984), which explores the experiences of working mothers, a major focus is on important psychological areas such as identity, self-esteem and depression.

Looking back perhaps I should have grappled more within the academic system, instead of avoiding it or merely moving in for brief

Turries of activity as I did. I have great admiration for all those women working within it who are constantly struggling for change while also teaching or researching and administrating. I'm not sure if psychology failed me in some way or if I failed psychology. I think rather it did not offer sufficient encouragement or support to anyone thinking of trying to step outside a traditional mode of researching or writing. It may have become a lot easier for women in psychology since the time I was studying, although the consistent cutbacks in education may be causing a retreat into orthodoxy.

I suspect that if I was a man I may not have been able to come to terms with my relative lack of career ascent. But although not unambitious, I have always been more concerned with doing something worthwhile and enjoyable than earning vast amounts of money, a view expressed by many girls in my initial research about choosing certain 'caring' occupations. Perhaps this 'idealism' sounds a bit dated now. I think it is very difficult to pursue less conventional research within psychology, or similar academic disciplines, without recourse to some form of personal financial support. I personally still feel quite interested in psychology but I don't see myself as a psychologist now, even though for the last few years I have been employed on an occasional basis in the department of psychiatry within a hospital medical school. Here it seems somewhat ironic that in order to subsist, I carry out often highly sophisticated computer analysis on a variety of research projects while working on my own qualitative projects. I'm not sorry to have moved out of the academic channel and I love the freedom of meeting and talking to people for my research and writing up their experiences in a sympathetic and meaningful way; but present circumstances will soon force me to look for something more secure.

II

Jane Jefferson

I've never called myself a psychologist. Psychology has never been the only subject of my work, though it has been more central at some times than others. When it's been a sideline it has often been interesting, but when it's been my major activity it has been frustrating. The frustration, I think, comes from the fact that one subject area – even an interesting one – can't satisfy my own way of seeing the world. I prefer a broad view, and one that takes political and historical context into account. Perhaps then, my dissatisfactions with psychology are from expecting too much of the wrong thing from psychologists?

What follows is a personal story of my experiment with psychology. I've tried to highlight those thoughts about it that have come from being a woman and a feminist, but many of my experiences would apply to other sciences and other academic disciplines. I just thought I could expect more from psychology . . .

At school physics was my forte, and with the only other girl in the class I gained a certain amount of pleasure from beating the boys – being just as good wouldn't have been good enough, as all the girls who dropped out earlier knew.

Choosing a career never seemed an immediate problem – for a girl. People were easily satisfied with 'going to university', and often didn't ask what subject I would do. A budding eco-mentality led me, after seeing a film on women engineers, to consider environmental engineering. This seemed to combine my traditionally female need to 'care' for something, with my smug, superior scientist's brain. The university interviews totally put me off – out of 200 people I was the sole woman, and my disillusionment deepened when I realized that the environmental approach was purely token too. I pulled out for a year and went to work in a women's hostel. This course of action made me think a lot more about what 'caring' really meant for women, and gave me respect for practice over theory.

Doing physics at university was a let-down. Exciting ideas were replaced by mathematics, while the pace of the work added anxiety to boredom. Luckily it was easy to change courses, so I was able to do biological sciences including psychology, and give up the 'hard' stuff. By then I had some ideas about the politics and sexual politics of science, and felt that the 'hard' tag was pure con, but I still felt I was giving in – choosing interest over ambition, and giving up the macho success I'd gained by sticking with physics. Somewhere along the line, 'd internalized the equation: biological (or worse social) science = asier = more feminine = less important.

Psychology was a new world. It fitted well with the biology I was also doing, to provide pictures of the way the brain worked through perceptions and cognitions, and explanations of how and why animals behaved in ways they did. I became fascinated with visual perception, and was absorbed, if repelled, by the experiments people did to understand it. Here was the hard science again – a way of understanding something by taking it to pieces and seeing what each little bit did. There were also a few ideas that fitted well with my political views, such as the basic idea that previous experiences affect current outcomes. After all, the same bright light seen after a dull one appears brighter than when seen after a brighter one, or kittens raised in a visually impoverished environment such as one consisting only of vertical lines, are unable to recognize more complex environments. My thoughts about this were still vague, and it wasn't until we did 'intelligence' that I realized what I really wanted to know, and what we weren't covering. This was anything to do with context, or interactions between causes of phenomena, or the influences of social factors. The perceptual stuff we did broke things down to look at the reactions of cells and the form and function of sensory organs, while the behaviour stuff was mainly from a behaviourist standpoint of stimulus and response, with little attention given to any other way of analysing things. When we tackled intelligence I realized that there were differing interpretations of evidence, different ways of asking questions, even different questions, largely depending on the views of the questioner. Here was an approach I wanted more of – asking why certain questions were important to psychology, and analysing evidence from individuals as part of a much wider view.

I discovered that there was a whole branch of psychology we had not touched on. Social psychology seemed to offer insight into how people interacted, why they acted in the ways they did, and how they became who they were. It also seemed to offer an awareness of itself as a science that had origins, with people involved in it doing research for stated aims, and including an analysis of how the framing of a question (at an everyday or research level) could and must have an influence on the answer. Unfortunately for my undergraduate choices, the two branches of psychology were totally divorced in Cambridge, and you could not study both experimental and social psychology together. This split, which totally blocks students wanting a more complete view of psychology, is the product of old animosities, and is reflected in the continuing arguments about whether social and political studies are real' sciences or not.

So, in my final year, I dropped experimental psychology along with straight science, and opted for the ever-'softer' but seemingly more relevant social sciences. It was made plain that this choice meant no longer being a 'true' psychologist eligible for membership of the British Psychological Society, and giving up any hopes of a career in clinical or educational psychology, but I felt that the political questions about the subject were more important and interesting. This time I felt I was giving up a safe path towards a career for a chance to look at psychology from different points of view, perhaps to discover something about women's position (mostly ignored in the other course) and to enjoy more enlightened teaching methods – even a module on Women in Society run by a collective of staff and students.

The courses I took that year provided some of what I was looking for. Issues around gender and psychology, such as 'sex roles' and their origins, were legitimate topics to study. Behind every topic there was always some sense of conflicting views and philosophies, for example around the importance of mothering, the causes of mental illness, or the ways in which children develop cognitively or emotionally. Theory and practice could be found to have histories, to involve interpretation and choice, and to reflect patterns of thought and power elsewhere in society.

Research itself was seen to have ethical and moral dimensions. But in terms of training us to be social scientists, there was no emphasis at all on the practicalities of research. We studied the methods used as topics to be analysed, but never came nearer to trying them out than reading second-hand accounts! When it came to getting research or other jobs at the end of the course, this left at a disadvantage those of us, especially women, without the self-confidence to plunge into unknown fields and get our hands dirty.

Though the theoretical content of the courses was usually satisfactory, we were a decade too late for attention to teaching methods! It seemed ironic that the most radical teaching unit in the university should still have the ancient teaching methods that some of its own courses revealed as inadequate. Only the course on women attempted to challenge this with discussion-based sessions, and to provide some student control over course content. Even this was kept in check by a course committee which ensured that the course was proper enough to satisfy university requirements and remained examinable. It was still sneered at for not being rigorous 'real' work, by a unit that was itself sneered at for not being 'real' science. As discussed in other chapters in this book, this seems to reflect the fate of women's studies elsewhere – ambitious female staff were wary of being associated with a subject that could have become a ghetto and was treated as an easily marginalized sideline.

Leaving university brought up the inevitable job worries.

Competition for research grants is high, and the chances of getting one to do something inspiring on women's issues seemed remote. In any case, research and teaching didn't attract me: I wanted to do something more practical.

Voluntary work done on the dole seemed to provide a way of doing caring and campaigning work without compromising my principles. However, it was hard to keep up the motivation with friends around me busily becoming doctors, lawyers, accountants or community workers, and maintaining an alternative lifestyle seemed increasingly difficult, and pointless. Going back to study psychology was a possibility, but general research still appeared irrelevant, and clinical or educational psychology – had I managed to get on a transfer course – seemed only to tackle individual problems without questioning their methods. Still wanting to do something 'useful', I considered social work, but was put off in the end by a group of feminist social workers – although most of them got something out of the personal contacts in their jobs, they felt they were able to do very little for women, and were paying a huge price in personal stress. Most were looking for other jobs.

I finally took a job (short-term, part-time) on a women's health research project. This was a stressful, under-resourced, low-status Community Programme scheme, but was very enjoyable and challenging. I learnt about research methods of interviewing and questionnaire design by doing them, and about how to get innovative proposals – that might actually change women's experiences of the health services – instituted in a health authority, by whatever means necessary.

When this work ended I thought again about doing more academic research. I was looking for something that questioned the role of science and technology in employment, defence, health and global politics. I wanted to move away from looking at women's needs in the health field alone, to consider the sexual politics of science – what counted as scientific knowledge, how was access to it controlled, how was it used, and what implications were there in all this for women?

I found an MSc course in Manchester that fitted many of my requirements and had funding available. Returning to academic life was something of a shock, with no student control over topics covered and all male lecturers. The first book-list had one book on science and gender – by a man – and there was little acknowledgement or knowledge of feminist critiques of science. There were, unusually, more women on the course, whose pressure helped produce an excellent module on genetics and reproduction, the only course to tackle our own experiences.

On the whole, the course had a lot in common with doing psychology: it promised much in terms of analysing the place of science in society, provided quite a lot of interesting material, facts and figures, but in the end the presentation of that material enforced academic hierarchies instead of revealing them, largely ignored gender, and failed to listen to or act upon its own criticisms of itself. In both cases the most rewarding and interesting work came up from women and men in modules organized around 'women's issues', and in both cases this gave the institutions concerned the greatest problems in student assessment.

I had half come to the conclusion that maybe the problems of psychology and of science policy, for me, lay less in their content than in the ways they were taught or instituted in practice. Out of the blue, I had the chance to see if I could do better. A friend working at a polytechnic told me they urgently needed someone to teach social psychology and interpersonal skills. Although dubious at first, I thought it could be exciting to try to teach things in a more open and critical way. I liked the prospect of working with groups of mature vocational students, had enjoyed doing counselling work and inter-personal skills in the past, and was finally won over by the idea of job-sharing with another feminist. The sheer quantity of work involved in a first-time lecturing post didn't quite seem to be halved by job-sharing, but it certainly helped to have my 'other half' around to talk about it.

Some of the pressures of this kind of work add to the excitement. Others just contribute stress and anxiety. Holding an audience's attention for a sustained period of time, and convincing them that you have something to say, resembles nothing so much as stand-up comedy. Not for nothing is that a traditionally male occupation – being arrogant and confident enough to feel you have the right to expect other people to listen to you non-stop for an hour! Find the right balance and it can be exhilarating, lose your grip and it becomes a living, perspiring nightmare. If you want to try a different method, it takes all your persuasiveness to get classes used to listening passively to split up into groups and discuss ideas. It is equally hard to convince them that their own opinions are important enough to consider, and that their experiences are legitimate sources of information.

Tackling teaching methods to try to encourage participation and a critical approach to the material presented is all the harder when you're a young woman – not a natural figure to command respect. It becomes tempting to bolster your own fragile feelings of worth by adopting a traditionally 'male' listen-to-me teaching style, rather than getting classes to question. Even dress can let you down if you refuse to, or can't, hide behind the smart two-piece, nylons and pearls. You can undermine your own security by refusing to dominate or predetermine the sessions, leaving you in the paradoxical and some-times terrifying position of needing but not having control. Add to this echnicians asking you to get your tutor's permission to use the video and the tendency of many male staff – young or old – to treat you in a patronizing way or find you totally invisible, and you find yourself undermined on all sides. Trying to do anything radical becomes another way of isolating yourself.

For all the strain I enjoyed teaching. Two things made me give it up. The first and most obvious was that we were on a temporary contract (more short-term, part-time work for women), and even with experience, without a PhD it's very hard to get a job in the academic world. On top of that, I still suffer from a typically feminine feeling that I'm not really qualified or worthy enough to compete in that world. The second reason has to do with psychology itself. Some of the frustration and difficulty of teaching came from my lack of respect for and increasing dissatisfaction with social psychology. Teaching is an excellent way of learning about a subject, but the more I learnt the more I felt that the social psychology I was being asked to teach had little practical application except in the area of personnel management! So much of it was trivial and simplistic enough to make students gasp or giggle, and much of the rest was dense and obscure. Teaching about the myriad approaches to and quantity of work done on attitude scaling made me feel quite embarrassed!

Teaching taught me to have confidence in what I could tackle. I'm now doing a PhD on the social impact of genetic screening, using all the approaches I've learnt in a mixed career. Psychology has its niche there, but it's a very small place. Although I feel the analysis I'm doing is important, and useful to 'women's issues', I still feel the need to get out and do something practical. But if I ever choose teaching again, it won't be psychology.

I cannot blame psychology for not offering sociological or other approaches to issues, but I regret the way we are chopped up into narrower specialties rather than taking broader views. Most science is taught only as a collection of facts and rules, so it seems a little unfair to damn social psychologists alone for not being self-aware. However, it seems to me that social psychology is in a unique position to analyse its own place in and effects on society. The fact that most of its practitioners duck this sort of question I think reflects a certain poverty of the subject.

I started this account wondering if I was expecting too much of psychology. My personal history traces a path undertaken to find out how the application of knowledge, particularly scientific knowledge, affects women's lives. Psychology, which covers how we think, learn, relate to each other and understand ourselves, should be in a good position to provide some answers, but failed to grapple with the relevant questions. So were my expectations unreasonable, or is psychology, as presently taught and practised, really unsympathetic to women and women-oriented work? Like many other women, for many different reasons, I had to move out of psychology to find what I wanted.

3

Choosing psychology or *Not throwing the baby out with the bathwater*

Jane Ussher

Beginnings: disillusion and discontent

How many budding psychologists go into the discipline with the misconception that it is about people, perhaps about women, only to find themselves immersed in an undergraduate, syllabus which concentrates on topics such as perception, learning, memory and meta-cognition, at the expense of anything more directly human? As a 'naive subject', in what appeared to be an experiment to see how infrequently psychology undergraduates would question the divide between their expectations and the harsh 'scientific' reality of mainstream psychology, I was disheartened and disillusioned. Positive reinforcement was meted out for acquiescence and acceptance of the principles of scientific rigour. The course was taught entirely by men, and was based solely on hypothetico-deductive analysis. It also seemed to be centred on the premise that undergraduates should be seen and not heard, and certainly should not disturb the academics' valuable research time with questions about the relationship between experiments on rats and psychological theory, or insight into how the disparate pieces of knowledge imparted fit together to make 'psychology'. In my frustration, I did try to leave: but I was told that transfer to another course was impossible, I must persevere: 'many undergraduates find psychology difficult or boring at first, you'll get used to it'.

I did persevere – while being made to feel that my discontent was due to my own inadequacy or lack of persistence, rather than any objective reality. It was perhaps the anger at this assumption that fuelled my motivation.

Positivism and science: no mention of women

I became a student whose life outside the psychology department was more important: one way of copying with the feeling of alienation towards psychology was to ignore it altogether, splitting it off into a compartment labelled 'endurance'. I produced satisfactory lab reports as required detailing the likes of reaction times in student volunteers, or the methods employed in validating an attitude questionnaire, while envying students on other courses who seemed to be studying something of interest and relevance. Why was it that sociologists, film theorists, or literature students could enjoy theoretical discussions about feminism and culture as part of their course, while I had to concentrate on mapping the layout of the brain? My exam answers on memory, physiology, perception, motivation in the rat, etc, were passable, if not stimulating. Psychology had become something that was to be consumed, rather like bran at breakfast, not for enjoyment or pleasure, but by necessity. The total absence of female staff members, and consequently female role models, contrasted sharply with the preponderance of women undergraduates. Where did they all go after qualifying? Psychology itself seemed to be a discipline taught by men, who discussed the work of other men, of real 'scientists': women were not merely marginalized, they appeared to be completely absent from the field. In quoting references, such as Wilson (1982), it was assumed that the person was a man, and in discussion the author was always referred to as 'he'. Imagine my surprise (and chagrin) years later to discover that many of these authors were women!

In my second year as an undergraduate I embarked upon what I anticipated to be the joyless task of a methodology essay, but while in the bowels of the university library I came across a paper that was a revelation: it was interesting, of relevance and had women as its central topic – a paper on the menstrual cycle. You may laugh at the very idea that menstruation could be the subject of serious study, as many have since, but this was a milestone in my career. At last psychology had something to say that seemed to be of relevance and importance, something which was of even greater interest than my burgeoning social life. Further examination of the literature convinced me that psychology could be both legitimate (in terms of being published in 'eminent' journals) and of direct relevance to women's experiences. I was later to challenge this version of legitimacy which heartened me earlier in my career, but at the time it validated and stimulated my interest in a psychology *of* women, *for* women. I was also heartened to discover that many of the authors in this field were women: almost the first evidence that it was not necessary to be gendered male in order to have a career as a psychologist.

My depth of interest in the subject of menstruation, seen almost as a form of deviance by some, was of sufficient endurance to lead me to carry out three years of postgraduate research on the subject, with the aim of achieving a PhD, as well as (in my naivety) producing some world-shattering piece of scientific knowledge. I was soon to learn that the latter is the exception rather than the rule, and if achieved invariably takes much longer than the prescribed three years of postgraduate study. Yet this myth persists, and leaves many postgraduates feeling inadequate as 'scientists', and must significantly contribute to the abnormally high drop-out rate in PhD students. This position is possibly more acute for postgraduates who choose to study the psychology of women, or to question traditional orthodox methodologies by using a feminist analysis, thereby finding it more difficult to be accepted as 'scientists'. This is illustrated by analyses of citations, a method of evaluation of worth which continues to be supported (Furnham, 1989), yet which indicates the limited impact of feminist psychology on the mainstream (Unger, 1982a, 1982b). As feminist psychologists are judged as not having made a significant contribution to psychology, it would not be surprising to find that feminist PhDs are less likely to be completed.

Splitting: science or feminism?

As a fledgling psychologist I found that my PhD subject, menstruation, was seen as an object of mirth or disbelief. As the only postgraduate in the department I had no peers to validate my work, or to provide feelings of legitimacy. I found the academics were engrossed in those traditional established areas of psychology: perception, cognition, or the study of hemispheric differences. In moments of weakness I began to wish that I'd chosen such a subject myself: that I could be accepted as a 'real' psychologist. I couldn't contribute to discussions about the possibility of producing 3D images on computer, or the extent to which lists of synonyms could be generated at random. I would now say 'so what!', but as an isolated woman postgraduate I was being continuously presented with the message that my own work was marginal, of little relevance and hardly worthy of inclusion in the discipline of psychology. How many other women are persuaded against studying the subject of their choice, of studying women, or of studying psychology with a feminist content? I felt that I was the skeleton in the cupboard for the department, to be kept out of sight and, preferably, out of mind.

I'd like to say that I ignored the prevailing disapproval and devaluation of my work and produced a PhD based on feminist principles, which pushed forward the frontiers of knowledge about women's experiences of menstruation. But I didn't. I carried out an empirical positivistic PhD studying physiological change, performance on computer tasks and mood during the menstrual cycle. The data produced from my enquiries was subjected to extensive and elaborate statistical analysis. Although I spent many hours with the individual women 'subjects', I did not collect their comments or opinions in any systematic way: this was seen to be of secondary interest to the 'objective' information I could obtain from the computerized tests. Interview material which I collected in the earlier days of research was seen to be of little relevance to the study and definitely not to be included in the thesis in any form. From a starting point wherein I wanted to learn about, and ideally add to, our understanding of women's experience of menstruation, I had evolved a series of experiments in which menstruation had become a variable on a par with stressors such as sleep loss, heat, noise, etc. It had become rationalized, compartmentalized as a stressor, and thus devalued. I knew in myself that women's experience of menstruation could not be meaningfully conceptualized in this limited way, given the negative social constructions of menstruation and the ease with which much unhappiness and discontent is attributed to it (Koeske, 1988). However, if I addressed these, more pertinent, issues, I was warned that I would not achieve the PhD in the specified three years and thus not be a 'good' psychologist. So I continued with my stress paradigm research, splitting off the feelings of unease with the type of work I was carrying out, and filing them away for later.

One could argue that my espousal of the (albeit temporary) mantle of 'rational scientist' was a necessary and effective compromise, as it allowed me to achieve the qualification I desired: I now see it as the outcome of successful brainwashing. A strong phrase perhaps, but I was the victim of a discourse which defined psychology in a limited positivistic way and decreed that all other types of investigation were invalid and therefore illegitimate. The purpose of my investigation had become solely the achievement of a PhD: that was seen as success within the academic game. The content of the work did not have to be particularly meaningful – in fact it seemed to me that the more removed from human experience (and particularly women's experience) the research was, the more acceptable it was. When I was undergoing my PhD viva the couple of pages I had included at the end of the thesis on the wider social and political implications of menstrual cycle research were the subject of much scrutiny. I was informed that to receive the qualification I would have to justify my comments and conclusions with reference to research – or take them out of the thesis (I did the former, reluctantly).

At this point the most likely outcome would have been to leave psychology, disenchanted again, to embark on a career which did not involve such splitting of my interests. Perhaps this is why there are so few women visible within psychology – they are gradually squeezed out, refusing to compromise any longer. If I were an orthodox, rational, highly motivated (male?) scholar, I would probably have sailed on into an academic career of some sort, devoting the rest of my time to perpetuating the system within which I had been schooled. What prevented either of these outcomes, and what still keeps me committed to psychology, was the involvement with other feminist psychologists, my involvement with 'Women in Psychology' (WIPS), the struggle towards the formation of the Psychology of Women Section (POWS) of the British Psychological Society and the continuing moves to establish the legitimacy of the Psychology of Women within the mainstream. Yet I sometimes feel a sense of *déjà vu*, when the distance between my earlier expectations and the reality of 'hypothetico-deductive' psychology is now reflected in the distance between my feminist beliefs and the dominant discourses within psychology in Britain today. Despite this, I strongly believe that feminists can gain much from psychology, as well as contribute much to it as a discipline. I believe that it is more important for us to work within the discipline than to leave it when disillusionment strikes, and although I respect the actions of those women who do leave, for me, that would be 'throwing the baby out with the bathwater'.

Women challenging: providing an alternative discourse

I am not going to chronicle the formation of the Psychology of Women Section in this account: it is described by Jan Burns and Sue Wilkinson in their chapter. However, my involvement with other women in this particular venture has been one of the major factors which has convinced me that it is possible to be both a psychologist and a feminist, and that change is not totally out of reach.

My discovery that there were many women psychologists, indeed feminist psychologists, carrying out research which was based on women's accounts, on feminist (or new paradigm) methodologies, was as important a revelation as my first reading of the paper on the menstrual cycle as an undergraduate. At successive conferences I met women researching areas such as gender identity, discourses surrounding sexuality, adolescent women's accounts of unemployment, and post-natal depression. For the first time I realized that I had nothing to be embarrassed about in my choice of PhD topic: the opposite, others were interested in it! However, I *did* feel some unease about the fact that my research was so positivistic: that I had not had the courage of my convictions and used women's accounts as a central component in my PhD. Yet I was relieved that my research had anything to do with women at all, as other women reported that they had been pressurized into researching topics much further from their interests than mine. Yet I still experienced a feeling of 'if only . . .': if only I had had a feminist supervisor; if only I had met other women in the same situation as myself earlier; if only I had persevered with my original interests; if only there were some forum, such as a BPS women's section which would have made meetings possible . . .

How many women have echoed these words, and then disappeared from the face of psychology? 'Psychology has nothing to offer us,' they say. 'It is a reactionary discipline, based on patriarchal assumptions, reinforcing women's oppression.' This is not surprising: in its drive to be accepted as a science psychology acts to isolate further those women who wish to carry out research using feminist paradigms. Women psychologists may find it easier to dismiss psychology, and to carry out their research or practice within other disciplines which are apparently more accommodating, such as within women's studies. Yet this perpetuates the system as it is, because these women are not available to become PhD supervisors for other women, are not affecting the structure of psychology as a discipline, are not publishing within mainstream psychology. This allows their work to be seen as marginal, as not being 'real' psychology. It also makes it much more difficult for other women coming after them to train in new paradigms of research, or to challenge the male-orientated structures, as the role models, mentors and precedents are not available. This is of the utmost importance, as it has been argued (Crane, 1972) that one of the reasons for the failure of theoretical frameworks is the absence of new individuals who acquire and retain their perspective.

It may seem that I am suggesting that feminist psychologists should become extremely altruistic: enduring conditions of difficulty and alienation (as outlined by other authors in this book) for the sake of other women, or for the state of feminist psychology as a whole. I would like to turn the argument round and say that challenging the orthodoxy, working with other women *within* psychology can be both personally rewarding and motivating, as well as ensuring that feminism is allowed to make an impact on psychology.

Psychology may, in its present form, represent much of what is anathema to feminists. The recent changes in the structure of psychology in Britain, with the introduction of the Register of Chartered Psychologists, are seen as further movement down the path to a regulated profession which is alienating to feminists. The BPS has the power to define what *is* psychology, in order to decide who may, or may not, call themselves Chartered Psychologists. One of the ways in which psychologists are judged to be 'legitimate', and thus eligible for chartering, is the presence of publications in established or 'eminent' refereed journals. The definition of 'eminent' is, as yet, limited – the likes of perception and behaviour therapy journals being acceptable, whereas psychology of women or feminist journals may be scrutinized or seen as marginal. Only by challenging this and producing equivalent publications in feminist psychology can these definitions of legitimacy be changed. Alternatively, feminists may choose to challenge the very nature of publication as the major criterion for acceptability as a psychologist, through revaluing the work which is a more accurate reflection of feminist psychologists' activities, such as teaching or clinical practice.

These current trends could result in further limitation on what is seen as legitimate psychology, with feminist theory or practice being left out in the cold. Or it could result in a growing acceptance of ways of working which are more feminist in orientation, among other changes, and an acceptance of new ways of working within the mainstream.

There is a precedent here within British psychology, in the experiences of social psychology as an established discipline. Now firmly part of the mainstream, social psychologists were previously a 'persecuted minority within the psychological hierarchy' (Robinson, 1989). It has been suggested by Robinson that there were three main reasons for the maintenance of high morale in social psychology, which must have largely contributed to its establishment and continuation: the fact that social psychologists in Britain knew each other, that they saw themselves as pioneers and that the discipline was popular with the students – thereby creating demand (Robinson, 1989, p. 22). Surely this parallels the situation in feminist psychology, or the potential situation if feminist psychologists become more visible. While we may not want the fate of feminist psychology to mirror that of social psychology, through becoming diluted in the process of assimilation, we can see that it is possible to move from a position of powerlessness and marginalization to a position of acceptability, in a relatively short time.

How can this visibility be achieved, you might ask. Change needs to take place at both an organizational level and at the level of publication (see Wilkinson, 1987, for a more complete analysis). Change is slow, but not impossible. In 1985 when the first meeting was held to lobby the BPS for a women's section, many people from whom one would have expected support said that it was a wasted effort because it would never succeed. The BPS is an immovable object, we were told, you'll never gain acceptance. A piece of more insidious advice was provided by those who warned against any association with a women's section, as it might be seen as feminist, as political, and thereby would exclude one from future academic appointments. Is this chapter going to put me in further danger of such an outcome – should I not become a secret feminist? I was told (by those with more sense and caution, as well as power) that I would be far better employing my energies in more established areas of psychology, where one would not be associated with such controversy. Is this not a parallel to advice given to earlier social psychologists? '... my brain was not pure alpha, but it deserved a far better fate than to waste its capacity on social psychology' (Robinson, 1989, p. 22).

Despite fatalistic warnings and rejections many feminists *are* active within psychology. Significant change is taking place, as is outlined elsewhere in this book. Now there is a BPS Psychology of Women Section with over 350 members. Although the psychology of women and feminist psychology are not totally overlapping categories (Unger, 1982a, 1982b), an important function of a section is to encourage and provide a forum for feminist analyses. The section has a twofold influence: ensuring that structural and organizational development cannot exclude women, or alternative methodologies, through having representatives on many of the BPS committees and boards, as well as making visible research and theory which is women-centred, through presentations at conferences, feminist invited speakers and publications.

Feminism and psychology: uneasy partners?

Feminist psychologists may agree on the need for women-centred psychology, but they often disagree on the meaning of 'women-centred'. Some writers seem to be arguing that it means all of women's experiences should be seen in a positive light. An example from my own research is the suggestion (Delaney et al., 1976, p. 24) that feminists should deny *any* effects of menstruation and reconceptualize menstruation in solely positive terms. To me, this seems to be denying that women are possibly affected in any way by menstruation. This would therefore be defining my own research interests as unacceptable. Others seem to go even further, suggesting that it is not acceptable for feminist psychologists to carry out research into experiences that are unique to women, either because this may act to reinforce beliefs that women are 'different', inferior or weak ('victims' of their biology) – or because it may imply that any differences between women and men are reducible to biology alone.

However, as Sayers argues, this negates important areas of women's lives:

> The denial, on grounds of abstract principle, that menstruation has any negative aspects ... does not ... as is sometimes implied, necessarily serve the interests of women ... Much of the scientific and often feminist-inspired research into the actual, as opposed to the assumed, effects of menstruation has been extremely useful in this way to the cause of women ... however, it is also essential to acknowledge that biology (menstruation, in this case), does have real effects on women's lives. (Sayers, 1982, p. 123)

Women's experiences have been ignored or denied by psychology for too long. If we shy away from studying certain aspects of women's experiences which may have some biological component (or have traditionally been conceptualized in a purely biological framework) on the basis that we may reinforce inequalities, we are reinforcing the dictum that women's experiences are less relevant and not appropriate as subjects of serious study or research. We are also perpetuating the systematic devaluation of research that cannot generalize to men as it is 'only' based on women (Bernard, 1973). This acts to reinforce the belief that the male is the norm and that women's experiences are only conceptualized in terms of deviation from that norm. It is important to validate women's experiences, and to do so within the mainstream, so that perception, cognition, etc, are not seen as being more valid as subjects of study than women's specific experiences such as menstruation, pregnancy or menopause. It is this belief that has motivated me to stay in psychology – as well as the belief that psychology has much to offer to feminist analysis.

My earlier frustration at not being able to present women's accounts in my PhD thesis was assuaged when I was asked to write a book (Ussher, 1989) which concentrated on those very feminist arguments which the traditional PhD excluded. Traditionally, women's reproduction has been seen as a burden or illness, acting to make women weak or unreliable. Conversely, reproduction has been completely ignored in studies of life-cycle development. In developing a feminist analysis of reproduction it is important to refute many of the myths pertaining to women's bodies, as well as to acknowledge the real effects of menstruation, pregnancy and menopause during the life cycle. A psychological perspective on women's sexuality and reproduction is not only relevant and pertinent, but I would say essential to this analysis. Traditional, empirical research has its place in being able effectively to reinforce the arguments that women are not inevitably debilitated by their reproductive system, as is suggested by 'raging hormone' theories. Other types of psychological investigation – such as discourse analysis (Hollway, 1984) or Q sorts (Kitzinger, 1987), as yet underutilized in this area, can develop the role of psychology still further. Thus a feminist analysis of the effects of social constructions of menstruation, pregnancy and the menopause on women's identity can very usefully draw on psychological research. If a psychological approach to this issue had been deemed irrelevant, and thus dropped, the arguments would have been less well substantiated, perhaps less meaningful. As with a growing number of similar volumes (Kitzinger, 1987; Squire, 1989; Wilkinson, 1986), a feminist analysis has been produced within mainstream psychology: published by an established academic publisher – as, indeed, is this very book! It is important not to underestimate the significance of this. Giving women's writing 'respectable' outlets provides a psychology from a feminist perspective for the undergraduate audience as a matter of course, and hence ensures its visibility within the discipline.

Clinical psychology: pathologizing or emancipating?

It is not only within academic psychology that dilemmas and compromises take place: practitioners are equally affected. As a clinical psychologist I have experienced a repetition of the splitting between feminist ideology and established practices. I was required to train and work within a system which traditionally pathologizes women, treats them as patients, and is orientated around changing the woman to fit in with the system. My motivation in training as a clinical psychologist was largely centred on the belief that direct work with individual women was the way I could most usefully develop as a feminist psychologist (as well as for the more pragmatic reason that there are many opportunities for career development in clinical psychology at present). I felt that I would be carrying out work that had direct benefit *for* women, rather than merely seeing women as the subjects of study. I also wanted to escape from what felt like the claustrophobic stupor of 'scientific' academia, to stop banging my head against the proverbial brick wall. But how wrong I was: it was 'out of the frying pan, into the fire'.

On my first clinical placement I saw a woman client, whom I shall call Helen, who was referred for agoraphobia. She experienced severe panic attacks upon leaving her home alone and could not travel any distance on the underground train. I was told that this was a 'straightforward anxiety management case', and prepared to 'treat' Helen with systematic desensitization (Wolpe, 1978), a form of behaviour therapy, as instructed. Yet when evidence of physical and sexual abuse of Helen on the part of her husband emerged, I was informed that it was not relevant to the referred problem and should be ignored. Discussion with my supervisor precluded any investigation of the ethics of continuing to treat Helen with a behavioural programme in these circumstances, or of alternative ways of working. As Helen's husband would not attend for 'couple' therapy, and Helen did not spontaneously express any wish to leave the violent relationship, I was informed that the most positive outcome was to help her to deal with the situation, conquer her fears, and that if she didn't like it, she wouldn't stay.

Thankfully, not all clinical psychologists react in such a manner as my supervisor: but in their quest for acceptance as 'scientist/ practitioner', many would adhere rigidly to their 'scientific' principles in therapy, noting the apparent effectiveness or ineffectiveness of one aspect of treatment, while ignoring the oppression experienced by their women clients. It is perhaps remarkable that a profession which is largely made up of women (with the exception of the top of the hierarchy) and which works with far more female than male clients, routinely fails to address the position of women in relation to a patriarchal mental health service, or the more general question of gender in clinical practice. If these issues were addressed, psychologists might look beyond their scientific rigour for explanations of women's distress. As Penfold and Walker argue in relation to psychiatry:

> There is little within the traditional discourse to build upon. What we as women know about ourselves we know from each other, from our novels, diaries, poetry, films, art, the work of our scholars, and from the sharing of the struggle towards a 'common language'. Those engaged in formulating knowledge of women will have to be prepared to tap these resources as well as their own clinical experience if their work is to prove itself relevant to women's needs. (Penfold and Walker, 1984, p. xi)

Mental health practitioners have often been grouped together under one umbrella by critics, the assumption being that psychiatrists and psychologists are equally guilty of pathologizing women, of attributing problems to the woman herself rather than taking a wider view which acknowledges the social and political context of women's lives. Yet while antipsychiatry arguments (Szasz, 1973) or social constructionist arguments (Laws, 1985) of women's mental health problems provide explanations that avoid biologically reductionist assumptions for *why* many women are distressed, they are of little help to the individual woman who feels that she is depressed. Theoretical analysis of the root of women's distress is vital to a reconceptualization of working practices in clinical psychology, and cannot be underestimated in its importance. However, there are many women who need direct help, which cannot be provided merely by reframing their problems as being the result of oppression, or theorizing about definitions of femininity as pathological. Clinical psychologists are in a position to provide direct work with women in this position, enhancing their power and responsibility, through providing therapy based on feminist principles, while avoiding pathologization or blame.

Clinical psychologists are not necessarily constrained by the medical model, and are increasingly challenging and reviewing the old concepts, developing new ones which serve rather than rule our thinking. Psychologists can concentrate on what a woman *has* achieved, such as managing to cope with young children in a difficult situation, rather than what a woman *hasn't* achieved, such as leaving a violent husband, even if they cannot counter existing oppression. More equal relationships in therapy, and open case-note policies, will challenge the role of woman as helpless patient and encourage self-advocacy. Primary care and community interventions, such as the Newpin befriending project in south London or the White City project (Hunt, 1986), can provide early intervention work for women in a way which is accessible and 'user-friendly'. Providing women with child management support, which does not 'blame' the mother for her difficulties, can increase self-esteem and feelings of competency which have direct benefits for mother and child. Validating the reality of a woman's perceptions, rather than changing them to fit in with her environment, can promote change without pathologizing the woman. As Christine Adcock and Karen Newbigging agree in their chapter, psychologists can also challenge the ideological basis of mental health practices which define women as ill if they do not fit in with the system, locating the problem within the woman, while ignoring the socio-political forces which create much of the discontent. Feminist clinical psychologists in policy-making positions can begin to alter the basis on which mental health services are provided. Through acknowledging the importance of gender in clinical practice, the medicalization of women's experiences can be avoided.

Paradoxically, I feel that I have only been able to carry out feminist therapy and be truly reflexive in my current clinical work, which is within an AIDS setting, for despite my expressed wish to work with women, I find myself working with a totally male client group. Other feminist clinicians have commented on the compromise they consider this must entail. However, I find that my therapy is truly empowering and egalitarian for perhaps the first time. This particular client group is generally articulate and politically aware and would reject any intervention which was not empowering. Perhaps if we can equip our other client groups with knowledge about the types of service they can receive, as these gay men have been equipped through their own networks, it will be more possible to practise feminist therapy through the demand for it. One of the reasons that it is possible to work in this way in my present setting may also be because there are no established practices or precedents in this area of clinical psychology. As AIDS is a new area for clinical psychology, there is little resistance to innovation from those who would normally dictate practice, and the very nature of the work means that it must be innovatory. Perhaps it is also because only now do I have the courage of my convictions. What it does suggest is that it *is* possible to carry out feminist therapy routinely in a National Health Service setting, thus not inevitably having to compromise principles in practice.

Future struggles

Although there are many pitfalls and stumbling-blocks inherent in working within psychology, I believe that it is possible to work in progressive ways in order to achieve disciplinary change, and to have feminist practice accepted as legitimate. This is not an easy prospect, but it can be both personally and professionally rewarding. Organizing with other women is potentially the most productive route, and is outlined later in this book by Sue Wilkinson and Jan Burns. But this is not without pitfalls, as we need to develop new practices in this area too. We may reject the traditional structures for organizing and decision making as being patriarchal and elitist, but are we able to forge new pathways in women-centred organizations, in order to avoid the problems of women in power becoming the new 'academic gate-keepers'? The need to find new ways of working, new structures for 'success', new ways of dealing with conflict, is a problem which is not unique to women in psychology:

> Because of the revolutionary nature and vision of feminism, and women's basic naivety, many women suffered their first defeats with surprise . . . women were very critical of the 'female' rules of handling conflict, such as politeness, tears and evasion. They were equally critical of the 'male' rules of handling conflict, such as logical or 'objective arbitration, compromise or violence'. (Chesler, 1972, p. 274)

Reflexivity in research and practice is advocated by many feminist psychologists (Wilkinson, 1987): I would argue that reflexivity in our activities within psychology, our activities with other feminist psychologists, is also vital. It is possible to work within psychology without compromising everything, but more difficult if individual women are attempting to do this alone. Rejecting old ways of working also involves rejecting the traditional elitist structure of systems within psychology: not working solely for our own advancement, but working with other women towards change and the development of new practices. We cannot always expect to share the same goal: there will be continuing arguments about the relationship between feminism and psychology, the ethics of having to compromise on some levels in order to advance on others, the question of integration or separation, the very nature of feminist research within psychology. Jan Burns discusses some of these issues in more detail in her chapter. However, this situation is healthy, as disagreement and debate should result in activity rather than stagnation and isolation. As Unger has noted: 'Those who identify with the psychology of women comprise the largest body of socially aware critics within organized psychology. Criticism of ourselves as well as of others will not destroy us. Refusal to do so may' (1982b, p. 132).

When I think back to myself as an undergraduate, when psychology equalled rats and pigeons, I am convinced that it is vital to open up the debate about feminism and psychology to those in a similar position. If more women undergraduates were involved in the discussions they might see a future in psychology, rather than opting for other professions, as many do at present (Ball and Bourner, 1984). Psychology can add to a feminist analysis in research and offer individual women in distress an alternative to the medical model. We can provide alternatives to hypothetico-deductive models, which are more meaningful for women, and perhaps see psychology as something that can add to a feminist perspective, rather than be at odds with it. In *not* throwing the baby out with the bathwater we can integrate a psychological perspective into feminist analyses as well as having a direct effect on the future of psychology in Britain as we become accepted as 'real' psychologists.

References

Ball, B. and Bourner, T. (1984) The employment of psychology graduates. *Bulletin of the British Psychological Society* 37, 39–40.

Bernard, J. (1973) My four revolutions: An autobiographical history of the ASA. *American Journal of Sociology* 78 (4), 773–91.

Chesler, P. (1972) *Women and Madness*. New York: Avon Books.

Crane, D. (1972) *Invisible Colleges: Diffusion of Knowledge in Scientific Communities*. Chicago: University of Chicago Press.

Delaney, J., Lupton, M. and Toth, E. (1976) *The Curse: A Cultural History of Menstruation*. New York: E.P. Dutton.

Furnham, A. (1989) Quantifying quality: an argument in favour of citation counts. *BPS Social Psychology Section Newsletter* 21, 24–8.

Hollway, W. (1984) Gender difference and the production of subjectivity. In J. Henriques, W. Hollway, C. Urwin, C. Venn and V. Walkerdine (eds), *Changing the Subject*. London: Methuen.

Hunt, H. (1986) Women's private distress – a public health issue. *Medicine in Society* 12, 2.

Kitzinger, C. (1987) *The Social Construction of Lesbianism*, London: Sage.

Koeske, R. (1988) Theoretical perspectives on menstrual cycle research: the relevance of attributional approaches for the perception and explanation of premenstrual emotionality. In A. Dan, E. Graham and C. Beecher (eds), *The Menstrual Cycle*. Vol.1. New York: Springer.

Laws, S, (1985) Who needs PMT? A feminist approach to the politics of premenstrual tension. In S. Laws, V. Hey, and A. Eagen (eds), *Seeing Red: The Politics of Premenstrual Tension*. London: Hutchinson.

Penfold, S. and Walker, G. (1984) *Women and the Psychiatric Paradox*. Milton Keynes: Open University Press.

Robinson, P. (1989) A la recherche. *BPS Social Psychology Section Newsletter* 21, 22–3.

Sayers, J. (1982) *Biological Politics: Feminist and Anti-feminist Perspectives*. London: Tavistock.

Squire, C. (1989) *Significant Differences: Feminism and Psychology*. London: Routledge.

Szasz, T. (1973) *Ideology and Insanity*. London: Calder and Boyars.

Unger, R. (1982a) Advocacy versus scholarship revisited: issues in the psychology of women. *Psychology of Women Quarterly* 7 (1), 5–17.

Unger, R. (1982b) The future of the psychology of women: separation, integration, elimination? Paper presented at the American Psychological Association, annual meeting, Washington DC.

Ussher, J. (1989) *The Psychology of the Female Body*. London: Routledge.

Wilkinson, S. (ed.) (1986) *Feminist Social Psychology*. Milton Keynes: Open University Press.

Wilkinson, S. (1987) Reflexivity: a central concept for feminist psychology. Paper presented at the Women in Psychology conference, Brunel University, July 1987.

Wolpe, J. (1978) *The Practice of Behavior Therapy*. New York: Pergamon Press.

4

Making a difference – questioning women's studies

Meg Coulson and Kum-Kum Bhavnani

As the 1980s grind to a close, and we look to the onset of the 1990s, there seems to be little of the political hope and collective confidence with which the struggles and debates of feminism were reopened some twenty years ago. Yet over the past two decades, women's struggles, feminist struggles and feminist analyses have become an identifiable social force in many parts of the world. But when we try to analyse the present situation of women overall, we are confronted with some glaring contradictions.

On the one hand, a greater public visibility for feminist issues can be observed, as well as a more visible participation of (some?) women in public – economic and political – life. At the same time, it is clear from the evidence, worldwide, that more women are working harder and getting poorer. This overall context reflects shifts in the structures of exploitation and oppression with a sharpening of inequalities within and between nation states, within and between North and South; and, as flexibility becomes the key to the labour market internationally, so great inequalities are generated among women (Mitter, 1986).

It seems important to us as two feminists – one black and one white, both of us taking the label of 'feminist', although not unreservedly – who are trained/working in psychology and sociology that we should try to make sense of this overall context and our place in it. In this piece, we want to examine the contradictions which have developed as women's studies courses have entered formal educational settings, and we want to consider the view that this entry has sometimes been marked by an exiting of feminism. As Currie and Kazi (1987) have asked: 'Is academic feminism the graveyard of radical ideas?' We share with other women writers the view that women's studies is going to be a contradictory project, and that this can be seen among many of the disciplines of the human sciences. We have chosen to look at women's studies in this book, which focuses on psychology, for we are aware that feminist psychologists are increasingly involved in the setting up and teaching of women's studies and that this is often linked to challenges to the epistemological and political bases of psychology.

One of the difficulties in trying to challenge the traditional bases of psychology involves overcoming the notion that psychology is the least progressive of the human sciences. While women's studies can be seen by feminist psychologists as an escape route from the confines of traditional psychology, there are dangers of leaping uncritically into the subject. Although the more radical image of sociology is rarely sustained in practice, and in these 'new times' more rarely defended, there has been some room in sociology for feminists to make their voices heard. We hope therefore that our arguments are strengthened by drawing on our different backgrounds.

The first question we raised when planning our contribution was 'What has happened, and is continuing to happen, to feminism?' Such an opening question may seem far from the central concerns of psychology, but we choose it as a way into a consideration of the wider political context against which we hope to discuss some of the present political and professional problems and challenges facing feminists in psychology, feminists in women's studies. There are numerous ways of approaching our question about the current state of feminism. For example, we could consider this question in relation to the fact that areas of Asia such as India, Sri Lanka and Pakistan have all had women prime ministers who also defined themselves as anti-colonialist in one way or another, and discuss whether this is an appropriate starting point for such a question. Or we can look at the protests about the 'disappeared' in certain countries in South America. Or we can look at the struggles of black women and women of colour in North America who organized support for the campaign of Jesse Jackson in the 1988 US presidential elections, and ask, how do such campaigns relate to a feminist project? However, if we look at the United Kingdom, we could begin from remembering the lively, if at times emotionally demanding, Women's Liberation conferences which were held annually from the end of the sixties to the late seventies and which now seem to be events of feminist history. Their demise has left a gap. It indicates the lack of a general women's movement which could, and did, provide the arena within which the necessary discussions and debates about theory and politics could be generated.

We do not want to romanticize the experience of national Women's Liberation conferences, but while they still existed it was less possible to forget that women's studies developed from feminist, and therefore political, struggles. But what happens now? Where and how does feminist debate occur? How is practical experience evaluated? How are new ideas generated? The situation has become more fragmented and debates occur in this context. They are more often related to specific campaigns, specialist conferences, and, often developed through print as in pamphlets, Women's Movement publications (such as *Outwrite*,

Spare Rib, Trouble and Strife), feminist publishers/publishing. The setting-up of women's units in a range of organizations and institutions has created, during the 1980s, another base for activity. There are also specialized subject groupings located within academic production; of these the British Sociological Association (BSA) Women and Sociology caucus has been established for many years, as have the groups of women associated with journals such as *History Workshop* and *Feminist Review*. The development of the Psychology of Women Section of the British Psychological Society (BPS) has been in line with these trends in the other social sciences, although more recent. That it is more recent suggests that the struggles to set up such a section and to have it recognized by the BPS is reflective of how psychology in Britain has been slow to acknowledge women's particular contributions.

Our concern is to explore some of the current problems which feminists, involved in higher education and in the development of women's studies, face in this situation of fragmented feminism and in relation to the wider social and political contradictions already noted. We see the issues raised here as part of a prolonged and multi-faceted struggle about the nature of education, of knowledge, of social relationships. This struggle has to be multi-faceted in the face of the complexity of the social relationships of the institutions of education. They are structured and constrained by prevailing economic and class interests, by neo-colonialist and racist assumptions and practices as well as by patriarchal traditions, all of which combine to prop up that tendency to reproduce social inequalities of, for example, gender, 'race', and class. It is our argument that as feminists we want to resist, undermine and ultimately transform these tendencies. Within this framework the development of women's studies in psychology and the concerns of feminist psychologists can be seen as a kind of microcosm of the political issues for women in education as well as for women's studies more generally. It seems important that we should try to identify the feminist problems (and possible solutions) around women's studies and more traditionally defined disciplines such as psychology so that we can have more understanding of where present problems, practices and struggles may lead us in the future.

Dilemmas

The lack of a coherent general political forum for the generation of debate has also meant the dilemmas associated with developments of women's studies need to be continually renamed. The most acute of these dilemmas relate to accountability, accessibility and political direction. Take accountability – for example in relation to feminist theoretical journals. If the accountability within such journals is to the academic community, it can operate to reproduce elitism and notions of expertise, 'better' consciousness and the notion of professional feminists. On the other hand, how else do we make inroads into the conventionally established disciplines? The challenge is how to sustain the connection to political struggles and the radicalism of such projects against the possibly corrosive influence of established academic standards, interests and competitive argument.

This links to the dilemma of accessibility. The lack of a Women's Movement within which debate can be presented can mean that such debates, especially if located within academic discussions, can become too abstract and thus prove incomprehensible to all except those who initiated the debate. The difficulty with this is twofold. First, this may mean that some of the women about/for whom the debate exists may not be able to participate in it. Second, a central premise of feminist analyses, derived from some of the struggles of black writers and debates (Farnham, 1987), is that theory is intimately connected to politics. By this account, theory must, itself, develop and take its lead from grounded/concrete/specific experiences. Abstract discussion may generate further abstractions and become divorced from specific historical material instances, so not only placing itself outside the feminist canon but also, if defended, locating itself within a vanguardist approach to politics – an approach we reject. But it *is* a dilemma. Sometimes, the complexity of the issues to be addressed is unavoidably reflected in a language whose terms are not accessible to everyone. Such issues have to be dealt with in ways which ensure that intellectual production is always just that; so that the productions of ideas and arguments is seen as part of an overall political project, and not only as a means of entering certain career structures or competing successfully among certain academic elites.

Accountability and accessibility can be seen as part of the problem of political direction. Given the protracted nature of the struggles to set up and sustain women's studies within formal academic settings, and the unavoidable compromises with malestream institutional practices, how do we assess what we achieve in relation to any notion of a feminist political project? The question appears to centre around a dilemma which has been present for a long time within many progressive struggles: 'Is the main aim to join the "academy", or to change it?' Although there is no consensus among feminists (or others) involved in women's studies in higher and further education, we need to clarify differences of political emphases and objectives.

As with equal opportunities policies, there is a vital political distinction between projects which enable previously underrepresented groups (black women and men, black and white women) to enter the institution and progress on equal terms with white men and transform the institution in that way, and projects which enable 'new' disciplines (such as women's studies) to enter the curriculum, and so transform the curriculum. Though this distinction is crucial in informing practices, we are clear that it is also necessary to liaise between such projects. For example, in the setting up of women's studies, is our interest to add women to courses and the subjects of study, or to increase the career prospects of women? How is it possible to change the kinds of social relations associated with intellectual work and transform what is understood as knowledge? And how far can women's studies contribute to such a process? How can education help in the realization of visions and the promotion of equality and social justice – how can it be harnessed to service political and social change?

We think that it is unfortunately not possible to assume a transition between joining and changing (academic) institutions unless the latter is persistently addressed. Fundamental to this is the further question: whose interests (which women? which men? which institutions?) are being addressed by, through, in women's studies? And who, within academic production will ask this question? These political dilemmas are not new nor are they unique to intellectual work. In part, they are the dilemmas of work within established institutions and the structures of white bourgeois patriarchal power. Our argument here is that as feminists we can never afford to forget these most awkward political questions, even if they are not being asked directly of us. The institution will not ask such questions of us – and, in fact, it blocks such questions being asked. In the absence of a coherent political forum we must devise some means of keeping these issues to the fore – a feminist ethics.

We are therefore suggesting that the lack of a Women's Movement within which debates can be generated and presented means that there is a gap which is not adequately filled by journals, nor by discussions only within higher education. This gap means that the dilemmas of accountability, political direction and accessibility assume a particular type of significance. Further, the difficulty of political/theoretical debates not being grounded can also mean that issues of accountability, political direction and accessibility are sometimes not seen, or are dismissed by the use of conventional academic, as distinct from feminist, arguments.

Women's studies in two senses

Besides exploring such double-edged problems, it may also be useful to think of women's studies in two ways. First, women's studies can be understood as women studying, women as students, women in education. In this sense it is placed in the context of the development of women's education both within and outside the formal schooling and academic systems. Some significant initiatives have taken place in recent years in the development of courses for women which, under the impact of feminism, go beyond the traditions of women's education in conventionally feminine subjects and skills. We include here the various kinds of courses offering women 'new opportunities' of access back into academic education or into employment, of access into conventionally masculine areas of expertise and skill such as technology, physics, science (projects like Women into Science and Engineering) and manual trades. There are also courses for women in, for example, creative writing, and courses mainly about white women in society/history/science/psychology. There are, too, courses about women and disability, lesbian writing and history, courses on women in therapy and so on. Some of these courses do try not to be exclusive, and include black women in their conceptualization – but still too few do so. There are also Access courses which attempt to encourage black people – both women and men – to enter institutions of higher education. We would argue that such courses do have to be seen as part of some project of feminism and, therefore, women's studies. This is because such courses not only facilitate, at times, the entry of some black people into higher education, but also because both black and white feminists will sometimes work on setting up and teaching these courses. And then, of course, black women will have a much greater presence in the institution.

This first sense of women's studies/women studying includes courses which have been organized by both state and non-state organizations; and many of the initiatives have come from outside higher education, from community-based groups including black groups of women and men, black women's groups, black and white feminist groups, the Workers' Educational Assocation, community and further education units and sections and so on. The often 'outsider' ('marginal') status of many of these initiatives, combined with the direct involvement of feminists in some of them, has meant that, in varying degrees, they have been able to break out of some of the conventions and constraints of the racially structured malestream education and academia. For this reason, we would argue, such developments are a central reference point for 'academic' women's studies while, of course, often being a route on to such women's studies courses. In this way, they are also a source of organic links between studying for degrees and an overall political project, part of whose aim is to empower women.

But women's studies can also be understood in the sense of the development of analysis of the world through women's eyes, in the growth of feminist intellectual work and the development of feminist theory. These developments claim a recognition within academic settings not simply on the basis that women's academic contributions are of the same weight as those of men, but on the notion that women's work in some areas has contributed, and is continuing to contribute, to a transformation of what is defined as knowledge. However, there continues to be a strongly Eurocentric bias in much 'western' feminist work, indicating a serious limitation to the transformation that so far has been achieved. In other words, women need to be discussed as a disaggregated category; this is not a point we will develop in this chapter but we want to draw attention to it. For example, there have been challenges by black and white feminists and feminists of colour about the exclusionary, if not racist, nature of some of the current feminist analyses and practices (Bhavnani and Coulson, 1986; Carby, 1982; Davis, 1981; Mohanty, 1988; Moraga and Anzaldua, 1981; Richardson, 1987). Such discussions have forced some white feminists as well as other progressives, within higher education, to take on challenges about the uneven and exclusionary nature of such feminist approaches.

Women's studies, women's careers?

Feminism, through both indirect and direct influence on women and on institutions, has had some (limited?) impact on academic career structures. The growth in women's scholarly work, the establishment of women's studies, the adoption of equal opportunities policies as well as higher and more diverse aspirations among some women, all these are among the trends contributing towards a situation where some women, almost always white, may gain a foot- (or do we mean toe-?) hold in the career positions most often held by white men. There are for example, women professors of psychology, sociology, social policy; women who hold positions as deans and as members of directorates in higher education. Yet these achievements are fraught with contradictions both for the successful women in such positions and for other feminists, potentially providing symbols of feminist victory or betrayal, a minefield for misunderstandings and lost illusions. Politically, it is useful to recognize that the career system is divisive and individualistic. At the same time, this system is also indicative of what is valued, of who, and what work, counts institutionally.

In the latter sense the movement of women into career and management positions can be seen as validation for women. In a discipline like psychology where the student majority is female while the majority of teachers and 'authorities' are male, such a transparently patriarchal arrangement must be challenged by endeavours to increase the representation and opportunities for women as teachers and in positions of power.

But while entry into career and management structures will carry with it material and status advantages at a personal level, as well as bringing entry into more powerful and privileged groups, it may be accompanied by pressures to adopt more careful, cautious, 'appropriate' perspectives and priorities. In the present political framework of enterprise culture and market forces such pressures can push towards the side of the so-called 'new times' and 'new realism'. Moreover, while it is mainly white women who rise into such positions, this apparent challenge to patriarchally organized institutions may actually replicate neo-colonialist political and economic relationships in which white people hold power over black women and men. We have each had to deal with these issues – working in and being judged by institutions which uphold masculinist, racialized, elitist and individualistically competitive values: all of which are antipathetic to our understanding of feminism. And it is in this context that collective work for change has to struggle endlessly against such odds.

In identifying these problems and contradictions, we want to emphasize that we are not simply being critical in a negative sense, but are suggesting that the very process of acknowledging the problems is a prerequisite of understanding and of disrupting the damaging effects. The question, 'What part does entry into management structures play in the feminist political project?' is important to discuss, leading to a consideration of, for example, how entry into the position of 'honorary-white-male' can be avoided and how feminist principles can be both protected and promoted. To carry this forward more positively, women's studies could be grounded in a more explicit awareness of the struggles and diversity in women's lives. The logic of this is that as we try to develop women's studies with this focus, such courses will have integral to them a sense of a system of accountability which goes outwards. The insistence on reference points outside institutions of higher education may also provide a means of sustaining the politics of women's studies.[1]

Women's studies – making a difference

When we were students (one of us more than three, the other less than two decades ago) there was barely a trace of feminist thought to disturb the curriculum offered to either of us. To the extent that women's studies has been set up and that feminist inroads into psychology and other disciplines and courses have been achieved, we can argue that women and feminist work have insinuated themselves/ourselves into the curriculum. Joining a women's studies course within or outside a formal educational setting has become one way of gaining access to a body of feminist ideas. Yet the very existence of these courses can obscure the feminist struggles through which such courses were created and on which they continue to depend (both for their inspiration and for their continuation). How is this history of struggle to be retained? Whose responsibility is it to ensure its visibility?

We have discussed two senses of women's studies. First, in the sense of women as students, women in education and, second, as promoting a woman-based world view. But we have also pointed to the relationship between them. For example, the organic links which may be forged by some women entering higher education, and the existence of women's studies courses are intimately related through the ways in which the teaching and assessment are organized. This may involve struggles with the academic establishment for the recognition of collective work both by students and teachers, and for greater diversity and choice in modes of assessment. Women's studies are often under-resourced, which can mean that students struggle financially to remain on such courses, and the teachers juggle already seemingly impossible workloads and teaching responsibilities in order to teach on such courses. While it is necessary to recognize that teachers have more power than students, and some teachers have more power than others, the teachers themselves may be under pressure and politically isolated. However, there will also be different combinations of class background, sexuality, 'race' and disability which may produce differing political priorities and which may also cut through the basic staff/student division.

In this chapter we have considered political challenges and dilemmas currently facing feminists teaching in higher education. We have discussed these issues in general terms in order to demonstrate their widespread and pervasive character. However, these issues seem to us to be particularly relevant to the present position of feminists in psychology. Psychology, a female-dominated (in terms of student numbers) discipline, has been less receptive to feminist initiatives than some other social sciences. As other chapters in this volume suggest, this may have something to do with its aspiration to be a science, and the meanings that 'science' is held to entail. But the situation is currently undergoing change, whereby some limited opportunities are opening up for women and for feminists. The concerns of this chapter have been to contextualize this development and to demonstrate how the possibilities of challenge or subversion – or co-optation, collusion and deradicalization, that follow from this change in structural

osition, call for a politicized understanding of what is involved in the
evelopment of women's studies.

We have suggested that as some women who define themselves as
eminists become promoted, so this promotion may itself be at the
xpense of other women, including, for example, black women. This
ffect of 'divide and rule' can be partly countered both within the
lassroom and within the broader life of educational institutions by
leveloping critical strategies. In this way, more women can then join in
reating a collective awareness of such processes and their potentially
liscriminatory consequences. As Corinne Squire's chapter in the next
ection of this book shows, women's studies is an increasingly
attractive option for feminist psychologists, although we have argued
ere that it has mixed effects, carrying with it the pitfalls of erosion of
adicalism, or else reproducing some of the inequalities that structure
igher education. We want to raise these questions now, when
eminists are beginning to make some impact in psychology, when
here is some movement away from being marginal to becoming
recognized within the academic and bureaucratic structures of
psychology.

Jan Burns documents in chapter 9 how questions such as 'inside vs
outside' have characterized the debates of feminists in other disciplines
or in professional organizations outside Britain for some time. In this
context (and in the same chapter), Sue Wilkinson emphasizes the
importance of consultation with, and accountability to, feminist
psychologists who position themselves outside the psychological
establishment. We have attempted, in this chapter, to broaden this
perspective and to identify some of the processes of fragmentation and
isolation of feminist academics, to comment on how they have
occurred and to argue for a wider accountability of feminist academics.
Such an accountability is not simply to the circle of feminists within a
particular discipline or interest grouping but to the wider national and
international feminist community. Such an overarching frame of
reference brings us face-to-face with the differences among women.
Thus, knowing these differences, and situating them within a framework for change, becomes part of the content and methodology of
women's studies.

We have argued that the future of feminism politically, and of
women's studies as an area of feminist activity, depends on recognizing,
analysing and confronting practices in relation to difference among
women. This can be done in a variety of ways which both interrogate
and extend central themes of women's studies. This would include
both welcoming the process of re-evaluating past heroines so as to
learn from the full complexity (and contradictions) of their lives and a
readiness to abandon the notion of an established feminist orthodoxy.

A significant factor in the current economic and political climate seem
to be that some women have opportunities opened up to them in a wa
which may not have been envisaged previously; and we are suggestin;
that this calls for the development of more reflexive discussions an(
approaches. As part of a feminist political project women's studies lay
claim to being different, to analysing difference, to making a difference
It is crucial to hold on to this radical vision, recognizing that th(
question of how 'we can lift as we climb' (Davis, 1988) has to be centra
for all feminists as we enter the last decade of the twentieth century.

Notes

Although our names are not given in alphabetical order at the head of this chapter, ther(
is no junior author. As our last article was published as Bhavnani and Coulson, w(
wanted to write this as Coulson and Bhavnani.

1   What does 'good feminist practice' look like in this context? The following list ma?
     provide a starting point for thinking about this:
     not cutting off from a broad base of awareness of women's struggles
     feeling/acting accountable
     being honest
     accepting challenges
     establishing a reference group
     not defending the indefensible
     always acknowledging the problems/the contradictions/the inequalities
     not losing sight of the possibilities . . .

References

Bhavnani, K.K. and Coulson, M. (1986) Transforming socialist feminism: the challenge
     of racism. *Feminist Review* 23, Summer.
Carby, H. (1982) White women listen! Black feminism and the boundaries of sisterhood.
     The Empire Strikes Back. Centre for Contemporary Cultural Studies, London:
     Hutchinson.
Currie, D. and Kazi, H. (1987) Academic feminism and the process of de-radicalization:
     Re-examining the issues. *Feminist Review* 25, Spring.
Davis, A. (1981) *Women, Race and Class*. London: The Women's Press.
Davis, A. (1988) Radical perspectives on the empowerment of Afro-American women:
     lessons for the 1980s. *Harvard Educational Review* 58 (3), August, 348–53.
Farnham, C. (1987) (ed.) *The Impact of Feminist Research in the Academy*. Bloomington:
     Indiana University Press.
Mitter, S. (1986) *Common Fate, Common Bond*. London: Pluto.
Mohanty, C.T. (1988) Under western eyes: feminist scholarship and colonial discourses.
     Feminist Review 30, Autumn.
Moraga, C. and Anzaldua, G. (eds) (1981) *The Bridge Called My Back*. Watertown,
     Mass: Persephone Press.
Richardson, M. (ed.) (1987) *Maria Stewart, America's First Black Woman Political
     Writer: Essays and Speeches*. Bloomington: Indiana University Press.

PART TWO

CHANGING DEFINITIONS OF PSYCHOLOGICAL KNOWLEDGE

The contributions in this part of the book show how feminist practice transforms conventional definitions of psychology in terms of what that knowledge is, its concepts and methods, and the changed relationships this involves.

Corinne Squire contrasts the expanding (feminist) market for psychological treatments of women's lives with the developing critique emerging from feminist psychologists of the very concepts those 'popular' accounts deploy. Taking up the oppositional character of feminist teaching alluded to in previous chapters, she explores how her feminist approach to teaching psychology generates and coexists with other critical approaches. A feminist commitment tends to dissolve psychology as a field of study, incorporating perspectives and criteria from outside the realm of what is traditionally defined as the 'psychological', and advances alternative methodologies and explanations. She highlights the contradictions faced by feminist teachers positioned simultaneously as both experts and critics within 'the system' (be it psychology or the Women's Movement). She argues for the need to theorize clearly the relation between teacher and student in terms of what each party can contribute to the 'psychology education' learning experience. By this means the teacher will be better positioned to empower the students through psychology, develop their feminist critique of psychology and will also be enabled herself to be open to the perspectives of her students, perspectives which are less constrained by institutional ties. The sense in which a course is 'antipsychological' depends on both the prior understanding of psychology and the experiences the students bring to the course. This does not happen in uniform ways. Commenting on her own teaching experience, Corinne Squire suggests that while for some women a feminist re-reading of psychology takes the form of validating and extending the domain of their experiences as women, for others it gives rise to a general critique of psychology. The way is opened up then for 'psychology education' to become a general tool of feminist enquiry as well as promoting a feminist re-working and re-evaluation of the psychology.

Ann Phoenix takes up this interrogation of both feminist and psychological practices through an account of work on early motherhood. She draws attention to the importance of processes involved not only in 'data collection', but also the procedures of support and accountability set up within a research team. Here the issues include not only who does the research and how it is conducted, but also who controls what happens to the material and what questions are investigated. All too often women researchers are employed on projects to carry out interviews whose rationale they have played no part in developing. The status of the 'conversations' that research with women by women has come to assume is shown to be problematic for both parties, as structural power relations are brought into research relationships through the inevitable roles it sets up as well as those of 'race', class, age and gender inequalities. There is thus a double challenge for feminists in psychology; just as the different positions of black and white women give rise to different feminisms, so feminist methodologies can also be diverse. In terms of practice, this account from 'social research' asserts the need to reclaim 'psychology' as a legitimate domain for feminist activity and enquiry by highlighting how there are still, albeit constrained, spaces within which progressive work can be carried out.

In the next contribution, Maye Taylor draws on her experience as a therapist to outline how feminist clinicians can use, challenge and change traditional psychotherapy. The feminist project to empower the woman 'client' rejects the standard intrapsychic interpretation of the problems brought to therapy, but takes these as a real reflection of her experience of oppression and subordination. According reality to a woman's fears carries particular theoretical significance in reinterpreting traditional accounts of incest, sexual assault and 'symptoms of paranoia'. Maye Taylor goes on to analyse how gender-typical roles give rise to the depression, despair and low self-esteem that characterize women's mental distress. She outlines the specific opportunities and advantages that a woman to woman service can provide. In particular this involves acknowledging and harnessing, rather than avoiding as in traditional practice, the power of both transference and countertransference relations, using the common identification and experiences of both woman therapist and woman client to build a therapeutic alliance which can secure the woman's sense of her own separateness, autonomy and self-worth.

So far the feminist psychologist is depicted as occupying a precarious position, sifting through and appropriating features of research and teaching that validate or explore women's experience, or seeking less hostile environments in which to do women-friendly work. The problem with this last position is that it leaves the definition and boundary of psychology intact. Celia Kitzinger highlights how the current project of feminist psychology is inherently contradictory: while feminism is committed to political activity and change, psychology is rooted in the scientific discourse of objectivity and detachment. She illustrates the challenge of feminism through reviewers' responses to papers she has submitted for publication and feedback from job applications, where politics is ruled out of the psychological arena. She extends the feminist challenge to psychology beyond the question of methodology – indeed she indicates how the 'hard/soft' polarization of quantitative and qualitative maps uneasily on to the psychiatric and sociological research on lesbians and gay men. Here we see that 'soft' research is not necessarily progressive, and if uncritically adopted as the criterion of feminist research may also serve to essentialize gender stereotypes.

What emerges is that the dangers for feminist psychology are twofold. On the one hand the expanding feminist audience for psychology incorporates notions of ego strengthening and identity formation as strategies towards the empowerment of women without questioning the political adequacy of their theoretical basis – and in particular the underlying heterosexism of this failure to critique psychology. On the other hand, as feminist psychologists we have to ask what it means to expunge politics from our organizations and theories, and what the significance is of the absence of writing by feminist psychologists in feminist journals. Overall Celia Kitzinger points out the limitations of posing the dilemmas facing feminist psychologists solely in the individualistic terms of personal ethical choices, arguing instead that we need to take a wider perspective on the definition and effects of psychology in order to be vigilant about what our involvement in psychology is doing to our feminism. As she concludes, we need to theorize clearly what our role is as feminist psychologists – we work as feminists within psychology, commenting upon its uses and effects on women, and use our involvement in psychology to demystify it for feminists and critique its depoliticizing effects.

5
Feminism as antipsychology: learning and teaching in feminist psychology

Corinne Squire

Feminist initiatives in psychology have met strong resistance from the traditional discipline. Feminists themselves have often neglected mainstream psychology, finding psychoanalysis's greater complexity and flexibility more helpful to them. As a result, feminism's influence in psychology is spread thin, its effects concentrated in specific areas like the psychology of achievement and moral reasoning, and in the specialist fields of the psychology of gender differences and of women. Nevertheless, feminist ideas are acquiring wider currency within psychological discourse, and feminist psychologists are increasingly recognizing the role their teaching can play in this expansion (Richardson, 1982; Russo, 1982; Walsh, 1988). This chapter discusses the importance for feminist psychologists of paying attention to teaching and learning practices. Then it explores a particular version of feminist psychology education, where psychology students and teachers extend feminist ideas into a kind of antipsychology. Such a development presents some problems. But it also has valuable implications for feminist psychology in general.

Why should feminist psychologists study psychology education?

Feminist perspectives on psychology are transmitted to their widest audience through popular books like *My Mother/Myself* (Friday, 1977), *Fat is a Feminist Issue* (Orbach, 1978), *The Cinderella Complex* (Dowling, 1981) and *Women who Love too Much* (Norwood, 1985). To conventional psychologists, such texts' commitments to feminism, their populism and their largely psychodynamic orientation, make their methods unreliable and their conclusions of limited validity. More significantly for feminist psychology, these very successful texts are all, despite their superficial variability, 'how to' books, with therapeutic or self-improvement aims. They all belong to an ego-psychoanalytically influenced feminist psychology, which, because it is concerned predominantly with personal change, skates over the social, economic, and political characteristics of gender relations, and neglects the irrational, fragmented and contradictory aspects of gendered subjectivities.

What about the mushrooming academic and applied psychological publications on gender differences, the psychology of women, and feminist psychology? Many feminist psychologists see these as the best indicators of feminist psychology's progress. But a relatively small group of psychology professionals reads the journals in which these papers are published. A much larger community comes into contact with psychology through a psychology course in a university, college, school, or adult education institute. Most courses do not require, and most students' circumstances do not permit, extensive reading of the primary literature where most feminist psychological work is to be found. Course textbooks' awareness of feminist issues, even in the areas of the psychology of women and of gender differences, is patchy, and seems likely to remain so. It is, then, through education practices in general, rather than just through reading and writing psychology books and papers, that feminist psychology education can currently reach the most people.

Courses in the psychology of gender differences and of women are obvious vehicles for feminist ideas, and they are increasing in number (Russo, 1982). But they are still uncommon in Britain, and they will in any case always make up only a small proportion of psychology courses. For feminist initiatives to have most effect, they need to address all areas of psychology education.

Traditional work on psychology education concentrates on improving the content and structure of courses, teaching methods, and student selection and assessment, all in an effort to raise student standards. Broader appraisals are rare. This is partly because teaching is seen as research's poor relation. But it is also because psychology education's clear connections with social and institutional factors tend to lead comprehensive accounts of it into radical criticisms of psychology as a whole. Many psychologists want to avoid such criticisms.

Some western feminist academics, too, view teaching as separate from and inferior to their 'own' work. But most, like radical psychologists, see an intimate connection between their academic or practical activities, and teaching and learning. They formulate this link either by picturing feminism as a body of knowledge which can be disseminated through education, or by equating the collective, experiential aspects of education with consciousness-raising in the western women's movement. But some feminists have a more complicated understanding of education. They recognize that feminist learning and teaching has to address not just obvious examples of women's oppression and self-derogation, but also subtler, unconscious expressions of dominant gender relations, and the social relations of, for instance, 'race,' sexuality and class, which are articulated with gender. These feminists see the perpetually renewed criticisms which students bring to 'established' feminist knowledge as encouraging the sensitive, wide-ranging approaches they need. Kaplan, for instance, says of feminist literary academics, that 'it is in and through their women students that they have to a great extent developed and expanded their critique of male-dominated culture' (1986, p. 65).

The complexity and breadth of feminist aims mean that feminist psychology should not be like any other field of psychology. It should criticize not just psychological objects, methods and theories, but also the institutional and wider social and political situation of psychology. This kind of eclectic analysis is particularly difficult in psychology; the discipline is so protective of its status that it resists criticism on any other than its own 'scientific' criteria. But the obvious involvement of psychology education, with extrapsychological as well as psychological factors, makes it a good place to try out such an approach.

This chapter, adopting an amended version of Fisher's (1982) list of the conflicts experienced by feminist academics, addresses not just the relationship between feminist psychology students and academics, and the discipline they are studying, but also the relationship between these students and academics; the relationship between both groups and the institutions in which they work; and the groups' relationships to the wider feminist movement, and to the social and political communities to which they belong.

The chapter is based on my discussions of feminist ideas about psychology with students from a wide range of educational, employment and social backgrounds, in a variety of contexts, from evening classes to postgraduate seminars; and from psychology degrees, to one-off short psychology courses on the one hand, and social science degrees and professional social work and nursing training courses on the other. The chapter concentrates on situations where gender has been explicitly at issue, and on women students' arguments, since it is in these circumstances that debate about feminist psychology becomes most intense. The chapter draws on my reading of papers on this subject, but also on taped and written records of students' and my discussions; on student presentations and essays; on my lecture notes; on course reviews; and on my own remembrance of events. There are many layers of selection involved in my representation of this material. The frame of the selection is an interest in the place that subjectivity, and psychological work on subjectivity, have in feminist theories. But the chapter is bound to contradict this alleged standpoint in various ways, some of which I can guess at, some of which I can't.

What is feminist antipsychology?

Many feminist psychology academics recognize that their courses produce anger in their students, and they argue extensively about how to direct this feminist consciousness most effectively. At the same time, they acknowledge that feminist psychology has a number of often-conflicting strands, which students have to learn to deal with (Walsh, 1988). This chapter examines how the anger which both feminist students and teachers feel is manifested in the development of different sorts of feminist psychology within psychology education itself.

Students and teachers react in a variety of ways to the role which discourses of gender play in traditional psychology. Sometimes they deny or ignore it. Sometimes they concentrate on analysing the dominance of discourses of masculinity, and working out how this might be changed. At other times, they reject the mainstream discipline completely, and start trying to construct an alternative, woman-centred psychology. And occasionally, they proceed from a recognition of the gendering of psychology, through a discovery of how other social differences, like those of class, sexuality and 'race', affect psychology, to what I shall call antipsychology, an approach which grants all psychological data and theories a severely limited validity, or even rejects them completely. These approaches often overlap with each other, or coexist on the same page or in the same sentence. But they can still be distinguished from each other. The antipsychological approach is the one which I shall argue offers most to feminist psychology.

Antipsychology and psychology

Psychology students' and teachers' attitudes to feminism emerge most clearly in the orientation they develop towards the discipline itself. Some explore feminist corrections of conventional psychology's neglect of women subjects and female-associated subject matter, and try to build on them. But this tends to leave them too close to the mainstream discipline to question fundamental aspects of it, like its insistence on developing scientific procedures and theories. Other students and teachers decide to put traditional psychology to one side, and devote themselves instead to imagining and searching out a gynocentric psychology, which uses women subjects, and women-identified subject matter, methods and theories. This approach is more dynamic, and it is often more in touch with feminist arguments outside psychology. But its notion of a culturally or biologically fixed female subjectivity makes it ahistorical, liable to play down differences between women, and prone to use the category of 'personal (women's) experience' in an authoritarian way (Squire, 1989).

A third feminist approach, which some teachers and more students develop, is an antipsychological critique of the way in which psychology addresses, not just gender, but sexuality, 'race' and class differences. What does this feminist antipsychology look like? Lott, teaching a feminist-oriented psychology of women course, gives a teacher's perspective. She uses non-psychological as well as psychological material, 'including poetry, literature, the popular and the mass media' (Walsh, 1988, p. 888), and gets students to write journals and do social problem-solving exercises as well as orthodox psychological literature reviews and critiques. In this way, feminist psychology becomes literary and sociological, as well as psychological. Among students, examples from my own courses include one who, discussing the different moral voice which some feminist psychologists ascribe to women, endorsed Stack's (1986) description of this voice's social specificity, and constructed an account of the social determination of all 'morality'. Another student punctuated an essay on the psychology of gender and achievement with denunciations of the class-specific nature of these debates. A third student dismissed the American and Eurocentric focus on the self preserved in Gardiner's (1987) careful recuperation of ego psychology for feminism.

In such cases, psychological factors lose their primary place, or are elbowed out of the explanations completely. How, then, is antipsychology valuable for feminist *psychology*? First, it questions the universality and timelessness that psychology asserts for itself, by detailing the social and historical determinants of psychological knowledge. This is especially important for feminists, because gender has a history in psychology of being reduced to a concern with the numbers of biologically female and male psychologists and subjects. Second, antipsychology presents a strong and flexible critical repertoire, which feminist psychology needs if it is to challenge the powerful and self-protective mainstream discipline. A single-issue critique is relatively easy for this discipline to assimilate. A feminist psychology that manifests itself in a range of social critiques, differently weighted according to the type of psychology it is addressing, stands a better chance of occasional success.

The third advantage of the antipsychological approach is that, as psychology is especially jealous of its boundaries and almost impermeable to ideas outside them, a feminist antipsychology which seems to have more to do with anthropology or sociology, or even history, politics or literature, is a useful development. It throws doubt on psychology's claim to be the ultimate source of knowledge about the human subject, by refusing to respect its boundaries, and drawing on knowledge from other disciplines. Fourth, feminist psychology's attention to social and historical differences matches contemporary western feminism's interest in such differences, and makes it able to exchange ideas with feminist initiatives outside psychology.

Feminist antipsychology is never entirely separate from psychology. Since it is formulated in reaction to mainstream psychology's account of its object, the individual subject, it always retains a focus on that object. Even if it analyses the individual subject out of existence by defining it as a social artefact, it does not thereby answer all the questions about subjectivity with which western twentieth-century discourses are permeated. Psychological concepts tend to creep back into even the most antipsychological of students' and teachers' arguments, through generalizations about female and male subjectivity, and references to 'human nature', for instance. These inconsistencies occur in every feminist psychological initiative. All of them try to account for gendered subjectivity, yet have also to accept its existence in order to address it. Greater reflexivity and theoretical caution let such difficulties be handled more gracefully than feminist anti-psychology can manage. But this disadvantage is outweighed by the special efficacy of its criticisms.

Antipsychology, students and teachers

A feminist concern with psychology education must address the relation which affects the transmission of psychological knowledge most directly: that between students and teachers.

Particularly at the start of their work together, feminist psychology teachers and students often see their relationship as an uncomplicated handover from one to the other of scientifically legitimated knowledge. They picture this happening within a democratically modified version of the formal lecture method, which allows students to make approved interventions, from questions and comments, to seminar papers. This straightforward liberal view of education is frequently accompanied by a psychological view of the teacher as a role model, for women students especially. Psychology's own interest in personalized accounts strengthens the tendency.

Sometimes, feminist students and teachers recognize the hierarchical, male-identified nature of this approach to education, but think its assertion of feminist psychological expertise makes it worth adopting – combined, perhaps, with a more woman-centred approach to psychology itself (see Hyde in Walsh, 1988). Other feminist psycho-logists try to conceptualize their educational endeavours differently, as a female or female-identified oasis within the larger patriarchal pedagogy, where power relations between students and teachers are dissolved, and each learns from and empowers the other. These feminist psychologists aim for knowledge which they, rather than mainstream psychology, judge to be significant. They try to work collaboratively, starting from their own experiences. Humanist psychological views of the progressive nature of student-centred education, and feminist trust in collective, experiential consciousness-raising, converge here into an equation of biological or cultural femaleness, with feminist and all radical education. In this scenario, every woman can be a role model. But in education and in feminism, experience, however deeply felt, can be as deceptive as theory. The collective imparting and getting of knowledge, however mutual it seems, is still structured by institutional and social differences between members of the group. Many feminist teachers of the psychology of women, for example, encourage students to investigate data for themselves and use their own experiences (Walsh, 1988). But they rarely participate in this process to an equal degree. Even if I talk in class about traumatic events in my childhood, my position makes me less vulnerable than students are when they do the same. If I disclose more, this only perpetuates the idea that a teacher can say more, and more significant things, than students. Woman-centred students and teachers play down such differences, in favour of a psychological account of their relationship.

The third antipsychological approach which feminist psychology students and teachers take, characterizes psychology teaching as an expression of gender and other social power relations, which imposes, rather than imparts, knowledge. Psychology teaching is a form of training, implicitly drilling students until they can understand and produce socially acceptable accounts of subjectivity. This approach defines the teachers as agents of social control, and their students as subjects of it. Given such an analysis, feminist students and teachers can only hope to gain some personal pleasure from psychology education, or to use it pragmatically, as a step towards educational, employment, or other goals. At best, they can put together a meta-psychological analysis of the discourses of psychology learning and teaching, of why certain things are taught and certain methods used. Many students develop comprehensive critiques of the sexuality-, class-, 'race'- and gender-marked nature of the series of influential investigations which a psychology course typically presents. Some students also demand that this series should not just be criticized, but should be abandoned for a course teaching the 'psychology' that is outside the mainstream, often not written down or even investigated. Where, they demand, is the psychology of black, white homosexual, and white, heterosexual, working-class subjects', especially female subjects', friendships and loves, but in certain kinds of sociological work, and in fiction? Where is the psychology of the majority non-nuclear family childcare experience, for example of grandmothers and grandchildren, except in their own accounts?

Such 'psychology' education might seem more like sociology or literature education, or just telling stories. But its continued interest in the individual subject preserves its psychological orientation. This is true even in the most socially directed field of psychology, social psychology. Teachers who persistently trash the social myopia of paradigmatic social psychology experiments often go on working with strong popular, rather than academic, ideas of psychology education, arguing that they should be teaching about 'relationships' rather than 'experiments', for instance. Students who consistently demand from me and each other information about socially relevant, non-psychological approaches to social psychological topics may still, when a new issue arises, want first to know from me what mainstream psychology says about it. I still try to tell them, and they still go quiet to listen.

Power never exists in the abstract, only in power *relations*. Psychology teachers have more power than their students, but the students have some, too. Antipsychological feminist students' satirical depiction of me as the person who is 'supposed to know' about psychology, expresses this unequal yet two-way relationship. Their rejection of mainstream psychology education for other discourses of the subject, and their assertion of equally problematic commonsense notions of psychological knowledge, converge in their rhetorical demands that I teach them psychologies which they also assert do not yet exist. All this generates the kind of bold, yet contradictory, unstable commentary on the nature of psychology learning and teaching, which an evolving feminist psychology needs.

Antipsychology and the institution

Psychology education is situated within educational and psychological institutions, which are licensed by, respectively, government and other public bodies, and psychological associations. In the largest non-professional field of psychology education, the input of psychological associations is achieved largely through their members' participation in educational institutions, and so it is the power of these institutions with which feminist psychology has to deal most directly.

Students' and teachers' first reactions to their discovery of the gendered structure of psychology is often to try to work within the discipline, subverting it from inside. Within psychology departments, for example, they attempt to include more material about women in courses; to make courses more accessible to women students; to enable these students to do better, especially at higher levels of psychology; and to get feminist-oriented work accepted as a serious part of psychology education. Other feminist psychologists take a justifiably pessimistic view of the chances of making major changes in mainstream psychology education, and set up their own educational institutions instead. In the short term, this might mean convening small 'women in psychology' discussion groups for students and teachers on a psychology degree. In the long term, separate structures can develop, such as women's therapy centres which run educational seminars and organize therapeutic training. Such initiatives retain more connections than they acknowledge with mainstream psychology education. The mainstream defines what they teach critically, or do not teach at all; and their own histories can be traced back to an initial training in it – in the case of women's therapy centres, for example, through an analytic lineage that returns ultimately to Freud.

When feminist students and teachers adopt an antipsychological approach, they are more able to deal with the ambiguous power which institutions of psychology education hold. They reject, along with psychology, all the educational structures through which it is transmitted: its admissions procedures, syllabuses, teaching methods and assessments. These, like the discipline itself, they see as impregnated with dominant discourses of gender, 'race', class and sexuality. Such a perspective is inconsistent with any participation in psychology education. Feminist antipsychologists get round this by pursuing limited aspects of psychology's institutional power, in a sceptical, self-critical way. Some students, for example, acknowledge the value of British Psychological Society-accredited exams enough to try to pass a required course, but decide at the same time to fulfil only the minimum course requirements, and to spend time instead on a topic that interests them, such as child abuse, reading psychological and non-psychological material, writing essays and autobiography, and talking intensively with friends. Such work, they know, the educational institution is unable and unwilling to assess.

Feminist antipsychologists also engage in more direct challenges to psychology's educational institutions. In a university psychology department, where the majority female student body is usually taught by a predominantly male staff, the hiring of female staff might be, for these and other feminist psychologists, a high priority. In a polytechnic social science department, where women are better represented among staff, gender issues are well recognized, and there is a high proportion of black students, feminist antipsychology among psychology students might centre on the lack of black faculty, and the Eurocentrism of the course structure, and be no less 'feminist' for this. In both cases, an antipsychological approach produces a continual awareness of the enormous gap between the educational institution's agreed equal opportunities policy, and that policy's full and voluntary implementation; of the low chances of making permanent or large changes to the institution; but also of the possibilities for resistance offered by the cracks in the institutional structure.

Antipsychology, feminist and other communities

Students and teachers who adopt an antipsychological perspective often spend time on projects that do not look like 'education' of any kind. This is where the distinctiveness of the approach comes into sharpest focus.

Feminist psychologists frequently act as psychologists first, importing feminist ideas into psychology and trying to work out how they apply there. This approach underestimates the complexity of feminist politics. Some students, and a few teachers, react to the conflicts it produces, by weakening their links with conventional psychology, and establishing stronger theoretical and practical affiliations with the Women's Movement. Hyde, for instance, wants the psychology of women to become important for her students through their discoveries, less of psychological bias, than of sexism in general; and she addresses their anger about these discoveries by discussing the achievements of the western Women's Movement since the 1960s (Walsh, 1988). Again, such a perspective tends to simplify gender politics, by omitting to ask which women the 'Movement' represents, and whether there is really only one movement.

Feminist psychologists who take an antipsychological line build a relationship not just with feminism, but with a number of forms of resistance. Their approach to psychology education draws on their understandings and experiences, not just of gender relations, but also of class, age and 'race' differences, of sexualities, of marriage, parenthood and education, and of political formations. Three examples should clarify this.

Williams (in Walsh, 1988) reports a shift in students' arguments about feminism, from a 1970s basis in gender, to a current grounding in fundamentalism or non-fundamentalism. By noting this shift, she also implicitly describes a modulation in the concepts of what 'feminism' and 'feminist psychology' are. This recognition of changes, beyond those brought about by feminism or psychology, is an important and unusual one for a feminist psychology teacher to make. Williams also uses clinical case material, in which the gendering of subjectivity is rarely consistent or unitary. She invites members of a variety of relevant organizations, not simply feminist ones, to take part in her psychology of women courses. And she encourages students to work not just outside the syllabus, but outside psychology: to 'build on their diverse backgrounds', and to attempt projects which include 'voluntary work or biographies based on oral histories' (Walsh, 1988, p. 890). This openness to non-psychological, non-academic, feminist and non-feminist communities operates, within a relatively traditional university environment, as a kind of antipsychology.

How do antipsychological feminist students address the world outside the educational institution? Imagine two groups, each containing twelve female students. In the first, the women, white, and aged between 30 and 50, are attending a non-examined university extramural course on psychology, held in the daytime at an adult education institute in a wealthy London suburb. The second group consists of seven black and five white students, aged between 21 and 45. This is a seminar group, studying psychology in the final year of a full-time social science degree at an inner London polytechnic.

Most students in the first group develop a conviction during the course that women's and men's intrinsically different subjectivities have a lot to do with gender relations. They picture women's subjectivity as nurturant, caring, pacifist and social. The group disagrees over whether it is biologically based, or so strongly culturally embedded that it is as good as biological. But some students – three, perhaps – start to question why they are studying psychology. They begin dismissing experimental evidence if it was obtained from college students; they carp at the undeclared class composition of many samples; one uses black American women's writing as her sole source for a paper on gender and 'identity'. In the other group, this state of affairs dominates, almost from the start. Students wave away feminist and other psychologists' preoccupations with scientificity, rail at the gender and other selectivities involved in more ethnographic psychological accounts, and demolish the male-identified and Euro-centric concept of the individual. But they retain interest in some sociological, political, and even philosophical approaches to psychological phenomena.

Why were the two groups different? Women in both groups came from predominantly working-class backgrounds. Most of the women in the first group looked after children and worked part-time, but none worked full-time. It would be too easy to attribute their relative partiality to psychological arguments to the time they spent in a domestic, 'psychological' environment. Many of them had extensive community interests, and the number who felt restricted by their lives was easily matched by the number in the second group who felt frustrated by their need to balance commitments to coursework, part-time work, children, ill or infirm relatives, and partners.

A number of differences remained. The black women, and to some extent the white women, in the second group, had an analysis of how 'race' and gender differences are articulated together, which they applied to feminist psychological arguments, and extended to take in class. The white women in the first group were much less likely to remind themselves of such differences. Discourses of 'race' and class were much less at issue in their largely white, high-income community. The local organizations and campaigns around, for instance, schools, hospitals, roads and libraries with which the women were involved, defined their problems as managerial, as much as political. By contrast, the women in the second group were engaged with a slew of clearly political local and national initiatives which put their housing, transport and daycare arrangements under threat, and aimed to cut and redirect their education. Perhaps it is not surprising that feminist psychology remained for the first group primarily a matter of personal, feminine experience, whereas the second group turned it into a critique of psychology as a whole, and an incipient politics of subjectivity.

I have implied in this chapter that feminist students and teachers of psychology are all feminist 'psychologists', but most of my examples of feminist antipsychology have come from students. This is because students seem to be better, though less powerful, antipsychologists than their teachers. Feminist psychology teachers have an insider relationship, either, like other psychologists, to psychology, or, sometimes, to 'the Women's Movement'. These allegiances weaken the demands they make of psychology and feminism, lessen the likelihood of their maintaining connections with communities outside them, and often put the forceful, persistent challenge of what I have called antipsychology beyond them. A final advantage of the antipsychological approach is that, unlike other perspectives, it makes it clear that feminist psychology teachers can learn a lot from their students, but that they will not do so until they try to work with more complex ideas about what a psychologist and a feminist is.

References

Dowling, C. (1981) *The Cinderella Complex*. New York: Summit.

Fisher, B. (1982) Professing feminism: feminist academics and the women's movement. *Psychology of Women Quarterly* 7, 55–69.

Friday, N. (1977) *My Mother/Myself*. New York: Delacorte.

Gardiner, J. (1987) Self psychology as feminist theory. *Signs* 12, 761–80.

Kaplan, C. (1986) *Sea Changes*. London: Verso.

Norwood, R. (1985) *Women Who Love Too Much*. Los Angeles: Tarcher.

Orbach, S. (1978) *Fat is a Feminist Issue*. London: Hamlyn.

Richardson, M. (1982) Sources of tension in teaching the psychology of women. *Psychology of Women Quarterly* 7, 45–54.

Russo, N. (1982) Psychology of women: analysis of the faculty and courses of an emerging field. *Psychology of Women Quarterly* 7, 18–31.

Squire, C. (1989) *Significant Differences*. London: Routledge.

Stack, C. (1986) The culture of gender: women and men of color. *Signs* 11, 321–4.

Walsh, M. (1988) Conference report: teaching and learning about the psychology of women. *Signs* 13, 886–91.

6

Social research in the context of feminist psychology

Ann Phoenix

Previous chapters have discussed the predominance of methods borrowed from the physical sciences in psychology, and the implications of this for feminist psychology. This chapter explores the intersection between psychology, feminist practice and policy-relevant research. It is suggested that in practice psychology, like feminism, is not unitary but represents a variety of viewpoints, methods and areas of study. Broad definitions, like those presented in introductory texts and dictionaries of psychology (for example, Taylor et al., 1982; Reber, 1985), therefore need to be taken into account in such a way that a variety of methods flourish within psychology. It is argued that method should not be seen as the defining feature of psychology and that research conducted by feminists has much to contribute to the discipline of psychology. The chapter makes particular reference to a study of motherhood in 16 to 19-year-olds.

Feminist research

There is no unitary 'feminist methodology' to which all feminists have to subscribe (Griffin, 1989). Feminists are themselves diverse, and have varied perspectives on feminism. This diversity affects the research they choose to do, and the methods they use. Nonetheless it is possible to pick out broad themes that feminist researchers are likely to agree with. Wilkinson (1986, p. 2) suggests that in feminist research 'A female perspective is to be regarded as central to the research, not as an additional or comparative viewpoint' and that feminist research entails a critical evaluation of the research process itself.

It follows from these themes that a feminist practice of psychology is likely to be different from a non-feminist one. It requires researchers, for example, to establish that research problems have not been constructed from androcentric viewpoints. Taking a female perspective seriously requires finding out what women's views are rather than inferring them from observation and experiment. As a result it may be necessary to interview women.

The necessity of using methodological tools (such as interviewing) which are considered low status in psychology, and of creating tools if traditional ones prove unsuitable, is in itself likely to lead feminists to evaluate critically research processes and to focus on the power relations that affect the lives of the subjects of their research (Griffin, 1988; Stanley, 1988). Thus, while 'feminism is a politics . . . directed at changing existing power relations between women and men in society' (Weedon, 1987, p. 1) feminist research is rigorous rather than polemical.

Feminist perspectives are not, however, the only ones which encourage critical evaluations of the assumptions underpinning research and a focus on power differentials in society. The critical analyses produced by black women and black men (many of which incorporate analyses of social class) point out that black people are generally in relatively less powerful positions than white people, and are either ignored or assumed in academic research to be deviant or pathological (Lawrence, 1982; Parmar, 1982; Brah, 1987; Gilroy, 1987; Marable, 1983; Phoenix, 1987).

In recent years there has been some debate (some of which has been acrimonious) between black feminists and white feminists. Black feminists have argued that white feminists have omitted black women's experiences and perspectives from their accounts and that it is unsatisfactory to treat the term 'woman' as if all women fitted into a unitary group (Davis, 1982; Issue 17 of *Feminist Review*, 1984; Bhavnani and Coulson, 1986). Feminism, they argue, is a theory and practice that aims to free all women and must therefore theorize differences between women as well as similarities among them. Furthermore, white feminists have been charged with sometimes contributing to the oppression of black women by either colluding with racism or being racist themselves (Carby, 1982; Parmar, 1982; Hull et al., 1982). Differences between black women and white women, and contradictions in their relationship, therefore, have to be addressed, and not rendered invisible in favour of stressing the commonalities that women share.

All women simultaneously have a class, 'race' and gender position. Class, gender and 'race' all have structural significance in a society which is differentiated by social class, patriarchy and racism. Analyses of the impact of each of these structural features is important to the understanding of individuals in social context. Such an understanding is now recognized as central if psychology as a discipline is to make progress in understanding individuals (Henriques et al., 1984; Richards and Light, 1986; Bruner and Haste, 1987).

It is, however, impossible for individuals to separate their experiences neatly into those which result from their social class position, those which are consequent on their skin colour/'race'/ethnicity and those which result from their gender. Indeed the fragmentation which results from attempts to identify the individual effects of these factors masks the specificity of oppression individuals experience. People are multiply positioned (Henriques et al., 1984) but they rarely experience that multiplicity as fragmentary. It seems likely, then, that black feminist psychologists bring different perspectives to bear on their research than do white feminists.

Feminist contributions to the understanding of individuals and social relations are not being minimized in the discussion above. A feminist focus on taking women's accounts seriously is crucial to psychological understandings. But feminist perspectives are not unitary, and are themselves permeated with other societal power relationships. Nor is an essentialist position, which suggests that *because* someone is a woman or black or working class, they will necessarily have different views from people who do not fit those social categories, being adopted. Nonetheless, the complexity of individuals' social positions necessarily affects their experiences, and thus needs to be theorized and taken into account.

Defining and researching social problems

This section looks at how definition of social problems is dependent on the social positioning of the definers; and at the ways in which research in social policy is perceived within 'mainstream' psychology.

Many critiques of social science methodology have challenged the assumption that research on people living their everyday lives can ever be value-free and objective (Henriques et al., 1984; Seidman and Rappaport, 1986). Researchers are not objective observers of social contexts and interactions, but are members of society who have specific social locations and who bring particular orientations to bear on their research.

The issues researchers choose to study and the frames of reference they use to structure their enquiries are often products of their individual interests and dominant social constructions of important issues. Funding, for example, is more likely to be given to projects on topics considered socially relevant than otherwise. The definition of social relevance obviously does not rest on researchers' personal definitions alone, but on those of the funding agencies, which in turn are informed by sociopolitical concerns. Hence definitions of social problems are dynamic rather than static (Seidman and Rappaport, 1986). The issue of who defines social problems and how they are constituted is not generally addressed.

Socially relevant research frequently focuses on 'social problems'. Hence there is a large body of policy-relevant research in the social sciences which addresses itself to 'social problems', aiming to provide a greater understanding of them and to ameliorate or eradicate them. The USA, unlike Britain, has a psychological society (the Society for the Psychological Study of Social Issues) geared to studying 'social issues'.

Feminist writing (by black and by white feminists), and writing by black academics (women and men), have made a significant contribution to thinking about the social construction of social problems. For example, Henriques et al. (1984) clearly document how psychological work on racial prejudice has focused on such prejudice as if it were simply a characteristic of pathological or misguided individuals. In explaining why psychology needs to take account of the structural nature of racism, Henriques et al. have redefined the nature of prejudice and made explicit the logical implications inherent in a focus on prejudice rather than on racism.

Similarly, Henley (1986) has pointed out how assertiveness training, originally designed to help women counter the disadvantages they face in employment, has, through its focus on changing individual women, come to be seen as necessary because of deficiencies in women themselves. Hence a measure designed to empower women has come to position them as social problems.

In the USA, where there are many more black psychologists than there are in Britain, black psychologists have begun to protest about the fact that black people have traditionally either been ignored in research (McAdoo, 1988) or have been treated as inferiors, passive victims or deviants. Research has thus served to sustain racist beliefs (Jenkins, 1982; Guthrie, 1976; Scott-Jones and Nelson-Le Gall, 1986).

It has so far been more common for black than for white psychologists to highlight the normalized absence/pathologized presence of black people in psychological research. Not surprisingly, members of devalued groups are more likely to question negative constructions of their group as a whole and to redefine formulations which treat blackness as automatically problematic. This illustrates the fact that those who define social problems tend to be socially distant from the problems they define and that their definitions tend to reflect only their own viewpoint (Seidman and Rappaport, 1986, p. 2).

The way in which research on social problems is perceived within psychology may also be regarded as problematic. Research in social policy fields often operates at the boundaries of psychology and other social sciences. Indeed, it is often influenced by disciplines other than psychology. The research produced tends to be seen as 'soft science' since it is often conducted in 'natural' settings which it would usually ɔe considered unethical to manipulate experimentally, and over which ʾesearchers generally have little control. The data generated is, there-ʾore, likely to be more 'messy' than that produced from neat experi-nental designs. The traditional psychological method of experiment s, therefore, rarely applicable, and observation is often not possible. Furthermore, it is frequently necessary to find out how respondents construct their own situation and to ask them about their life histories. In practice, interviews often provide the main source of data.

In addition, policy-relevant research is frequently perceived to be applied, rather than pure or theoretical science. Hence it is considered atheoretical. Yet many psychologists (some of them feminist) are engaged in policy-relevant research. They use theoretical and methodological tools produced within as well as outside psychology in their research, and their published work feeds back into psychology. The distinction between basic and applied research arguably represents a false dichotomy.

The 16–19-year-old mothers study

The remainder of this chapter provides an extended example of a feminist-influenced, policy-relevant research project.

The starting point

Work on motherhood in the under-20s is published both in psycho-logical journals and in journals with no particular disciplinary base. Researchers from a variety of disciplines undertake work in the area. However, most research reported shares a common orientation to the 'problem of teenage motherhood'. It is usually taken for granted that it is undesirable for women in their teenage years to give birth (Simms and Smith, 1986). Research reports as well as professional statements in Britain and the USA all generally take a negative orientation to this age group of mothers and their children. There has also been a depressing catalogue of findings which suggest that early motherhood is causative of a 'gloomy adumbration' of socioeconomic ills (Wells, 1983).

'Teenage motherhood' has, for example, been associated with anaemia and toxaemia for pregnant women, low birth weight, perinatal mortality, physical abuse, accidental injury and poor educational performance for children born to women under 20 (Butler et al., 1981; Alan Guttmacher Institute, 1981; Bury, 1984).

The context in which the study started in 1983 was, therefore, one in which teenage motherhood was generally devalued as a social problem. The study was initiated by a senior researcher at the Thomas Coram Research Unit and funded by the (then) Department of Health and Social Security. As is generally the case with research units where individuals are only salaried if research funds are generated, the proposal had to be generated at high speed. As a result the rationale and aims of the project were couched in standard terms for research in this area. The study was originally called the 'Unmarried Mothers' project, and it was intended to focus on different age groups of women who gave birth without following the normative prescription of marrying first. However, before the study started it was decided to focus on mothers who were under 20 years of age, and the name was changed to the 'Young Mothers' project. It was also decided to follow a common research format and to compare a group of 'indigenous' mothers under 20, and an age-matched group of 'West Indian' mothers.

The research team and the black advisory group
The rest of the research team were appointed after the study had been funded. The team then comprised two project directors (one from social policy, the other a psychologist), a senior researcher (a sociologist) and two research officers to do the data collection (one a psychologist, the other an experienced interviewer with a journalistic background). The project directors were male, the rest of the research team were female. The research officer who was a psychologist was the only black member of the team.

Research in Britain is generally hierarchically organized. The model within which research agencies operate is that of senior academics applying for sufficient funds to enable them to employ junior assistants for the duration of data collection and sometimes analysis. Those who design studies often do not collect the data or (in the case of social policy research) see the circumstances in which respondents live. Assistants/interviewers are more often women than men who are more likely to be working for men than for women and by virtue of their status and relatively late appointment within research projects have limited opportunities for influencing the course of research projects. A replication of societal gender hierarchies is often, therefore, inherent in many research projects.

In a parallel manner, the handful of black researchers in Britain are more likely to be appointed to posts which explicitly require black researchers. This is potentially exploitative in that the concern of those directing such research projects is generally to give their projects academic validity by matching colour of interviewer to that of respondent. Such colour matching is designed to forestall criticisms that black respondents are unlikely to talk openly to white interviewers and to guarantee successful data collection.

Black and other minority ethnic group academics in the USA are beginning to detail their dissatisfactions with the fact that, when they apply for tenure track jobs, they find that their 'overspecialization' in research on their own ethnic groups is seen as over-subjective and questionable (de la Luz Reyes and Halcon, 1988). Only white academics are believed to have the necessary objectivity to do research on black people. The recruitment of black researchers to collect data on black people is thus, at least in the USA, not likely to enhance black academics' careers. Such employment is also potentially exploitative because, as junior members of research teams, most black researchers (like most women interviewers) have little opportunity to influence the published interpretations of the data that only they were considered able to collect.

A particularly unusual feature of the study was that it had a black advisory group composed entirely of black women, most of whom were feminists who were either involved in or interested in research. Their disciplinary backgrounds were in psychology, sociology and education. Their contribution to the project went beyond that usually expected from advisory groups because they met several times each year, read everything they were sent very carefully, and consistently evaluated the project. Their contribution proved both supportive and stimulating; their advice was not, however, always followed.

The eventual focus and methodology

As usual when research is being conducted the existing literature on teenage motherhood was discussed within the research team before the methodology was finalized. It soon became apparent that although the literature almost uniformly stressed the problematic nature of 'adolescent motherhood', the reported findings were not entirely worrying. The difficulties of those found to fare badly were over-extended to mothers under 20 as whole.

The desire to take women's experiences seriously, which is a central tenet of feminist work, and to avoid reproducing by default the view of black people as pathological, led to critical thinking about the focus of the literature. As a result attention was given to the social construction of early motherhood itself. In common with research on other 'social problems' (Seidman and Rappaport, 1986), literature on motherhood in the under-20s stresses individual motivation and responsibility for the incidence of teenage motherhood (Phipps-Yonas, 1980; Arney and Bergen, 1984).

Even when researchers concluded that 'sweeping condemnations of early motherhood are now unwarranted' (King and Fullard, 1982), they nonetheless made assumptions that women who became mothers while they were in their teenage years were pathological. King and Fullard, for example, found that most of the mothers under 20 they studied fared well. Yet they continually compared 'teenage mothers' with 'normal mothers'. The use of the word 'normal' in this context is arguably unproblematic since it is a commonly used psychological term for describing what, in effect, is no more than a comparison or group. Yet the fact that mothers under 20 are contrasted with 'normal mothers' betrays King and Fullard's easy acceptance of the widespread beliefs that 'teenage mothers' are abnormal.

It is usual for research in this area to compare black mothers in this age group with white ones. In these comparisons qualitatively different types of 'explanations' tend to be produced for the two groups of mothers. The incidence of motherhood in young black women is generally explained via sociocultural factors, while for white young women, psychological explanations are favoured (Phipps-Yonas, 1980). The explanations put forward, that black women become pregnant for cultural reasons while white women do so because of their individual deficiencies, are inherently unsatisfactory since they assume rather than demonstrate the validity of those differences (Phoenix, 1987).

The main resulting shift in the focus of the project was from an attempt to establish whether 'young mothers' and their children fared badly, and whether young black women fared better or worse than white ones, to an attempt to understand the processes which lead some young women to become mothers as well as the processes by which some young women and their children come to fare well while others fare badly. As a result it was decided not to have a comparison group at all. The study was longitudinal. Women were interviewed in late pregnancy, 6 months after birth and 21 months after birth. Children were given developmental assessments at 21 months (see Phoenix, forthcoming, for a more detailed description of the study).

As in any research project there were difficulties and compromises. The sample, for example, proved difficult to find at home, and as a result attrition was higher than the research team would have liked (only fifty of a potential seventy-nine women were interviewed in-depth on three occasions). There were sometimes also internal disagreements. The use of standardized developmental assessments was, for example, disputed by the black advisory group and within the research team. One argument against them was that their in-built comparison to a constructed normal score was unsuitable for a project concerned with intra-group processes. Yet, because standardized tests produce data quickly and easily, it was eventually decided to use the Bayley Scales of Infant Development. Because the project did not have a standard design for research on mothers in this age group, it was necessary to explain and justify the project to colleagues and peers more frequently than would otherwise have been the case.

The relationship between psychology and the project should not be seen as undirectional. The project itself contributes an understanding of the context in which motherhood, early in the life course, occurs and the effects it has on young women and their children. In addition, the project highlights the ways in which radical (feminist, anti-racist and social stratification) approaches to social policy research can produce psychological material. Women were not, for example, only studied in relation to their children (as is common in psychology). Hence they were not constructed 'exclusively as mothers' (Fraser, 1987) but as individuals with multiple positions and 'careers'. The tendency within psychology to define people in an individualized way denies the complexity of their experiences. Despite its claim to objectivity and value freeness, psychology is political in that, for example, it constructs and maintains ideologies which 'blame the victim' (Seidman and Rappaport, 1986).

Interviewing: a feminist research tool?

Interviewing is a useful feminist and psychological tool for the understanding of women's own evaluations of their lives and experiences. Oakley (1981) pointed out how traditional 'cookbooks' on interviewing deny the two-way interpersonal relationships it is necessary to establish in the interview situation and are based on masculine paradigms of objective research. Brannen (1988) suggests that the relationship between the researcher and respondent varies with social class (and hence the power relations between them) as well as with the nature of the topic being studied.

The study described here was reliant on in-depth interviews of a socially stigmatized group of women who came predominantly from lower working-class backgrounds. The circumstances in which the women lived and their social class positions necessarily influenced the data collection. The context in which the interviews occurred was one in which it was difficult to find many women at home in order to interview them. Each post-natal interview took, on average, four visits, and many women received seven unfruitful visits before being dropped from the study. Respondents did not generally break appointments in protest at their inclusion in the study, although this may have been true in some instances. In one situation, for example, eighteen visits were made to secure one interview – yet the respondent was genuinely very pleased to see the interviewer and reported that she enjoyed the interview. Since most interviewees were not on the telephone, it was very difficult to make subsequent appointments if respondents were consistently out.

The likely explanation for the difficulty of finding respondents at home seemed more likely to be that the research process was not important in respondents' lives. Most respondents did not keep diaries and had no reason to consider the research interview more important than their daily activities, which, for many, included going out from their (frequently depressing) home environments for long periods each day.

Because interviewees often lived in cramped conditions with other members of their family, it was sometimes difficult to interview women in privacy. On one occasion, for example, a father marched into the room where his 17-year-old pregnant daughter was being interviewed and forbade the interviewer to ask any further questions about himself or his wife. The general poverty in which most respondents lived was tangible in interview visits. Some women were happy to be interviewed over lunchtime, claiming they never ate in the middle of the day. When interviewers were offered drinks, food cupboards were sometimes strikingly empty of anything other than one packet of tea. Milk was often in short supply and furniture and fittings were often sparse.

The interviews were not generally interactive or conversational. Women usually answered the questions they were asked without demanding information from the interviewer. This did not mean, however, that they did not enjoy the interviews or were monosyllabic in their responses. On the contrary most women reported themselves as enjoying the interview and interviews lasted between one-and-a-half and six-and-three-quarter hours (done in three visits).

The one-sided nature of the interviews was related to the social distance between researchers and the researched. Although the interviewers were, like the respondents, women, they were materially better off than the women being interviewed. The social power differentials between the dyad involved in the interview situation could not be left outside the interview situation or dispensed with. A conversational style of interviewing was, therefore, not appropriate since the participants in the interview were not of equal status. Respondents are more likely to make the interview a two-way process if they feel themselves to be of equal status with interviewers (Brannen, 1988).

Women did spontaneously ask their interviewers some questions. These were mainly to do with whether interviewers were married and/or had children themselves. At the end of the study respondents were asked how they felt about taking part in the project and it became clear that most interviewees enjoyed being interviewed.

Interviewer: How did you feel about taking part in the study?
Respondent: Interesting.
Int: What was interesting about it?

Res: Well, it's not every day you get to sit down and sort of tell people your problems . . . Makes you feel quite interested you know – I'm an interesting person.

Res: I usually sit and listen, so it makes a change to talk.

Res: I can say what I want. It gives me a chance to say what I want.

Although the research was explained to all women (verbally and in writing), some women were confused about what the study was about and why they had been chosen to take part. For example one woman asked after the last visit, 'Well, Ann, how are you? Are you a qualified social worker yet?' This misunderstanding is not surprising since most women were not familiar with research professionals and did not really know what to expect. This raises general questions of how psychologists may be seen as one of a whole army of welfare professionals.

Res: Um, I found it very confusing . . . And I'm not really sure why the research is doing. It's okay. I enjoyed it. It's been quite, you know, it's been good . . . I always wanted to know – I still would like to know why this research has been taken part.

Res: I don't know why I'm being interviewed or you know – maybe I was told, but I can't remember. [*Laughs*] Why did you pick on me?

A minority of women felt that they had been asked questions which were too personal, or that the interviews had lasted too long.

Res: Very nosey they are . . . about your housing and how much money you earn and things like that.
Int: Did you mind being asked those questions?
Res: Well, I didn't really mind, but I think they are a bit personal.

Res: Um, I think the last interview was a bit tiring. It seemed to go on for ever and ever and ever. But um, I thought oh God, when's it gonna get to the end of it you know.
Int: What about this interview?
Res: No, this one's all right. Weren't as long as the middle one. It seemed to go on for *ever*.

(The last interview lasted three hours, and was longer than the middle one.) Asked about their preferences for interviewers, the great majority of respondents said that they preferred to be interviewed by women rather than men. Some also said that they preferred to have the same interviewer over the three visits.

Res: I don't know. I find it hard to talk to men, I suppose. They don't seem to see things the way women do.

Res: I mean I'm getting to know the person that's been coming and I mean the first time I met you you know I was a bit strange. I didn't know what to say . . . I mean it's easier today than what it was on the first visit.

Most respondents said that the colour of the interviewer made no difference to them. This may have been partly because with the decision not to compare black and white respondents, no attempt was made deliberately to match respondents and interviewers for colour. Respondents may have felt diffident about expressing colour preferences to an interviewer of a different colour from themselves. But many interviewees who were, incidentally, colour matched expressed no colour preference. The following response from a black woman was, therefore, rare but demonstrates how respondents' perceptions of and experiences of racism are part of the interview situation, whether explicitly acknowledged to make a difference or not.

> If —— had been doing the interview I would have had to tell her that the questions were too nosey because white people don't understand what a typical black family is like. Therefore while white people might feel they shouldn't ask too much about certain things because they're strange, black people would understand.

In summary, the interviewing relationship in this study could not be claimed to be an equal one, although it was in many instances reciprocal. Many interviewees enjoyed having an uninterrupted opportunity to discuss their feelings and to be really listened to in confidence by another woman. Nonetheless, however pleasant interviews were, they were not simply friendly visits but represented attempts to obtain information for purposes beyond the interviewee's (and sometimes the interviewer's) control. Furthermore, gender was only one of the societal power relationships present in the interviewing relationship. 'Race', class and (although often denied by respondents) age were also important components and may partly have accounted for the respondents' lack of commitment to keeping appointments with the interviewer. The impact of structural features other than gender on interview situations remain to be theorized in discussions of feminist methodology.

In recognition of the unequal relationship, and in order to give something tangible back to respondents who were visibly poor, interviewers left copies of the National Council for One Parent Families' guide to the state benefits available for those women (single or married) who wished to have it. However a consideration of the power relations inherent in interview situations raises wider issues.

One of these is the suggestion that future research on women who are impoverished *should* include within their budgets a sum designed for paying respondents. Respondents should be given at least a token sum of money for contributing to research which is providing salaried positions for researchers who are dependent on their respondents' accounts. It can be argued that this might simply be a ploy to increase response rates in groups which are difficult to obtain and that accounts are likely to be falsified as a result. The potential for exploitation inherent in interview situations would, however, be reduced (although not removed) by such payment. It also seems that payment of respondents makes no discernible difference to the accounts they give (Rutter, personal communication).

Conclusions

The aim of this chapter has been to demonstrate that feminist and black perspectives can make a useful contribution to psychological research. In particular the insistence that women's perspectives be taken seriously, and that implicit assumptions in research be made explicit, allows theoretical advances to be made and new methodological approaches to be tried.

The chapter has used the example of social policy research in the area of motherhood in teenage women to argue that it is important for such research to be informed by feminist and black perspectives and analyses of the impact of social class. The research described also, however, used psychological concepts, and contributed to the development of psychological theory. It is therefore argued that broad definitions of psychology should be used rather than limiting the definition of psychology to a narrow range of methods or topics. In addition it is suggested that interdisciplinary work can usefully assist the psychological understanding of the individual in context.

It may be argued that the perspectives described above are political, and hence not likely to produce objective research. Research which is apparently objective can, however, serve to maintain the devalued status of people constructed as social problems, and hence has an implicit political orientation.

The response of those trained in psychology who felt critical of many of its inherent assumptions used to be to define themselves as outside the discipline. With a growing number of psychologists informed by feminist and other radical perspectives, however, this is no longer the case. Psychology now has to accommodate psychologists with a wider variety of approaches than hitherto, and to change in accordance with them.

One positive feature of the project described here is that it produced new ways of thinking about motherhood in the under-20s in a mixed (female/male, black/white) research group. Feminist, black and class perspectives were incorporated by researchers who are white, middle class and some of whom are men. In this case this was partly due to the individuals involved and partly due to the influence of the black advisory group. Such co-operative ventures are essential in a climate where some men now believe they know what a feminist perspective is and have made enough concessions to it, and when debates between black feminists and some white feminists appear deadlocked. One of the challenges that lies ahead for feminist psychology is in establishing successful alliances between black and white feminists, and between feminists and sympathetic men so that the development of feminist psychology continues.

Note

The black advisory group was a beneficial and supportive influence on the project. Thanks especially to Bebb Burchell, whose idea it was, and to Yaa Asare, Kum-Kum Bhavnani, Reena Bhavnani, Ronny Flynn, and Irma La Rose. Without Peter Moss, the project would not have taken place. Thanks to him and to the other members of the research team: Julia Brannen, Ted Melhuish, Liz Gould, Mary Baginsky, Ruth Foxman and Gill Bolland. The project was supported by a grant from the Department of Health and Social Security.

References

Alan Guttmacher Institute (1981) *Teenage Pregnancy: The Problem That Hasn't Gone Away*. New York.

Arney, W. and Bergen, B. (1984) Power and visibility: the invention of teenage pregnancy. *Social Science and Medicine* 18 (1), 11–19.

Bhavnani, K. and Coulson, M. (1986) Transforming socialist feminism: the challenge of racism. *Feminist Review* 23, 81–92.

Brah, A. (1987) Women of south Asian origin in Britain: issues and concerns. *South Asia Research* 7 (1), 39–53.

Brannen, J. (1988) Research note: the study of sensitive subjects: notes on interviewing. *The Sociological Review* 36 (3), 552–63.

Bruner, J. and Haste, H. (eds) (1987) *Making Sense: The Child's Construction of the World*. London: Methuen.

Bury, J. (1984) *Teenage Pregnancy in Britain*. London: Birth Control Trust.

Butler, M. (1981) *Teenage Mothers*. Report to the Department of Health and Social Security.

Carby, H. (1982) White woman listen! Black feminism and the boundaries of sisterhood. In Centre for Contemporary Cultural Studies (eds), *The Empire Strikes Back*. London: Hutchinson.

Davis, A, (1982) *Women, Race and Class*. London: The Women's Press.

de la Luz Reyes, M. and Halcon, J. (1988) Racism in academia: the old wolf revisited. *Harvard Educational Review* 58 (3), 299–314.

Fraser, N. (1987) Women, welfare and the politics of need interpretation. *Thesis Eleven* 27, 88–113.

Gilroy, P. (1987) *There Ain't No Black in the Union Jack: The Cultural Politics of Race and Nation*. London: Hutchinson.

Griffin, C. (1988) Feminist research: theorising experience and experiencing theory. Paper presented at Economic and Social Research Council Field Research Workshop on Feminist Research and Qualitative Studies.

Griffin, C. (1989) 'I'm not a women's libber, but . . .' Feminism, consciousness and identity. In S. Skevington and D. Baker (eds), *The Social Identity of Women*. London: Sage.

Guthrie, R. (1976) *Even the Rat was White: A Historical View of Psychology*. London: Harper & Row.

Henley, N. (1986) Women as a social problem: conceptual and practical issues in defining social problems. In E. Seidman and J. Rappaport (eds), *Redefining Social Problems*. New York: Plenum.

Henriques, J., Hollway, W., Urwin, C., Venn, C. and Walkerdine, V. (1984) *Changing the Subject: Psychology, Social Regulation and Subjectivity*. London: Methuen.

Hull, G., Scott, P. and Smith, B. (eds) (1982) *All the Women are White, All the Blacks are Men, But Some of Us Are Brave*. New York: The Feminist Press.

Jenkins, A. (1982) *The Psychology of the Afro-American: A Humanistic Approach*. Oxford: Pergamon Press.

King, T. and Fullard, W. (1982) Teenage mothers and their infants: new findings on the home environment. *Journal of Adolescence* 5, 333–46.

Lawrence, E. (1982) In the abundance of water the fool is thirsty: sociology and black 'pathology.' In Centre for Contemporary Cultural Studies (eds), *The Empire Strikes Back*. London: Hutchinson.

McAdoo, H.P. (ed.) (1988) *Black Families* 2nd edition. London: Sage.

Marable, M. (1983) *How Capitalism Underdeveloped Black America*. London: Pluto Press.

Oakley, A. (1981) Interviewing women: a contradiction in terms. In H. Roberts (ed.). *Doing Feminist Research*. London: Routledge and Kegan Paul.

Parmar, P. (1982) Gender, race and class: Asian women in resistance. In Centre for Contemporary Cultural Studies (eds), *The Empire Strikes Back*. London: Hutchinson.

Phipps-Yonas, S. (1980) Teenage pregnancy and motherhood: a review of the literature. *American Journal of Ortho-psychiatry* 50, 403–31.

Phoenix, A. (1987) Narrow definitions of culture: the case of early motherhood. In S. Westwood and P. Bhachu (eds), *Enterprising Women: Ethnicity, Economy and Gender Relations*. London: Routledge.

Phoenix, A. (forthcoming) *Young Mothers?* Cambridge: Polity Press.

Reber, A. (1985) *The Penguin Dictionary of Psychology*. Harmondsworth: Penguin.

Richards, M. and Light, P. (eds) (1986) *Children of Social Worlds*. Cambridge: Polity.

Scott-Jones, D. and Nelson-Le Gall, S. (1986) Defining black families: past and present. In E. Seidman and J. Rappaport (eds), *Redefining Social Problems*. New York: Plenum.

Seidman, E. and Rappaport, J. (1986) Framing the issues. In E. Seidman and J. Rappaport (eds), *Redefining Social Problems*. New York: Plenum.

Simms, M. and Smith, C. (1986) *Teenage Mothers and their Partners*. London: HMSO.

Stanley, L. (1988) Paper presented at Economic and Social Research Council Field Research workshop.

Taylor, A., Sluckin, W., Davies. D., Reason, J., Thomson, R., and Colman, A. (1982) *Introducing Psychology: Second Edition*. Harmondsworth: Penguin.

Weedon, C. (1987) *Feminist Practice and Poststructuralist Theory*. Oxford: Basil Blackwell.

Wells, N. (1983) *Teenage Mothers*. Liverpool: European Collaborative Committee for Child Health of the Children's Research Fund.

Wilkinson, S. (ed.) (1986) *Feminist Social Psychology: Developing Theory and Practice*. Milton Keynes: Open University Press.

7

Fantasy or reality? The problem with psychoanalytic interpretation in psychotherapy with women

Maye Taylor

This is unashamedly polemic, a feminist psychotherapist's personal view of some of the issues surrounding women and psychotherapy. It takes as axiomatic the subordination and oppression of women, and that psychiatry has played a part in that process. It posits that women have historically acquired the role of patient, and that men have largely taken on the position of doctor, thus contributing to a popular view of women as mentally unstable and men as mentally healthy.

There will be no attempt here to rehearse the numerous theoretical arguments, or to do any kind of literature review as that has been done well in other publications (Showalter, 1987). Instead, I will start from practice and although very little explicit reference to individual women will be made (I have a personal reluctance to objectify women as 'cases', stemming from my experience of case presentation by male psychiatrists), the whole chapter is based on ways of understanding the problems of women whom I have met in therapy. There will be no denial that men suffer emotional distress, but simply the acknowledgement that the aetiology of women's distress is different, and that understanding this requires looking at what is going on for all women psychologically within the present conditions of patriarchal societal relations. Since most current theory and practice is imprisoned within this conventional patriarchal ideology, it is logically inevitable that psychotherapy partakes of that ideology, and therefore that it is permeated by sexism.

To challenge this position we need a different response. Over the years it has become increasingly apparent that the rigid application of classical psychotherapeutic rules fails to take into account essential differences between men and women's actual *experiences*. Feminist psychotherapy therefore involves a way of seeing, understanding, and making connections between our psychological state and the structural position of women.

The writings of the psycho-radicals of the sixties, Laing and Cooper, (Collier, 1977) in conjunction with the emerging feminist thinkers,

uggested that problems presented for psychotherapy were, in the final
analysis, not pyschopathological in origin, but the psychic expression
of social pressures and tensions. For example, it is entirely plausible
that a deserted wife, isolated in a northern housing estate, unable to
cope with her three traumatized children, and with a totally inadequate
income, will exhibit depressive symptoms of clinical intensity. She will
certainly experience acute feelings of guilt for her failure as a wife and
or her failure to cope with the situation which anyone from the outside
can see is an impossible situation. So what would be an appropriate
treatment response?

Radical sociologists would follow the tradition derived from C.
Wright Mills and his original distinction between private troubles and
public issues (Mills, 1959), and they would argue the need to make
visible the relationship between these, if the sense of despair and
entrapment of the disadvantaged person is to be overcome. This
constitutes a powerful indictment of mere intrapsychic 'causal'
explanations, and taken in conjunction with the feminist position,
provides us with a different platform for formulating appropriate
responses. So in feminist psychotherapy the incorporation of the
apparently conflicting claims of the psychodynamic and sociological
explanatory system can be integrated into a powerful interpretive
system which allows us to locate the wider roots of the problems which
women bring into psychotherapy. Emotional distress and misery can,
under this different scheme, be seen to derive from personal psychopathology or family pressures, or from the social system and
combinations of these.

One can use and adapt the Maslow-type hierarchy and produce five
levels where we can locate the presenting 'problem' (Maslow, 1954):

1 Existential, i.e. life choices.
2 Personality, i.e. psychopathology.
3 Interaction, family relationships, etc.
4 Predicament, the person's immediate situation.
5 Material deprivation, money, shelter, food.

All of these possibilities need to be taken into consideration in the light
of the significant gender differences which will apply at all levels. A
manifestation at any of the five levels may be the outcome of
disturbance at any of these levels; women may move from one
attribution to another in their own attempts to account for their
current situation, and so, rather than limiting itself to ego defence
mechanism interpretations, feminist psychotherapy acknowledges and
works with the possibility of reality in women's predicaments without
denying the existence of psychological process.

The legacy of the female role

It is evident that women have internalized the messages from thei female stereotype and thus will bring, to any situation, much materia that women can share of a biographical and historical nature; yet, a the same time, it is evident that many of the current issues in their lifε result in their being lost in a sea of personal troubles which they finc difficult to identify or resolve. If the actual trouble is to be addressec we need to know what it is, and to discover what really is the trouble we have to start with the client's own definition of the situation.

The risk in psychotherapy is that in focusing on one aspect, 'sick psychopathology, we may turn this into a real aspect: 'I didn't know was depressed until I saw the doctor; I thought I had backache!'

The rigid application of the Freudian principle that the real problem lies in whatever the client is most unwilling to reveal can produce psychotherapeutic myopia: with the reality of the awfulness of the woman's actual situation being lost. Freud himself quotes a question put by a patient: 'Why do you tell me yourself that my illness i probably connected with my circumstances and events of my life anc that you cannot alter these in any way?' (Freud, 1895). Freud' response is to talk about transforming hysterical misery into commor unhappiness and learning to live with that and not being able to change the circumstances. With the emergence of feminism we can envisage that those circumstances could be changed, through structural change and by the empowerment of women. Individual psychotherapy car certainly help a woman gain strength in order to change those aspect of her situation which she identifies as needing changing. Interestingly returning to Freud, the vital aspect of dealing with depression by hi account involves acting constructively on the anger that people fee about their social lot and not turning this anger destructively against themselves; in short undoing the defence of introjection (Freud, 1917). But to do this the woman must feel she has a chance of achieving some change in her 'social lot'. As definitions of mental health derive from *feelings* of well-being, dependent on a positive self-concept, then the problems for women of internalizing the female role, which denies them the possibility of a positive self-concept, become evident.

Women's early experience sees us expecting the same freedom of action as men initially, but then learning the reality of the limitations of women's actual freedom of action. In theory, children are brought up as *children*, in reality as girls and boys. Freud helpfully draws our attention to those contradictions, albeit very tangentially, and yet at the same time, paints a grotesque picture of women based on their so-called genital inferiority (Freud, 1931). However, as the clinical goal of psychotherapy is to help people to become more fully conscious of the contradictions in their life, and then perhaps being able to deal with them, this is particularly relevant to the consciousness-raising of feminism.

Here I must acknowledge that there is an essential difference between those personal changes that an individual can achieve through psychotherapy, and the need for those structural changes which are necessary to bring about substantial change in the practice which systematically assigns children to one gender category or another. The emphasis placed on sexual differentiation, name identity, type of occupation, kinds of behaviour and access to resources, seems vital only for the continuation and preservation of a certain kind of status quo: that which is male-dominated. Is it any wonder that actions and self-descriptions are genderized and taken to be a coherent, natural and inevitable reuslt of biology, which become generalized as psychological traits? Yet we know that femininity and masculinity *are* ideological practices, the more effective *because of* the taken-for-granted nature of the assumptions about what is properly male and what is properly female. These assumptions have clearly been taken into psychotherapy and emerge as normative statements and codes of conduct. Put even more bluntly women have been put into the position of being economically dependent within patriarchal structures and then being pathologized for that dependence.

Clearly the relationship between economic dependence and personal dependence needs to be articulated as a structural process rather than as individual free choice. Without this perspective, traditional psychotherapy, with its emphasis on individual rather than structural processes, holds the danger that these dependency processes will be repeated in therapy to the detriment of women. This does not consider that structural forces per se are responsible for women's problems but demands that they are brought into the equation. The consequence of this for therapy requires that women are contextualized within their social roles and not amputated from the consequences of them. Through our roles as wives and mothers women largely act as the emotional caretakers and nurturers of society. Yet women are caricatured as dependent in the sense of being clinging, helpless and weak; their assigned role thus containing a contradiction and a pejorative label.

The stereoptype goes further and encourages this contradiction in the form of classical femininity. For example, it is acknowledged that men bring their emotional lives to their wives but that men's dependency is not often made explicit but, more often than not, is met within marriage so that their emotional worries are processed and laundered by their wives. Current research indicates that it is not just women per se who are overrepresented in the mental health statistics

(Gove, 1972), but rather that it is *married* women who experience more emotional distress. It is evident that marriage works better for men than women and one is left asking the question: where do women take their dependency needs if they are so busy caring for the needs of others?

Emerging from my work with women who are in a state of depression are two major themes: their sense of powerlessness, where there is a lack of alternatives in the face of overwhelming and seemingly unsurmountable odds; and intense frustration, not simply at the awfulness of their situation, but rather at the discrepancy between their life and their idealized conception of others. It certainly seems probable that women are more likely to undergo experiences which generate those feelings, which is why it is women who, in spite of rigorous attempts at change, still tend to occupy the subordinate roles in relationships with men. It is the women who, for a variety of reasons, are more likely to be inhibited from forming strong social ties outside those relationships, developing other interests or pursuing occupational achievement outside the home. When things go drastically wrong in the home they thus have fewer avenues of escape open to them. When domestic arrangements break up, it is women who are left in a financially insecure position. The discrepancy between average earnings of men and women has a very real effect. Modern women are now facing an even worse situation, where on the one hand society encourages them to believe that they are in every respect equal to men and should think of themselves as such, while on the other it systematically denies them the opportunity to compete on equal terms. To address only the internal dynamics as orthodox psychotherapy prescribes is to ignore the external factors.

Why feminist psychotherapy? A critique

It was inevitable that with the increasing awareness and greater understanding of women's social position, women would demand psychotherapeutic services that specifically addressed women's needs, took into account and understood women's experience and history, and supported women's struggles. The establishment of the Feminist Therapy Centre in London in 1976 is one such result. Feminist psychotherapy takes as a major starting point the assumption that existing treatment practice in all psychiatry has real shortcomings and is biased against women as individual people, because it is gender-based. In 1986 a prominent male clinician said with passion, and without being savaged by his audience, in an address to a large psychiatric conference: 'When women grow up without a dread of their biological functions and without subversion by feminist doctrine, and therefore enter upon motherhood with a sense of fulfilment and altruistic sentiment, we shall attain the goal of a good life and a secure world in which to live'. When such statements can be made it is reasonable to conclude that oppressive sexism exists both at individual and structural levels within psychiatry.

It is ironic that the appeal in his statement is to women's altruism and self-sacrifice. There is no doubt that psychiatry prides itself on being benign and compassionate, but it is predominantly male, and men, in spite of claims to 'objectivity', cannot be neutral. There is, then, an obscuring of the psychiatric function as an apparatus through which society is ordered, and in which the subjugation of women is crucial. Women are seen as synonymous with family, a normal and natural progression from *what is* to *what should be* – the perfect ideological straitjacket. The function of much psychiatry for women has been to get them to accept their position more comfortably; use of tranquillizers has kept women within the very situation which is causing us distress. This mental distress experienced by many women is linked to violence caused by men. The secrecy surrounding incest, rape and wife battering has begun to be broken, and alarmingly high rates of such violence are being reported. I can recall a case where a male clinical psychologist had enlisted the husband as 'co-therapist' in setting up a behaviour modification programme for his wife, the function of which was to modify and reward domesticity. It later emerged that the man beat his wife: it is not surprising then that a woman to woman mental health service is sought by many women.

Feminist psychotherapy

Feminist psychotherapy challenges the social control function that psychiatry performs; it highlights how the concentration on prescribed roles neglects the person, and it is this neglect that feminist psychotherapy addresses. It certainly challenges any therapy which rewards the female for carrying out her stereotyped domestic role which in fact may intensify rather than relieve her distress.

Psychotherapy itself has two components: a specific body of theory, i.e. psychodynamic psychology, and a treatment method that at its simplest involves trust, talk and understanding. This, in Freudian terms involves the forming of a therapeutic alliance with the healthy part of the patients's ego to bring about 'cure'. It is the nature of this therapeutic alliance and the interpretations made which feminist practice has seen fit to modify. Feminist psychotherapy can be seen to be a logical development arising out of the fusion of this treatment method with psychodynamic psychology, social psychology and sociology. The Women's Movement has made big inroads in challenging taken-for-granted assumptions about women, contributing to the establishment of feminist psychotherapy, which is perhaps better viewed as a perspective rather than a set of specialist techniques.

Parameters of feminist psychotherapy

One basic ground rule of feminist psychotherapy is that the feminist therapist is able to, and does, identify with a woman client and yet still maintain the essential boundaries. This identification is a valuable aid to understanding. The woman therapist will have experienced similar pressures and been subordinated by the same structures and processes. This does not mean that the therapist automatically colludes with the woman's perceptions. But it does involve a very powerful identification through which the therapist will be able to help the woman identify for herself those persistent stumbling-blocks to change in her *own* life. She can be helped to separate out those which have their roots in unconscious processes and thus militate against her own attempts to change her life. So the existence of psychic life, as a powerful determinant in the politics of everyday experience, is not denied; it is an integral part of the woman's experience; but feminist psychotherapy rejects any view of self which is conceived outside patriarchal culture; rather, seeing women's individuality, personality and reality as shaped by the material world and certainly currently influenced by it.

Women do sometimes feel possessive and insecure and jealous which can lead to extremes of dependency, and these responses can readily be seen as repetitive and enduring. But to see these qualities solely in terms of individual pathology is to ignore the social factors. Feminists argue that apart from the reality of woman's biology and sex, in her capacity to menstruate, conceive, give birth and lactate, and man's capacity to impregnate, the attributes we associate with femininity and masculinity are culturally constructed. The construction of women's personality is intrinsically linked to our gender identity. For a woman her social identity and 'unique self' will have emerged together and will reflect the dominant culture.

Yet these constructions are held up in society as natural, right and proper. 'Psychopathology' needs to be interpreted in this context. Women already experience enormous guilt. How often have I been faced with a woman who opens the session with: 'I shouldn't feel depressed, I have a nice home, a good husband and three lovely children.' She demonstrates little sense of self, and as we know, healthy self-regard is vital for mental health. The 'making a virtue of service' ideal for women in the family often gets translated to self-abnegation of bizarre proportions and with tragic results.

A typical scenario is of a woman diagnosed as chronically depressed.

She has four children, the youngest 5 months old, and a husband who works long hours to provide a materially good home. Her life is about looking after others, wiping bottoms, feeding from breast, spoon and table, anticipating demands, reacting to demands, reassuring, playing, taking enormous responsibility for the lives of five other people. She has tried to make space for herself, she says: 'My husband is very good to me; he lets me go out with my friends on Monday nights' – this is said with no resentment or understanding of the inequality as a possible basis for her depression. In order to go out she has to prepare everything beforehand. This plus the resentment from her husband when she does go out takes away much of its benefit. She has therefore given up and now finds herself trapped in an endless service treadmill and cannot see why she feels the way she does. For me, rather than seeing this woman as depressed, it makes more sense to see her as emotionally bankrupt, exhausted. She is constantly paying out physically and, more importantly, emotionally. Because she does not find it all the totally rewarding experience she was told it would be, she compensates even harder, because the failure must be her fault.

Role requirements and mental health

This demonstrates the first of the three generally acknowledged major ingredients in a woman's social roles which have massive implications for her mental health. She must always defer to others, follow their lead, and articulate her needs only in relation to others. In essence she is not to be the main actor in her own life. The role requirements of wife, mother and daughter determine the rules. In psychotherapy time and time again I see women who have no sense of their own self, no separate existence; they believe they are not important in themselves, for themselves. They are frequently self-deprecating, having come to systematically undervalue themselves. I work with them to help them recognize and acknowledge their own needs, but having lost any sight of these needs over the years it can be a long and painful process; hiding from their own needs and desires has been developed as a coping strategy. Having experienced the frustration of ambition early in life, women who come into therapy are characterized by feelings of inadequacy and lack of confidence and often cannot imagine that other women feel like that. They subscribe to the mythology that other women's lives are completely fulfilling and blame themselves for not finding fulfilment and for feeling discontented. Their level of explanation obscures the social milieu and the family interaction; it is difficult for the woman to acknowledge what is going on and stay in it, so that often she will prefer to locate her distress in terms of her own psychopathology.

By looking at the level of existential life choices, we can identify the second of the major role requirements. This articulates that a woman must always be connected to others and shape her life accordingly. A woman's social status is indeed located in her husband's/father's status (according to the Registrar General's classification). Socialization has led her to look for a man to complete her, give her an identity and a purpose. Women who form lesbian relationships will be largely viewed as deviant by the psychiatric profession – and their lesbianism per se will be targeted as the pathological problem irrespective of whatever emotional issues the woman herself presents.

Women find it difficult to see 'aloneness' as worthy of a celebration. Single women's independent lives are often the envy of their married sisters yet those single women struggle with feelings of incompleteness expressed as 'there's something missing' and often in terms of 'feeling unwanted and therefore unwantable'. In therapy this can be exposed as an acquired inability to be able to nurture themselves, their nurturing always has to be of others. This is often traditionally pathologized as dependency! In this context spinsterhood is seen as not chosen and hence sick whereas bachelorhood is seen as chosen and hence healthy. The significance of the rhetoric of 'choice' in the current political climate should not be underestimated.

Interestingly, contrary to the popular myth of the carefree bachelor, the mental health statistics suggest that single men suffer more than single women. However, the image for women persists and has its consequences in the way in which they experience their lives and the way in which their lives are perceived by others. Indeed it is not so long ago that 'old maid's mania' was used as a term to describe a clinical condition. The structural pressures against women becoming or existing as autonomous are well internalized and therefore frustrate and prevent women from coming to terms with their own predicament. There is a self-fulfilling prophecy aspect to all this which manifests itself in despair and misery.

The question of whether there can ever be free choice for women in the face of such powerful structural, ideological and cultural forces often emerges for married women as a personal crisis in their early thirties. This crisis manifests itself primarily with a sense of frustration that their lifestyle is not of their own choosing and that they are living their lives to a prepared script. The limited role repertoire open to women of this age, given labour market forces and career possibilities, tends to focus on the 'time-honoured' roles of wife and mother which, unlike a job, cannot be easily abandoned.

A third cost from women's social role can be articulated as 'having to have emotional antennae' and always behave in a 'responsible manner'. Preparation for this commences at an early age with young girls at play being described approvingly as 'good little mothers' and often being expected to take care of younger siblings, ultimately resulting in their being expected to anticipate needs as well as respond. How often, too, severely depressed women are advised to take on charity work and look after and think of others! This constitutes another dose of being everybody's caretaker and nurturer, as a response to their own needs not being met.

There is an imbalance in the emotional giving and taking: women's own deep feelings of neediness get repressed and replaced by guilt feelings when they allow themselves to recognize that they have needs of their own. In therapy this manifests itself after it has been identified and acknowledged, in a very powerful transference which emulates the mother–daughter relationship in reverse. The mother–daughter relationship can be a very competitive one, with both competing for scarce emotional resources. The mother often finds herself envious of her daughter's ability to express her needs when she herself cannot acknowledge her own, she expects herself only to *gratify* others rather than demand fulfilment of her own needs.

In feminist psychotherapy this can, and does, produce an intense relationship, but as it is a professional relationship between women who share similar experiences, it is relatively unambiguous and safer than real life relationships. Within this women can express their ambivalent feelings about their own daughters; they can explore their envy and dislike, and their anger at the expectation that they should prepare their daughters for their place in society by socializing them into conformity. The pain of this is often projected into the therapy session with a woman alternately trying to please the therapist and exhibiting quite murderous feelings towards the therapist who refuses to make her 'special' and break all the rules for her.

Women in therapy struggle with feeling they ought to nurture and take care of the therapist and take responsibility for her; they need to do this in order to keep their relationship with her. If a woman's life history has not prepared her to take caring from another woman on a consistent basis, her relationship with the therapist becomes very significant indeed. Initially she will find it very difficult to negotiate between two extreme images; the idealized mother – all good and all providing; and the bad rejecting mother of her own experience – withholding and disappointing. This kind of splitting needs to be confronted in a real relationship so that she can re-learn things misheard in childhood about her lack of worth.

But perhaps 'misheard' is not the case; it is clear that many of the messages which bombard women have the consequence of preventing any separate sense of self or of self-worth. Take, for example, the woman who consistently heard that she was not worth loving, that being a girl she must be pretty, that she must please others with her appearance; who spent large sums of money on plastic surgery for breasts and face and still it didn't work, she still didn't get 'the' man to love her. Highly efficient in her job, with lots of good women friends, always well groomed, she came into therapy acutely depressed with a sense of failure. She was obsessed with the fear of getting fat, messages from childhood continued to echo, 'You don't look nice with a fat face dear' – hence she had long since lost any enjoyment in food, a common theme. If she does achieve the longed for and prized relationship, and it does not bring the fulfilment she expects, she will be left feeling inadequate and empty. Tensions mount and as women find themselves alternatively curbing and exposing their dependency needs, the men they are involved with become alternately confused and angry and intimidated. Feminist therapy can provide an emotional climate of security and freedom, allowing the woman to express her dependency needs and desires while still allowing her to experience herself as an individual in her own right. This experience of being close and still separate, in an intense relationship, is a vital component in the woman's progression towards personal autonomy and ability to form more equal relationships.

Transference

The transference relationship becomes central within feminist psychotherapy, starting from accepting the classical psychoanalytic interpretation of transference feelings as originating in the compulsion to repeat. The women may continually repeat a form of behaviour as a way of coming to grips with it; so feelings belonging to significant others are displaced and projected on to the therapist, who is then able to direct the woman's attention to what is happening. Feminist therapy, therefore, here departs from the position of simply working with traumatized early family relationships, by incorporating the notion of 'splitting' as that phenomenon which makes up sexism, racism and homophobia by dividing attributes into good and bad comparisons (Malan, 1979). It assumes that this will have been internalized and will appear within the transference and needs to be handled as affecting the woman's perception of herself as stereotypical.

Any psychodynamic formulation which fails to take into account the external factors in the woman's situation and bases transference interpretations solely in intra-psychic compulsion, without reference to gender specificity, denies the possibility that the woman is grappling with actual reality. I reject Oedipal interpretations which concentrate exclusively on how a woman is relating, say to her husband, in an incestuous way. I cannot envisage making any interpretation that focuses exclusively on the woman without also considering what satisfactions the man in question is obtaining from the relationship. Failure to at least consider the interactional function of the relationship in interpretation serves to locate the responsibility for the situation entirely within the woman, finding its echoes in her servicing of the family.

Psychodynamic interpretations which serve to reinforce the requirements of a woman's stereotyped world do not acknowledge the differentiated power relations which exist there. Feminist therapy acknowledges a sharing of experience which at a very basic level allows a transference to develop which can shed light both on what is unique to each woman and on what is shared. It can also allow the therapist to actually validate the woman's experience, and more importantly it allows women to focus on what is *real* in the political situation of women.

Another departure from mainstream psychotherapy concerns the concept of resistance and the need to allow for possibilities other than psychopathology. Take the situation of a woman in therapy who has always had to be a 'good compliant girl', whose mother could never give her much time because of the demands of a manic depressive father and a 'delinquent' older brother who had to be serviced. She existed by never making any demands for herself. She learnt her place in the hierarchy very well. Perhaps when this woman failed to attend a therapy session one sunny day, having decided she would rather walk in the park, it might be more helpful to see this as a first step towards personal autonomy. Pleasing herself and not just pleasing others, and to handle it as such – rather than interpreting it as resistance or as some other unconscious psychological mechanism of self-defence. A woman who has to change her sessions because she cannot find childcare, is not automatically seen as acting out aggressive rejecting feelings within feminist psychotherapy. It is possible she has real problems with childcare! The point being made here is one of allowing for the operation of other processes than simply the intra-psychic. Thus a feminist psychotherapist can use her identification in facilitating her client to locate the problems more realistically.

Counter-transference

Moving to the woman therapist specifically, one of the important issues to arise is the question of disclosure. Traditionally, a therapist's disclosure is seen as spoiling the transference and to be avoided at all costs. However, in feminist therapy disclosure can open up the relationship to a real exchange and need not be merely about gratifying needs. Disclosure on the part of the therapist, of course, carries the risk that the therapist will form quite a strong relationship with the 'client' and that this then carries the risk of pain and loss to the therapist. Perhaps the appeal of Freudian detachment lies in the protection of the therapist, the non-personal interaction of the conventional response to questions for personal information ('Let's look at why you are interested in my experience'), leaves the person in therapy taking all the risks and the therapist in a position of absolute power.

This is one way of progressing but it can be counter-productive if you are trying to downplay transference which feeds on helplessness, mystery, distance and remoteness. Most women in therapy have had too much emotional remoteness and too little power already. Relating to a real person in the therapeutic alliance and coping with the feelings engendered in this alliance are an integral part of the process of empowerment of women. The idea that the therapist is simply a mirror who can and does just reflect back ignores all that we know about the dynamics of human interaction. It is impossible to be totally neutral. When the therapist is male and the client female her previous experiences of helplessness in the face of male power, and living in a culture which *celebrates* male power, will make the encounter another version of subordination. We need to ask whose needs would be being met in such a situation. It is professional dishonesty to claim that all values can be kept out of the therapeutic alliance; values underpin the way the therapist actually relates to the person and the inter-pretations that the therapist makes (and vice versa). It has been well demonstrated that all therapists have a predilection to interpret within their own autobiographical preference and that this will influence the nature of the relationship in an implicit way (Hobson, 1985). Giving the woman some information enables her to engage with the therapist, and with the interpretations made, within a more enlightened framework. This involves there being a more equal relationship between 'client' and therapist than is perhaps acceptable to main-stream psychiatry.

Of course within feminist therapy strong feelings are generated. Listening to women talk about their experiences can create extremes of sadness and anger in the therapist. She can identify with much of what she hears – this is clearly counter-transference (which at its simplest is all the feelings that the therapist experiences towards the person in therapy). Rapport can be established at a deep level and this can form the basis of the therapeutic alliance. Feminist therapists accept their response, are not frightened by it, and certainly do not automatically render it problematic. The constructive identification involved between women allows for a better understanding of what is uniquely female in the interaction. Often the emotionally charged reactions in the therapist cannot be linked to the specific content of sessions and thus would indicate the existence of interactive patterns stemming from the therapist's own unconscious forces.

By examining her own counter-transference responses the therapist is in a stronger position to understand the 'client's' experiences outside therapy and, as indicated before, this enables the therapist to target what is uniquely the 'client's' *own* developmental heritage. Without an understanding of what is common to all women there is a danger of blaming the victim as a result of the therapist's own hostile responses. Sadly this is well illustrated by the issue of women's fear of sexual assault. The threat of sexual assault is very real and the experience of it very common in women who come into therapy. Many women bring to therapy intense anger towards men. They are frequently in situations where they are sexually harassed and intimidated both at home and at work. The therapist can validate that part of the woman's experience which is based on living in a culture where men do not respect a woman's sovereignty over her own body, where men do not have respect for women's sexuality, and where women's bodies are seen as existing for male pleasure. This is not gratifying or colluding; the therapist addresses the reality of her situation and her anger while at the same time addressing the woman's internal fears, both expressed and unexpressed. The reality of this would seem to challenge classical interpretations of hysteria and paranoia as being particularly insensitive and certainly not particularly constructive. Indeed the use of this interpretation may well reveal more about the defensive stance of the male therapist when faced with the stark reality of the impact of male oppression on women.

Feminist psychotherapy, then, involves a powerful alliance which does not, as is often alleged, automatically translate itself into a collusive identification keeping the woman in the very patterns which are causing her distress. This is clearly not the purpose of feminist psychotherapy which aims at the empowerment of women. It signifies a perspective which accepts the concept of women's shared experiences while working towards a dynamic understanding of their unique selves. By using counter-transference the feminist therapist avoids the danger of objectifying the 'client'. In feminist therapy there is no taboo on tenderness.

References

Collier, A. (1977) *R.D.Laing: The Philosophy and Politics of Psychotherapy.* Brighton: Harvester Press.

Freud, S. with Breuer, J. (1895) *Studies on Hysteria.* Pelican Freud Library Vol.II. Harmondsworth: Penguin.

Freud, S. (1917) *Mourning and Melancholia.* Pelican Freud Library Vol.XI. Harmondsworth: Penguin.

Freud, S. (1931) *Female Sexuality*. Penguin Freud Library Vol.VII. Harmondsworth: Penguin.

Gove, W. R. (1972) The relationship between sex roles, marital status, and mental illness. *Social Forces* 51, 34–44.

Hobson, R. E. (1985) *Forms of Feeling the Heart of Psychotherapy*. London: Tavistock.

Malan, D. H. (1979) *Individual Psychotherapy and the Science of Psychodynamics*. London: Butterworth.

Maslow, A. H. (1954) *Motivation and Personality*. New York: Harper & Row.

Mills, C. Wright (1959) *The Sociological Imagination*. Cambridge: Cambridge University Press.

Showalter, E. (1987) *The Female Malady*. London: Virago.

8

Resisting the discipline

Celia Kitzinger

My resistance to psychology began when I was 16, and involved for the first time in a sexual relationship with another woman. Desperate for information, and far too embarrassed to ask anyone, I embarked on a literature review of psychological, psychiatric and psychoanalytic research. It was the early 1970s, and although the professional psychology journals were beginning to tell a different story, the information available to a lay reader at the time was firmly rooted in the pathological model. Lesbians were described as jealous, insecure and unhappy, the sick products of disturbed upbringing suffering from unresolved castration anxiety or oedipal conflicts, pursuing other women in a futile attempt to substitute a clitoris for a nipple as a result of their unresolved weaning problems. I remember particularly two Penguin paperbacks, these being, of course, among the most accessible to me: D.J. West's (1968) *Homosexuality* and Anthony Storr's (1964) *Sexual Deviation*. Both books include sections on treatment, prevention and cure of homosexuality, and both paint a sorry picture of lesbian life. 'No one in his [*sic*] right mind would opt for the life of a sexual deviant', says West, 'to be an object of ridicule and contempt, denied the fulfilments of ordinary family life, and cut off from the mainstream of human interests' (p. 220). Anthony Storr asserts that 'to be a woman who is loved by a man and who has children by him is the first and most important aim of feminine existence' (Storr, 1964, p. 73) and that consequently lesbian relationships are 'always *faute de mieux*, and those lesbians who protest that, for them, this kind of relationship is better than any possible intimacy with a man do not know what they are really missing' (pp. 79–80).

Resisting these theories was a matter of self-preservation. I stubbornly refused to believe that they applied to me, or had any relevance to my own life. Maybe *other* lesbians were like that, but my lover and I certainly weren't. As I began to meet other lesbians I simply dismissed this entire area of psychology as 'rubbish', a pseudoscientific reflection of the prejudices of society generally – prejudices which had already resulted in severe personal sanctions against me personally (including being expelled from school). Psychology did not reflect what I knew to be true about myself and my world: it denied my most important relationships, and obliterated my personal experience.

For many women, both lesbian and heterosexual, submission to psychology and psychiatry has meant defeat and self-hatred: an obstinate resistance has been essential for our survival. The lesbian and feminist movements of the early 1970s constituted an important part of the organized resistance and the initial emphasis was on resistance to psychology's *results*. Lesbians disputed the results which 'proved' that we were sick and both lesbian and hetero-feminists challenged the systematically degrading and oppressive portrayal of women in the psychological and psychiatric literatures. Gay and Lesbian Liberation groups in the United States disrupted meetings of the American Psychiatric Association until, in 1973, this body decided on the basis of a majority vote (and virtually no scientific evidence) that homosexuality was no longer to be considered a pathological diagnostic entity. By the end of the decade, the scientific evidence to support this decision had been constructed in accordance with the accepted rules of positivist-empiricism, and the overwhelming assumption was that the lesbian was really no different from the heterosexual woman: a great deal of time, energy and research money was spent proving this to be the case by psychologists who believed that in so doing they were demonstrating their own broadmindedness and contributing towards the alleviation of prejudice against gay people (cf. Kitzinger, 1987b). Bell and Weinberg (1978) showed that there were more differences *amongst* lesbians than between lesbians and heterosexual women, and Masters and Johnson (1979) demonstrated, through exhaustive laboratory research, that there were no differences in physiological response between lesbian and heterosexual women.

A scattering of articles in the core refereed psychology journals reflected this changed perspective (Davison, 1976; Freedman, 1975; Henley and Pincus, 1978; Morin, 1977), and the focus of psychological research shifted away from homosexuality to the new 'disease' of 'homophobia' (prejudice against gay people), and towards an exploration of ways in which psychology could be used positively and creatively by lesbian and gay therapists to 'assist lesbian identity integration' (Masterton, 1983), to 'help lesbians to come to terms with their sexuality' (Sang, 1978, p. 268) and to 'help the members of the couple achieve a more satisfying relationship with each other and with the heterosexual world in which they live' (Decker, 1983). In the early 1970s, a new journal was founded to cater for this interest in so-called 'gay/lesbian affirmative' research (*Journal of Homosexuality*), and there is now a well-established genre of 'lesbian psychology' written by lesbian feminist professionals and addressed to the lesbian community, which details ways in which lesbian well-being can be promoted through psychology (Loulan, 1984; Boston Lesbian Psychologies Collective, 1987; Clunis and Green, 1988).

This shift from lesbian resistance ('antipsychology') to 'lesbian psychology' is paralleled, over much the same period, by a similar development within (hetero-)feminist psychology. As with lesbian resistance, the hetero-feminist resistance began with an attack on psychology's *results*, challenging their validity and seeking to 'correct' psychology's errors. Unlike much of lesbian psychology at the time, hetero-feminist psychology also resisted psychological *methods*, characterizing the 'hard' statistical and psychometric approaches as 'masculine', and seeking to replace them with the 'soft' (qualitative) 'female-identified' approaches. It is worth noting that this methodological critique was much less popular among lesbians, partly because, compared with heterosexual women, they had less investment in being 'soft' or 'feminine', and partly because quantitative methods had in fact been very little used in research on lesbianism: before 1969, about a quarter of all studies on sexual 'orientation' relied exclusively on face-to-face interviews (a paradoxical 'benefit' of the psychiatric case study), and interviews and questionnaires together accounted for about three-quarters of research in the area (Shively et al., 1984). While hetero-feminist (and humanistic) researchers claimed that qualitative methods are more likely to respect the meanings of the research participants, lesbians were only too aware that some of the most virulently anti-lesbian investigators had never sullied their work with a dehumanizing statistic or contaminated their intuitions with a controlled experiment. Some of the earliest work by lesbians challenging the results of the pathologists came, therefore, from psychometricians (e.g. Hopkins, 1969).

Subsequently, an important strand of both lesbian and hetero-feminist theorizing concluded that it was not simply the results, or the methods, of psychology that were at fault, but rather that psychology as a discipline was inherently problematic. In fact feminists outside the discipline had been arguing this point since the early 1970s, and argued it against not just established and clearly oppressive psychological theorizing, but also against the new breed of 'feminist psychologist' with her talk of 'sex roles' and 'conditioning'. Radical feminists pointed out that these approaches depoliticized women's oppression, and that 'the field of psychology has always been used to substitute personal explanations of problems for political ones, and to disguise real material oppression as emotional disturbance' (Leon, 1970). Expression of this view is now commonplace in 'feminist psychology', although detailed analysis of the political processes at work is rare outside grass-roots feminist theorizing.

Having identified psychology as incompatible with feminism

because of its refusal to deal with political realities, and its pretence at objectivity, feminists with a professional involvement in the discipline then sought to redefine and harness psychology for the feminist cause: henceforth it would acknowledge its own subjective and political status. As with 'gay psychology', lobbying was set in motion, new journals were founded, new discoveries debunked long-established 'findings', and mainstream psychology was forced to adapt at least to the extent of 'permitting' 'Psychology of Women' sections within its professional bodies in the US and UK (see the chapter by Sue Wilkinson and Jan Burns in this volume). The British Psychological Society is now actively encouraging Psychology of Women courses to be incorporated into the undergraduate curriculum as a 'high priority' (Scientific Affairs Board, 1988, pp. 21–8).

The overt anti-lesbianism displayed by feminist psychologists has been documented elsewhere (Fontaine, 1982; Frye, 1982; Zimmerman, 1982; Kitzinger, 1988a), and 'feminist psychology', like 'lesbian psychology', and psychology generally (Moghaddam, 1987; Levidow, 1988), is also severely limited by its commitment to a white, middle-class, North American/western vision of the world. Nonetheless, despite these acknowledged deficiencies, both 'feminist' and 'lesbian psychology' have achieved widespread acceptance within the lesbian and feminist communities of the cultures from which they originate. We are inundated with popular psychology paperbacks purporting to provide a 'feminist' and/or 'lesbian' psychological perspective on everything from slimming diets to sexual fantasies, from our relationships with our mothers, sisters and friends, to explorations of 'ego development' and 'sex role identity'. Many lesbians and hetero-feminists are now avid consumers of the new pop psychology culture. They actively employ the language of psychology – words like sex role, homophobia, conditioning, inferiority complex, empowerment and the real me are common parlance – and the 'consciousness-raising' group, vital to the early years of second wave feminism, has been replaced with various forms of therapy. In this sense there is now a widespread 'practice of psychology by feminists' which extends far beyond the professional boundaries.

In summary, the psychological scene now is very different from that which I confronted, and resisted, as a woman and a lesbian more than fifteen years ago. Whereas, at the beginning of the 1970s, lesbian and hetero-feminists led vigorous protests against psychology, which they condemned for its heterosexist, androcentric, and apolitical view of the world, today these same groups are actively employing the language of psychology and using or promoting psychological and psychiatric services. In place of the lesbian and feminist 'antipsychologies' of my pre-university and undergraduate days, there is now a degree of acceptance for hybrid conceptual entities called 'feminist psychology' and 'lesbian psychology', both within feminism generally, and within parts of psychology as a discipline, as evidenced by the establishment of the Lesbian and Gay Division within the APA (in 1984) and the Psychology of Women Section in the BPS (in 1987). Is there then, now, any need to 'resist' psychology? Or can I take my place within the discipline as a 'lesbian-feminist psychologist'?

As this book illustrates, for many feminist psychologists there remains a sense of tension between feminism and the professional practice of psychology. At any gathering of feminist psychologists, there is always urgent discussion and self-questioning about 'selling out', or using feminism to 'scale the ivory tower'. Can we maintain our feminist convictions in the face of the huge socialization pressures brought to bear on us by institutionalized psychology, or are we being subtly corrupted and sucked into the system? When invited to give papers, or convene symposia, or sit on committees, are we being used to give a false legitimacy as token feminists, or is our self-doubt and uncertainty a reflection of our 'typically female' distrust of our own abilities and self-worth? If we accept posts within the BPS, are we invading the citadel of male privilege and making it easier for women who come after us, or are we advancing our own careers on the back of the feminist movement? Despite the intensity of such discussions – in which I, too, participate – I believe they address the wrong questions. They are phrased in terms of individual ethical dilemmas. Far more important is an exploration of the relationship between psychology and feminism in terms of its social and political features. How can we account for the shift from feminist 'antipsychology' to 'feminist psychology'? What is 'feminist psychology', and what relationship does it have with the rest of the discipline (?'non-feminist psychology'), and with feminism as a political movement?

Several feminist researchers have pointed out the limited impact of feminist psychology upon the discipline as a whole: 'conservative social scientists reacted by closing the ranks of the brotherhood and bolstering their position with increased stress on hardcore approaches emulating the natural science' (Meyer, 1988). In the United States there is an ongoing debate about the coherence of psychology as a discipline, and the perceived threat of psychology's approaching demise has led some professionals to recommend an increased emphasis on teaching a logical positivist value system focusing on operational definitions, antecedent-consequent relationships, and universal and generalizable laws – the sort of psychology that omits altogether a political perspective and denies its own political location (Aitkenhead, 1988). At the same time, there is increasing professionalization of psychology, both in the United States and in Britain, in the process of which careful definitions are being drawn up concerning who counts as a 'proper' psychologist, and what constitute legitimate topics for psychological research (Aitkenhead, 1988). 'While feminist work may be a current item, within many domains of inquiry', comments one feminist psychologist (Morawski, 1988), 'the actual acceptance of this work is not secured.' She describes the way in which feminist scholars are denied jobs or promotions on the grounds that their research does not fit into any of the existing disciplines: 'In such cases we are reminded that disciplines are constituted by procedural rules, by protocols for developing understanding of some phenomena and not others. The production of knowledge is thus rule-bounded, and questioning of the rules will be resisted' (Morawski, 1988).

One of the rules fundamental to the traditional construction of psychology is that it is an apolitical domain of technical expertise. In becoming psychologists, feminists have often had to submerge their political commitments under a concern for objective science. Their research may have political *implications*, but it is not in itself political.

The group formed by feminist psychologists before they achieved a section within the BPS was called Women in Psychology. It was women-only and explicitly political. That group appears to have disbanded now that a section has been formed, under the name Psychology of Women (which is supposed to sound more 'objective, detached and impersonal') (cf. Nicolson, 1987), although the section can apparently be neither explicitly political, nor women-only (Burns, 1988). Indeed, the first open forum held by this new section raised a question about whether or not feminist psychology was necessarily political: '*Is* the psychology of women political?', it was called. And this is at the root of the problem: the core of psychology's disciplinary definition includes some concept of objectivity and neutrality; it is an apolitical science. As long as 'feminist psychology' confined itself to arguing about the correctness of certain findings, or even the validity of certain methodologies, it did not necessarily violate this definition. But if 'feminist psychology' is avowedly political then it becomes a contradiction in terms. Engaged in feminist practice, we are excluded from the category of 'psychologist'; practising as 'psychologists' we are no longer acting as feminists. Let me illustrate how this definitional process has worked in my own experience.

My own experience is that I am not permitted to be 'feminist psychologist' because, when I write as a feminist, I am defined out of the category of 'psychologist'. When I speak of social structure, of power and politics, when I use language and concepts rooted in my understanding of oppression, I am told that what I say does not qualify as 'psychology'. Because those who control the definition of 'psychology' act as gate-keepers for the professional refereed journals,

I cannot be published in them. Although I am constantly asked to contribute chapters to edited books and articles for the radical press, and even to write for *The Psychologist* in a 'journalistic' capacity, my work is generally rejected by the editors of refereed journals – often for precisely those reasons which lead to invitations beng extended from other quarters: it is 'political' or 'journalistic'. In terms of employment and promotion within psychology, refereed journal articles count for much more than chapters in books, articles in the non-refereed journals, or even single-authored books (Reicher, 1988): as Ziman (quoted in Mahoney, 1979) has said, 'the journal referee is the linchpin about which the whole business of science is pivoted'. I have also found it extremely hard to get employment: after 112 applications during the last year of my PhD research and during the subsequent year of unemployment, I was eventually offered a temporary research fellowship in an education department. When that expired, another period of unemployment and 44 applications (both in this country and abroad) were necessary before I obtained a probationary lectureship in a polytechnic.

Analysis of rejection letters from refereed journals (I have received eight to date, plus eleven anonymous referees' reports) offers an intriguing insight into the professional definition of psychology and the processes whereby the gate-keepers reinforce this disciplinary definition. In what follows I draw on these rejection letters from journal editors and referees' reports (the journals range from some of the prestigious core journals of social psychology, to more specialist social and educational journals), from personal letters written to me by other psychologists concerned about my apparent unemployability, and from conversation and interviews. (The rejected journal articles cover all three of the major topics on which I have worked: lesbianism, human rights, and injustice in schools.)

A constant theme running throughout the rejections is the complaint that I am politically motivated. Sometimes it is explicitly feminism that is objected to: one sympathetic (male) member of a psychology department which had rejected my application for a lectureship told me that his department already had a feminist and that, as far as some members of the department were concerned, she was 'one too many'. The advice I was given when I discussed my applications with other feminist psychologists already in secure employment and anxious to help me was pretty uniform and reflected their understanding of the difficulties involved in being both 'political' and a psychologist (the following quotations come from personal letters).

> I would advise that you moderate, just a little, your political statements, until you have a secure position.

> About your application: I think I know what you are doing. You do it very well . . . There is just my question then about the tactic form. You can imagine that I am going to say something about engaging in some degree of ingratiation. At this stage, you understand, I do not mean to talk about selling out.

> My instrumental advice is – if you want to get a job, compromise. I do think you face an uphill battle unless you compromise – how much only you can decide. I'm not suggesting it, just saying that you may need to do it *or* give up.

Interviewers and journal reviewers alike insist on the contrast between 'objectivity' (the presentation of factual evidence and empirical data), on the one hand, and 'politics' (ideology, polemics) on the other – in so doing, reasserting precisely that disciplinary definition of psychology as positivist-empiricist that I was trying to undermine. At one job interview, I was asked to explain my stated interest in 'social constructionism' to the panel. After presenting my understanding of 'science' and 'objectivity' as social constructions used to mask psychology's legitimation of status quo ideologies, I was asked to 'reassure the panel that you are committed to discovering objective facts'. The editorial board of one international conference accepted my paper on lesbian identities, in which I argued for a radical feminist theory of lesbianism in preference of alternative liberal humanistic theories, but made the following recommendations:

> [We] would like to suggest you concentrate your paper on empirical data . . . We would like to ask you to treat the radical feminist theory of lesbianism in the same way as the above mentioned theories . . . We would like to ask you to pay attention to the difference between theory and ideology.

A book proposal on subjectivity did the rounds of publishers, and was rejected by all of them: one wrote saying. 'I fear that the bulk of psychologists are not ready to accept your message yet', and another sent back an anonymous review by a psychologist:

> The proposed book is highly polemical, and for that reason is likely to raise the hackles of conventional psychologists . . . Most psychologists would not like to be told that they are trapped in a 'traditional positivistic paradigm': apart from the clichéd jargon, most psychologists think of positivism as a discredited doctrine of the Vienna Circle, abandoned by psychologists in the 1940s or early 1950s . . . the style could perhaps be moderated.

Other rejection letters were more explicit in their criticism of my avowedly political perspective:

> My main objection to the article is the style of argument. What we are offered is a single perspective with no attempt to represent other views as having any validity . . . Regretfully then I classify this article as an attempt to persuade the reader to adopt a point of view by presenting only one side of

an argument . . . Quotations are of individual opinions . . . rather than hard data. (anonymous reviewer)

I thought that the minimal requisite of a fair presentation of any case, however ignominious it may be, was balanced presentation of the case, leaving the reader or jury to make up their own minds . . . I feel that a lot of the replies to your research must suffer from a lack of objectivity, and will surely come from people who have an axe to grind. I presume that as someone involved in serious research, you will take full account of this parameter before drawing your conclusions. I'm sorry that I cannot accept your paper in its present form . . . If, however, you can produce a more balanced paper, giving the other side of cases mentioned, then I should be most pleased to consider it for publication since, as I said at the outset, the subject is definitely interesting. (editor's letter of rejection)

Central to these rejections, then, is the sense that my work is not 'balanced' or 'objective', that it is an attempt to 'persuade' the reader of a particular point of view (something no 'serious researcher' would dream of doing!), and that it is politically biased – 'polemical' or 'ideological'. And it is not just *what* I say, it's the way that I say it. Suggestions about my writing style are frequent: that it should be 'moderated' or 'toned down' – that it should be less 'journalistic' or 'emotion-laden', that I should 'avoid the jargon of the radical sociology of the 1960s'. 'The text is replete with value-laden words' commented one anonymous reviewer; 'a more scientific presentation is needed', wrote another.

In many cases the critics suggest that I do what I do very well, but that they don't want that sort of thing in their journal (or department). This is often because what I am doing is not seen as 'psychology'. The editor of one of the most prestigious European-based social psychological journals returned a submission with the comment that 'we try to minimize as much as possible papers which are essentially descriptive . . .' Clearly worried lest I should take offence at this attitude to descriptive research he continued:

I hope you will not derive from this comment a depreciation for descriptive research, that would certainly be a misunderstanding. On the contrary, I believe that for a number of purposes descriptive research is much more relevant and important than more nomothetic oriented research (and probably also more difficult to do). I only explain now our Journal policy and I'm sure that there are several more sociologically oriented Journals which would be a very good outlet for your present study. (editor)

The advice to go for a more 'sociologically-oriented' journal suggests that my work is seen as not quite 'psychology'. This is made explicit in a letter from the editor of an international journal of applied social psychology who made the comment: 'the emphasis is not sufficiently social psychological to justify publication in the journal'. Both of his anonymous reviewers had made the same point, one saying that 'there is very little reference to social psychology', the other complaining that the paper is 'generally too light on social psychological substance'.

The editor of another widely cited social psychological journal also based in Europe queried the same point about another paper: is my work really 'psychological'?

> Essentially you provide a 'cartography' of issues, views, opinions, beliefs, etc., about human rights. This in itself is fascinating. However, I am not convinced about the psychological or social psychological relevance of it ... Interesting social philosophy and ideology, no doubt, but what does it mean psychologically?

Again, my work was seen as 'not psychology' – perhaps social philosophy or ideology, or sociology, but not psychology. (This research was finally published, in an abbreviated form, in a small-circulation journal (cf. Stainton Rogers and Kitzinger, 1986), and a full copy of the research project is lodged with the Council of Europe who founded the research (Stainton Rogers and Kitzinger, 1985).

At the time when I received this latter rejection letter, I was working on an analysis of psychological rhetoric (cf. Kitzinger, 1987b, chapter 1) and decided to test my own theoretical analysis by putting it into practice. I resubmitted this same paper on human rights to the BPS annual conference (which, ironically enough, had rejected my previous submission on 'rhetoric in psychology'). But the resubmitted version was disguised in the rhetorical garb of positivist-empiricism. (Actually, this started as a joke – could I produce a convincing parody of social psychological writing? – and was elevated to the status of a test case when a colleague suggested submitting the paper.)

'How do people construe their rights?' the title demands: questions make good titles, because it suggests that science is about to provide an answer (Kitzinger, 1987b, pp. 22–3; Stainton Rogers and Kitzinger, 1988). I follow the question mark with a colon (grammatically incorrect, but accepted and reproduced in the conference programme), and the subheading, 'a study of alternative schematisations'. This last word is an example of 'terminological oversophistication' (or 'big words', Kemeny, 1959), and the use of the colon ('titular colonicity') has been described as 'the primary correlate of scholarship' (Dillon, 1981): 72 percent of published research titles contain a colon (Dillon, 1981). My summary begins with a sentence containing two passive verbs (contributing to the aura of objectivity) (cf. Kitzinger, 1987b, p. 24) and I list five references in the first two sentences (cf. Gilbert, 1977, on the use of references as persuasion). By suggesting that the reported research builds on what has gone before. I contribute to the 'up the mountain' account of scientific progress (Rorty, 1980; Kitzinger,

1987b, pp. 7–10), and the use of visual imagery ('illuminate', 'focus', 'clarification') contributes to the 'discovery account' in scientific rhetoric (Woolgar, 1983, p. 246). The last sentence of the first paragraph ends with the (outrageously rhetorical!) claim that contemporary social and political debate over human rights issues 'is conducted in strident and highly-charged ideological terms to which rational and objective scientific inquiry could bring much-needed clarification' (the mythologizing of expertise: Kitzinger, 1987b, pp. 10–14). A paragraph on methodology and an outline of the results follow in much the same vein, and the paper ends with a sample of 'utility accounting' – the presentation of psychology as useful, nay indispensable, for human well-being (Kitzinger, 1987b, pp. 20–22): 'it is suggested that social psychological research into alternative schematisations offers an important input for those working on rights issues and other domains of human welfare where a plurality of models are operative.'

The paper was accepted.

Unfortunately, I was never able to discover *why* this parody of a scientific paper had been allowed to enter the hallowed halls of a BPS conference. I had already been told (on the occasion of my previous rejection) by the Chair of the Standing Conference Committee that no correspondence would be entered into regarding submissions. So perhaps it wasn't because of the rhetoric – perhaps they were able to see through to the truly interesting ideas camouflaged beneath it? At the conference my co-researcher (Rex Stainton Rogers) presented the paper without the scientific rhetoric, and journalists (Tysoe, 1988) translated back into sensible and politically relevant language the ideas that I could have presented that way in the first place, had the system allowed.

No one familiar with recent work on the rhetoric of science (Nelson et al., 1987; Simons, 1989; Kitzinger, in press) will be surprised by this outcome. Older studies within the framework of the sociology of science have also examined editorial decisions, and illustrate certain systematic biases towards preferred results or methodologies, and towards certain authors at the expense of others. One researcher, for example, sent the same manuscript to 75 reviewers from the *Journal of Applied Behaviour Analysis*, a well-respected periodical. The papers had identical introductions, methods and references, but the results and discussions were different: half were favourable to behaviour modification, and the other had the graphs and tables reversed so as to make them unfavourable to behaviour modification. When reviewers read manuscripts in which the data supported their own perspective they rated its methodology as 'adequate' or 'excellent' and recommended publication: when it didn't, they rated it 'inadequate' and recommended rejection (Mahoney, 1979). In another study twelve articles from highly prestigious journals, by authors at top rank institutions (Harvard, Oxford, etc.) were resubmitted in superficial disguise to the same journals that had just published them with the author affiliation changed to a low prestige institution. Three of the twelve were recognized; eight of the remaining nine were vehemently rejected as being severely substandard (Peters and Ceci, 1982, reported in Standing and McKelvie, 1986). Researchers able to cite their own published and 'in press' papers in submitted articles also stand a better chance of publication (Mahoney, 1979), illustrating Merton's (1968) famous Matthew effect ('unto everyone that hath, shall be given and he shall have abundance: but from he that hath not, shall be taken away even that which he hath'). Finally, a disproportionately high percentage of editorial appointments are held by men (Over, 1981). Overall, authors' satisfaction with the fairness of their treatment at the hands of journal editors is often low (Bradley, 1981) but hard to express – it can sound like 'sour grapes'. Publicly flaunting one's failures is also not good for career prospects – as was pointed out to me by (otherwise sympathetic) colleagues in the course of my writing this chapter.

Several critics have made suggestions for improvements in the submission and refereeing process. (Standing and McKelvie, 1986), and a few journal editors have written about the trials and tribulations of their job, and openly discussed their reviewing procedures (Manstead, 1985) – but I think it would be wrong to scapegoat individual editors, or referees, as the villains of the piece, or to expect that clearer guidelines would solve the problem. The 'problem' is institutional psychology as a discipline. Its rejection of feminist research as 'political', 'polemical' or 'journalistic' is surely not a mistake, but central to its maintenance of disciplinary boundaries.

Sue Wilkinson (1988) concludes that feminists should study the conditions which govern the acceptance or rejection of feminist psychology 'in a self-conscious attempt to increase the impact of their work on the mainstream'. So perhaps I should now sit down and cynically translate all my rejected papers into PsychSpeak, submit them to the journals and improve the look of my CV. There is that temptation. Or perhaps, on the grounds that my work would then no longer be 'feminist' (as I understand that term), I should give up on the idea of publishing in the mainstream journals altogether: 'It is the demand feminist thinkers place upon themselves to adhere to disciplinary practices – to speak in certain orderly, intelligible and legitimate ways . . . that necessitates their reinscribing in their speech the very patterns of patriarchal relations they wish to undermine (Shotter and Logan, 1988).

All the disciplines define their boundaries and censure those who stray beyond them – and politics is decidedly out of bounds for the psychologist. Other researchers have illustrated this same point, documenting the way in which questions about links between professional organizations (such as the BPS) and South Africa are successfully relegated to the classification of 'politics' and hence considered an illegitimate area of concern (Aitkenhead, 1988), or describing the fate of researchers who become politically involved in their research (Reicher, 1988). Feminist research is not perceived by the mainstream to be legitimate science primarily because feminism is seen as political, and because psychologists have been socialized into the belief that advocacy and scholarship are incompatible. When feminist research is characterized as purely political, this 'provides the mainstream researcher with grounds for dismissing it as illegitimate; politics has nothing to do with science' (Wilkinson, 1988). To be intelligible as psychologists, feminists are forced to adhere to disciplinary practices which undermine feminist politics.

I am left with some uncomfortable questions – questions which I do not hear being discussed among feminist psychologists today.

While the last decade has seen an explosion of 'feminist psychology' and 'lesbian psychology', its impact on the mainstream of those societies which have founded it (primarily the US and UK) has been negligible. Over the same period, the percentage of people in Britain believing homosexuality to be wrong has risen steadily (*British Social Attitudes Survey*, 1980, 1985, 1986, 1988) and Clause 28 – restricting the civil liberties of lesbians and gay men – has been passed. We are witnessing the return to 'Victorian values' (or the rise of the 'moral majority') with all that implies for women and for lesbians. And yet although I meet academics from other disciplines – sociologists, historians and anthropologists – on the marches and vigils I have never yet met a psychologist colleague at a feminist campaign meeting or on a picket line. Nor do feminist psychologists publish (as other feminist academics do) in the feminist press – journals like *Trouble and Strife, Lesbian Ethics* or *Radical and Revolutionary Feminist Newsletter*. What, then, is the relationship between the academic 'feminist psychologist' and those parts of the Women's Liberation Movement that get their hands dirty doing real political work?

The effect of the recent outpouring of 'feminist psychology' is also problematic despite, or perhaps because of, its huge popularity. Quite apart from the clearly legitimate criticisms of this work for its white, heterosexual, gentile, middle-class and western bias, many radical feminists characterize it as an attempt, on the part of privileged liberal feminists, to undermine the radical foundations of the movement, by relocating the political in the psychopathology of the personal, and by individualizing or depoliticizing the issues involved (Cardea, 1985; Penelope, 1984; Mann, 1987). This is the same criticism that was made by feminists in the early 1970s (Sarachild, 1974; Serre, 1973), and this critique achieves a new urgency at a time when, with the rise of the 'new right', many erstwhile activists seem tempted to swap their exhausted political ambitions for therapeutic ideals. There is increasingly an encroachment, into the political language of radical feminism, of terms derived from or based in psychology, and the spread of psychobabble throughout the lesbian and feminist communities restricts the possibilities for political dialogue. Feminism today is becoming *not* a political but a *psychological* movement concerned with struggling against 'sex roles', overcoming women's 'inferiority complexes' or 'fear of success', counteracting our 'conditioning', and combating 'sexist attitudes' or 'homophobia'. Instead of subverting or supplanting psychology, as feminists initially intended, many have accepted its language as their own, and it has often been professional feminist psychologists who first offered these personalized concepts to the feminist communities (cf. the critiques by Jackson, 1985; Strega and Jo, 1987; Kitzinger, 1987a): in consequence, feminism has been translated from a political movement into a 'lifestyle' or 'state of mind'. Psychology is, if not an agent of, at least a willing participant in the depoliticization of feminism.

The hybrid 'feminist psychology' can be made conceptually coherent *either* through the politicization of psychology, *or* through the depoliticization of feminism. Many radicals have charged that the latter notion is prevalent. I have heard of and participated in a great deal of discussion among 'feminist psychologists' about how feminist psychology should respond to criticism from the *psychological* establishment. I have heard very little discussion about how we might respond to radical *political* criticism from the grass-roots of our movement(s). And I wonder: are 'feminist psychologists' reading feminist political journals with the same attention they devote to professional psychology journals – and if not, why not? Do they attend feminist conferences, workshops and summer schools as they do psychology conferences and meetings? Are they prepared to engage with political arguments from feminists as seriously as they do with psychological arguments from professional colleagues? Or is the process of socialization into the position of 'psychologist', combined with the harsh realities of (un)employment and promotion prospects, such that 'feminist psychology' will always be much more 'psychology' than 'feminism'?

As I have already illustrated, feminism has had a severely limited impact on psychology as a discipline: if we have resisted psychology, it has resisted us back. Nonetheless, some have pointed to the establishment of the Psychology of Women Section as a partial concession to feminism. An alternative perspective is to see the section as a way of bringing into the BPS a splinter group of latent antipsychologists whose popularity (as Women in Psychology) was potentially threatening to the discipline. This suggestion smacks of the conspiratorial, but the Scientific Affairs Board of the BPS, in its recent document on *The Future of the Psychological Sciences*, announces its concern about 'diversity' within psychology, and recommends that the Society try to 'minimize its negative effects on the discipline' (13, 13, 3). 'We believe that the discipline should resist splintering of psychological knowledge into groups which identify themselves as separate from the mainstream of psychology and seek to deny their psychological origin' (SAB, 1988, 13, 13, 2). To give such splinter groups representation within the BPS is a risky strategy: will 'feminist psychologists' be absorbed into the mainstream as a result of this development, or will we insist on our political origins?

For me, being both a feminist and a psychologist means to be responsible to other feminists for my psychology, and, equally, to be responsible to other psychologists for my feminism. To remain identified with each group, I need to be able to offer something positive to each. To feminism I offer my analysis of the dangers of psychobabble invading the women's movement, my criticisms of so-called 'gay affirmative' psychology, and my 'insider' knowledge of a patriarchal discipline (Kitzinger, 1983, 1987a, 1987b, 1988b, 1988d, 1988e). To psychology I offer my analyses of the role of rhetoric within the social sciences, a radical social constructionist perspective as an alternative to positivist-empiricist approaches, and my 'insider' knowledge of lesbianism and feminism (Kitzinger, 1986, 1987b, 1988a, 1988c, 1989; in press; Kitzinger and Stainton Rogers, 1985).

Although rejecting the label 'feminist psychologist' as a contradiction in terms, I am passionate in my commitment both to feminism and to psychology. The intellectual excitement and the practical impact of my research and teaching are lodged in the space created by this contradiction – and the challenge of contradiction seems infinitely more creative than the comfort of compromise!

References

Aitkenhead, M. (1988) Official morality and the regulation of research: dilemmas of deviance. Paper presented to the Annual Conference of the British Psychological Society, 15–18 April, Leeds.

Bell, A.P. and Weinberg, M.S. (1978) *Homosexualities: A Study of Diversity among Men and Women*. London: Mitchell Beazley.

Boston Lesbian Psychologies Collective (ed.) (1987) *Lesbian Psychologies: Explorations and Challenges*, Chicago: University of Illinois Press.

Bradley, J.V. (1981) Pernicious publication practices. *Bulletin of the Psychonomic Society* 18, 31–4.

Burns, J. (1988) Letter, *Psychology of Women Section Newsletter* 2, 37.

Cardea, C. (1985) The lesbian revolution and the 50 minute hour: a working-class look at therapy and the movement. *Lesbian Ethics* 1(3), 46–68.

Clunis, D.M. and Green, G. Dorsey (1988) *Lesbian Couples*. Seattle, Washington: Seal Press.

Davison, G.C. (1976) Homosexuality: the ethical challenge. *Journal of Consulting and Clinical Psychology* 44, 157–62.

Decker, B. (1983) Counseling gay and lesbian couples. *Journal of Social Work and Human Sexuality* 2, 39–52.

Dillon, J.T. (1981) The emergence of the colon: an empirical correlate of scholarship. *American Psychologist* 36, 879–84.

Fontaine, C. (1982) Teaching the psychology of women: a lesbian feminist perspective. In M. Cruikshank (ed.), *Lesbian Studies: Present and Future*. New York: The Feminist Press.

Freedman, M. (1975) Homosexuals may be healthier than straights. *Psychology Today* 8, 28–32.

Frye, M. (1982) A lesbian perspective on women's studies. In M. Cruikshank (ed.), *Lesbian Studies: Present and Future*. New York: The Feminist Press.

Gilbert, G.N. (1977) Referencing as persuasion. *Social Studies of Science* 7, 113–22.

Henley, N.M. and Pincus, F. (1978) Interrelationship of sexist, racist and anti-homosexual attitudes. *Psychological Reports* 42, 83–90.

Hopkins, J. (1969), The lesbian personality. *British Journal of Psychiatry* 115, 1433–6.

Jackson, C. (1985) Fat is a feminist issue – a classic diet reviewed. *Trouble and Strife: A Radical Feminist Magazine* 7, 39–44.

Kemeny, J.G. (1959) *A Philosopher Looks at Science*. Princeton, NJ: Van Nostrand Reinhold.

Kitzinger, C. (1983) The politics of orgasm. *Radical and Revolutionary Feminist Newsletter* (Women Only) 12, 15–18.

Kitzinger, C. (1986) Introducing and developing Q as a Feminist methodology: a study of accounts of lesbianism. In S. Wilkinson (ed.), *Feminist Social Psychology: Developing Theory and Practice*. Milton Keynes: Open University Press.

Kitzinger, C. (1987a) Heteropatriarchal language: the case against 'homophobia'. *Gossip: A Journal of Lesbian Feminist Ethics* 5, 15–20.

Kitzinger, C. (1987b) *The Social Construction of Lesbianism*. London: Sage.

Kitzinger, C. (1988a) 'Lesbian theory'. Paper presented to the London Conference of the British Psychological Society, 19–20 December.

Kitzinger, C. (1988b) Sexuality: cause, choice and construction. *Lesbian and Gay Socialist* 15, 18–19.

Kitzinger, C. (1988c) Individualism and the feminist challenge. *American Psychological Association Social Division Newsletter (CSP)* September, 38–46.

Kitzinger, C. (1988d) Developing lesbian theory (4-day course). *International Lesbian Summer School*. Lesbian Archives, Wesley House, London.

Kitzinger, C. (1988e) Feminism and lesbian separatism: the relationship. Talk given at Conway Hall, London, November.

Kitzinger, C. (1989) Liberal humanism as an ideology of social control: the regulation of lesbian identities. In J. Shotter and K. Gergen (eds), *Texts of Identity*. London: Sage.

Kitzinger, C. (in press) The rhetoric of pseudoscience. In I. Parker and J. Shotter (eds), *Deconstructing Social Psychology*. London: Routledge.

Kitzinger, C. and Stainton Rogers, R. (1985) A Q methodological study of lesbian identities. *European Journal of Social Psychology* 15, 167–87.

Leon, B. (1970) Brainwashing and women: the psychological attack. Reprinted in Redstockings (1978) *Feminist Revolution*. New York: Random House.

Levidow, L. (1988) NonWestern science, past and present. *Science as Culture* 3, 101–17.

Loulan, J. (1984) *Lesbian Sex*. San Francisco: Spinsters Ink.

Mahoney, M.J. (1979) Psychology of the scientist: an evaluative review. *Social Studies of Science 9: 349*–75.

Mann, B. (1987) Validation or liberation? A critical look at therapy and the Women's Movement. *Trivia* 10, 41–56.

Manstead, A.S.R. (1985) Editing the British Journal of Social Psychology: the first two years. *The British Psychological Society Social Psychology Section Newsletter.* 14, 39–45.

Masters, M.A. and Johnson, V.E., (1979) *Homosexuality in Perspective*. Boston: Little, Brown.

Masterton, J. (1983) Lesbian consciousness-raising discussion groups. *Journal for Specialists in Group Work* 8, 24–30.

Merton, R.K. (1968) The Matthew effect in science. *Science* 159, 56–63.

Meyer, J. (1988) Feminist thought and social psychology. In M. Gergen (ed.), *Feminist Thought and the Structure of Knowledge*. New York: New York University Press.

Moghaddam, F.M. (1987) Psychology in the three worlds. *American Psychologist* 42, 912–20.

Morawski, J.G. (1988) Impasse in feminist thought. In M. Gergen (ed.), *Feminist Thought and the Structure of Knowledge*. New York: New York University Press.

Morin, S.F. (1977) Heterosexual bias in psychological research on lesbianism and male homosexuality. *American Psychologist* 19, 629–37.

Nelson, J.S., Megill, A. and McCloskey, D.N. (1987) *The Rhetoric of the Human Sciences*. Wisconsin: University of Wisconsin Press.

Nicolson, P. (1987) The Women in Psychology Society. *Social Psychology Section Newsletter* 27, Spring, 19–22.

Over, R. (1981) Representation of women on the editorial boards of psychology journals. *American Psychologist*, 36, 885–91.

Penelope, J. (1984) The mystery of lesbians: Reprinted in S.L. Hoagland and J. Penelope (eds), *For Lesbians Only: A Separatist Anthology*. London: Onlywomen Press.

Reicher, S. (1988) It's not what you say it's the way that you do it: the forced abstraction of psychological research. Paper presented to the annual conference of the British Psychological Society, 15–18 April, Leeds.

Rorty, R. (1980) *Philosophy and the Mirror of Nature*. Oxford: Basil Blackwell.

Sang, B. (1978) Lesbian research: a critical evaluation. In G. Vida (ed.), *Our Right to Love: A Lesbian Resource Book*. Englewood Cliffs, NJ: Prentice-Hall.

Sarachild, K. (1974) Psychological terrorism. Reprinted in Redstockings (1978) *Feminist Revolution*. New York: Random House.

Scientific Affairs Board (SAB) (1988) *The Future of the Psychological Sciences: Horizons and Opportunities for British Psychology*. Leicester: British Psychological Society.

Serre, C. (1973) Terrorisme psychologique. Reprinted in Redstockings (1978) *Feminist Revolution*. New York: Random House.

Shively, M.G., Jones, C. and DeCecco, J.P. (1984) Research on sexual orientations: definitions and methods. *Journal of Homosexuality* 9, 127–36.

Shotter, J. and Logan, J. (1988) The pervasiveness of patriarchy: on finding a different voice. In M. Gergen (ed.), *Feminist Thought and the Structure of Knowledge*. New York: New York University Press.

Simons, H.W. (1989) *Rhetoric in the Human Sciences*. London: Sage.

Stainton Rogers, R. and Kitzinger, C. (1985) *Understandings of Human Rights*. Report to the Council of Europe.

Stainton Rogers, R. and Kitzinger, C. (1986) Human rights. *Operant Subjectivity* 9(4), 123–30.

Stainton Rogers, R. and Kitzinger, C. (1988) How do people construe their 'rights'? A study of alternative schematisations. Paper presented to the annual conference of the British Psychological Society, 15–18 April, Leeds.

Standing, L. and McKelvie, S. (1986) Psychology journals: a case for treatment. *Bulletin of the British Psychological Society* 39, 445–50.

Storr, A. (1964) *Sexual Deviation*. Harmondsworth: Penguin. (Reprinted 1974.)

Strega, L. and Jo, B. (1987) Lesbian sex – is it? *Gossip: A Journal of Lesbian Feminist Ethics* 3, 65–76.

Tysoe, M. (1988) Human rights . . . natural right or legal contract? *The Psychologist* 1(6), 219.

West, D.J. (1968) *Homosexuality*. Hardmondsworth: Penguin.

Wilkinson, S. (1988) Feminist research: reconciling advocacy and scholarship. Paper presented to the annual conference of the British Psychological Society, 15–18 April, Leeds.

Woolgar, S.W. (1983) Irony in the social study of science. In K. Knorr-Cetina and M. Mulkay (eds), *Science Observed*. London: Sage.

Zimmerman, B. (1982) One out of thirty: lesbianism in women's studies textbooks. In M. Cruikshank (ed.), *Lesbian Studies: Present and Future*. New York: The Feminist Press.

PART THREE

STRUGGLES AND CHANGE

The final part of this book describes the struggles of women working in different areas of psychology to challenge and change their practice.

In their joint chapter, Sue Wilkinson and Jan Burns provide a detailed account of the context and implications of setting up the Psychology of Women Section of the British Psychological Society. Sue Wilkinson's contribution locates the events and terms of the debates in relation to corresponding international struggles of women psychologists to gain formal recognition in other professional organizations. The three main questions she identifies as structuring the British debate reveal much about the resistances and fears to which the organization of women within a male-dominated profession give rise. The resistance can perhaps be seen as an institutionalized version of the defences deployed by individual male educational psychologists described in the next chapters.

In the case of the BPS, rejection of the section on grounds of 'politics' underlines its own implicit politics, while we also see now-familiar story of women's issues and women's organization almost by definition challenging prevailing structures. The structural necessity of making the section open to men (to meet the demands of the BPS) serves, as both authors indicate, both to legitimate (and constrain) the 'psychology of women' as an academic area of study (because men claim to do it too), and also makes the section even more dependent on external feminist and feminist psychologist political activity to maintain its accountability.

In a more personal vein Jan Burns tells how her involvement in organizing the first Women in Psychology conference in 1985 and the Psychology of Women Section of the BPS influenced her developing feminist politics and changing relationship to psychology. She ends the chapter by indicating the key areas of promise and compromise for women psychologists affirming and using our positions to advance the political situation not only of feminist psychology and psychologists but also to make some progressive intervention in the wider political arena.

Two complementary accounts of the experience and position of women in local educational psychology services follow. Both comment on structural issues of the organization of each system and service as well as highlighting the generalized effects of the masculine values and ways of organizing that constrain their work. Both contributions describe attempts within local educational psychology or schools psychological services to set up women's groups, and each account highlights the empowering and validating effects this had for the women concerned, together with the uniformly defensive reaction from their male colleagues.

The first account systematically analyses the various ways gender issues are structured within educational psychology, from acknowledging the positive features for women working in the profession to pointing out the disadvantaged position of the (mainly female) part-time staff. In particular, it highlights how gender-typical assumptions structure models of management, intervention and relationships with clients and serve to remove any emotional involvement. The emphasis on strong management, on distanced client relations and on consultancy-based work has led to behaviourist approaches being favoured over individual counselling or psychodynamic approaches. The consequences of failing to incorporate equal opportunities issues as a central feature of educational psychology training and practice are also described. These range from an institutional reluctance to support in-service training in this area, to the resistance from teachers in schools to address these issues, to the reproduction of inequalities in the workplace in terms of the gendered hierarchy of the service. The authors also comment on the response to the organization of a local women psychologists' group. While the group brought its members support and confidence, the male staff's hostility seemed to derive from envy, since they also wanted the same degree of support. However, the attempt to set up an 'equivalent' men's group was unsuccessful. As the authors note, it is a sad reflection on both the structure of masculinity and psychology that even within the so-called caring professions it is so difficult for men to offer each other support.

Set initially within a context which highlights the differential allocation of resources within educational psychological services, a second contribution was to have traced a personal account of the experience of training and becoming an educational psychologist for women who come to identify themselves as feminist. The account focused on events within a local educational psychology service following a meeting to consider the Association of Educational Psychology's *Guidelines on Sexism*. This culminated in the setting-up of a women-only group to consider how to implement its recommendations. Meeting together the women became aware of how they both supported and were backgrounded by their male colleagues. I say 'was to have traced' because this second contribution has been removed at a very late stage in the production of this book. That anonymity was not, it became clear, sufficient to guarantee the security of these women is symptomatic of the predicament of women in educational psychology. In spite of the backlash which led to the group gradually dissolving, the legacy of that confidence-building exercise remains and the women went on to highlight and challenge the everyday ways in which educational psychology colludes in the perpetuation of inequalities. These include rendering invisible the work done by women in developing good relationships and creating a harmonious atmosphere; the cultural chauvinism that permeates testing and assessment; and the key 'diagnostic' category of 'special needs' which is applied overwhelmingly to working-class boys, a disproportionate number of whom are black.

The final contribution identifies dilemmas and tensions in developing a progressive approach to clinical psychology. Christine Adcock and Karen Newbigging's account echoes some of the central concerns already identified. They tell how disquiet with the scientific models of investigation, knowledge and clinical relationships they experienced in training came to develop into a political critique informed by feminism. They highlight the effects and futility of taking, as psychology has traditionally done, the individual as the unit of intervention. As in Maye Taylor's earlier chapter, they identify the ways in which a feminist approach to clinical practice envisages and transforms relations with 'clients'. But taking these issues further they point out that the progressive models for practice upheld by feminism do not fit easily with the realities of working with women who are multiply disadvantaged by mental health problems or by learning disabilities. Indeed the very assumption that gender and gender identification is the key dimension for reconstructing a radical psychology practice can be construed as at best reinforcing in another form the intellectualism of the expert who knows best. Furthermore this emphasis on common gender identification, although it may serve to help the psychologist empathize with the woman she is working with, may also deny or reduce the other disadvantages and differences to which the intersection between gender and disability gives rise. Denying these differences serves to mask the power relations within which the woman 'client' is positioned, and thus runs the risk of effectively disempowering her further. Equally the best-intentioned clinician who uses her professional power in the interests of her client may also stigmatize her further by doing so. The authors conclude by identifying some of the key issues facing clinical psychologists in constructing a feminist practice.

9

Women organizing within psychology

I

Sue Wilkinson

The focus of this contribution is the struggle of women psychologists to achieve representation and recognition for their work within national psychological societies. Although I will be most concerned to 'tell the story' of the British Psychological Society's Psychology of Women Section, I will also make some comparisons with events in other countries (particularly Australia and the USA, but also Canada and New Zealand), where these serve either to illustrate frequently raised objections to feminist action or to highlight the processes involved in major disciplinary change. Finally, I will raise the question of whether the costs and compromises of such a struggle outweigh the benefits – part of the broader issue of whether feminist objectives can be met within the constraints of institutionalized psychology.

I hope that this account can be viewed as feminism in practice: that is, as being essentially 'for' women. I would like it, particularly, to be for the women who have been involved in the formation of the British Psychological Society's Psychology of Women Section, and also for the women who are just beginning the struggle (having heard recently of three more countries where women are currently seeking representation within their national psychological societies: Israel, Argentina and Italy).

This account is inevitably personal, in that I was involved in particular ways within the unfolding 'drama': others would no doubt have other emphases, or even completely different versions. Nor do I doubt that the story changes in the telling, depending on context, audience, and the events themselves receding into the past. Such stories are easily lost (in any form): often women simply do not know their histories (sic), let alone be able to learn from them.

Early days

This contention may be illustrated by what were (as far as I am aware), the earliest attempts to form an organization to represent women's concerns within the British Psychological Society, in the mid-1970s.

The British Psychological Society (BPS) is the main national organization representing psychologists in Britain – and, since the recent admission of psychology to Chartered status, it is also the body which maintains the Register of Chartered Psychologists, that is, those who are defined as 'properly qualified and experienced' (BPS, 1988a). The Society's membership includes both academic psychologists (represented by 'sections' of the Society – for example Social, Developmental, Cognitive) and psychologists in professional practice (represented by 'divisions' – for example, Occupational, Clinical, Educational). There are also 'special groups', representing other areas where psychologists provide a public service – e.g. Teachers of Psychology, as well as geographically based 'branches'.

Although it seems that women began to organize within the BPS as recently as ten or twelve years ago, it has not been possible to reconstruct any clear picture of the events of the time, despite contacting many of the people who were involved. Certainly there was a BPS symposium, convened by Jane Chetwynd in 1975, on sex-role stereotyping and psychology, which produced the book *The Sex Role System* (Chetwynd and Hartnett, 1978); this was followed by an international conference at the University of Wales Institute of Science and Technology in Cardiff in 1977, which generated the book *Sex-role Stereotyping* (Hartnett et al., 1979).

Also, in September 1976, in response to a request from the Division of Occupational Psychology, the BPS Professional Affairs Board set up a working party on the new legislation represented by the 1975 Sex Discrimination Act. This reported in May 1978, and a footnote in the report (BPS, 1978) attests to some of the problems that the working party experienced – this has been borne out by the recollections of one of its members (Phillips, personal communication, July 1987). However, the members' memories do not tally regarding whether a formal attempt at establishing a section was made (Hartnett, undated, c. 1987; Pearson, July 1988; Phillips, July 1987 – all personal communications). One possible source of confusion – although this is only my speculation – is the similarity of procedures in establishing this working party and the general procedure for setting up a scientific section, in that both entail obtaining signatures of support for a proposal.

My own first public forays into the arena came in 1983 and 1984, when I convened symposia on feminist research at BPS Social Psychology Section conferences (these subsequently became the book *Feminist Social Psychology*, Wilkinson, 1986). At the second conference four of us – Mathilde de Jong (now Mathilde Idema), Paula Nicolson, Alison Thomas and myself – talked about the possibility of a Feminist Section (and Paula wrote a 'background' article for the *BPS*

Bulletin – which was rejected): however, we did not take any further action at that time, beyond collecting some information.

The 1985 section attempt

Things got moving at the Easter 1985 postgraduate psychology conference, when a group of twelve women met and agreed to initiate the necessary procedures for forming a new BPS section; Jan Burns and Mathilde Idema acted as co-ordinators and main proposers of this – and at the same time they began to organize a one-day conference on Women in Psychology, to be held at University College, Cardiff, in November 1985. Jan's article, which follows, provides a more detailed account of the work entailed and of the conference itself.

The formal procedure for establishing a BPS section entails writing a proposal, which has to be supported by the signatures of at least twenty Fellows (sic) or Associate Fellows of the Society; this has then to be approved by the Council; then at least 100 Members of the Society must express an 'intention to join' the new section; and finally a General Meeting of the Society must approve formation of the section (BPS, 1988b). However, this is typically supplemented by various 'advisory' procedures, ranging from 'informal' contact with BPS officers, to more 'formal' advice from the Scientific Affairs Board (SAB) – and sometimes other committees. The two together form a well-nigh impenetrable barrier for anyone not thoroughly 'socialized' into BPS affairs and also give the Society considerable scope for scrutinizing and directing its members' activities.

The chronology of activities in 1985 was as follows: during April, May and June the postgraduate group, bullied and cajoled by Mathilde and Jan, advertised the initiative and canvassed for support, held consultative meetings in Cardiff and London, liaised with the BPS, and drafted a proposal. In July the proposal went to a Scientific Affairs Board meeting, and various changes were suggested (some of these were echoed when it was also discussed at a Social Psychology Section committee meeting); and in September, at another meeting, the SAB expressed its support for the formation of the new section. However, in October, the Council voted against the proposal, by 21 votes to 7 (with 4 abstentions): a move unprecedented in the history of BPS sections.

Why did it happen?

In order to understand more clearly what lies behind the rejection of the proposal, it is instructive to look at the 'advice' and opinions offered by various BPS officers and committees in the preceding months, particularly in terms of themes and issues which repeatedly recur, and which can also be seen in examining similar materials from the other countries in which 'grass-roots' movements have tangled with the psychological establishment. This analysis is constructed from a complex mix of recollections, correspondence, published papers and other documents – and I am very grateful to the many women who have contributed materials and memories. I am especially grateful to Jan and Mathilde for meticulous record-keeping relating to the 1985 section attempt.

I have space here only to discuss three key issues, which I will frame in terms of questions which appear to be posed by the psychological establishment about the proposed new organization. These are: (i) Does it 'fit'? (ii) Is it 'separatist'? (iii) Is it 'political'? Jan considers these issues more explicitly, both from a personal point of view and in terms of their wider implications. It is particularly interesting to note the way in which all of the issues seem to mirror internal debate within feminist psychology (or 'the psychology of women', as it is usually termed in the US) itself: see Basow (1987) for further discussion of this, as well as Jan's contribution.

Does it fit?

In the early correspondence between the section proposers and BPS 'advisers', there is extensive reference to the definitions of the various Society subsystems (sections, divisions and special groups), in an attempt to determine exactly what the proposal is for, e.g.: 'it does not look like a Special Group as I cannot imagine that a women's section would be providing advice, tuition or services to the public. It might be a Section if the main emphasis was to be on the scientific study of the psychology of womanhood, presumably in comparison with men?' (BPS to section proposers, May 1985). Even once it has been classified as closest to a section, the question is raised of how it will 'fit' with other sections, e.g.: 'There are physiological, cognitive, social, developmental, occupational and other applied aspects to the study of the psychology of women which cut across the concerns of all existing Sections . . . the study of the psychology of women (will) always remain orthogonal to the other theoretical perspectives in psychology . . .' (BPS to section proposers, October 1985, and circulated to section supporters).

Very similar arguments surface in Australia, where the proposal for a Women and Psychology Board was regarded as cutting across the activities of existing boards within the Australian Psychological Society: neither the Scientific nor the Professional Division saw it as fitting entirely within their province (Gault, personal communication, undated, *c*. 1986). They also appear in Canada, where the Canadian

Psychological Association rejected a conference symposium entitled 'On Women, By Women' on the grounds that 'it didn't fit in anywhere' (Greenglass, 1973).

Thus, one major criterion for acceptance of a proposal is the 'fit' with the existing structures of the parent organization (not its academic value and/or interest of members). It is well worth relating this to the contention of women's studies proponents that reorganization of the structures of knowledge is necessary for feminist work, because existing disciplinary structures cannot accommodate it (Spender, 1978).

Is it 'separatist'?

The second question relates to the issue – identified by Kahn and Jean (1983) – of whether the field should seek to develop autonomously, or locate itself within the 'parent' discipline, in an attempt to stimulate change. For the national psychological societies, this issue has focused on separatism, i.e. whether the proposed organization will be open to both women and men, or 'restricted' to women only. For feminists, separatism is only part of the wider issue of how (or even whether) they can operate within the highly bureaucratic and patriarchal structures of a traditional discipline like psychology. Here I will be concerned mainly with separatism, returning to the wider issue later; Jan also discusses the issue of autonomy versus integration more broadly.

Most of the women I contacted, while often expressing a desire for separatism, felt it had no chance of success within their national psychological associations. In fact, only in New Zealand was an attempt made to establish a women-only division: however, male members of the New Zealand Psychological Society managed to obtain a ruling that this was against the Human Rights Act (Ritchie, personal communication, May 1988).

In the UK, the 1985 proposal (which was for a Women in Psychology Section) was wrongly inferred to be for a women-only organization. Informal 'advice' from the BPS office suggested that 'this would be going against the Society's own recently approved *Code of Conduct*, which bans discrimination on the grounds of race, sex, etc.' (BPS to section proposers, May 1985). Both the Social Psychology Section committee and the Scientific Affairs Board (meeting in July 1985) suggested to the proposers of the section that a change of name might be considered, while one of the Society's officers went as far as to suggest an alternative: the 'Psychology of Womanhood' (BPS to section proposers, July 1985). With some reluctance, the proposers agreed on the Psychology of Women: principally because this was the name of Division 35 of the American Psychological Association, successfully established twelve years earlier, and therefore setting a useful precedent.

However, the change actually proved counter-productive, in that at the crucial Council meeting, it was admitted that: 'awareness of the evolution of (the) proposal led to speculation (beyond the document under consideration) about the intentions of those behind the proposal' (BPS to section proposers, October 1985, circulated to supporters). Furthermore, the arguments used against the section continue to assume separatist aims: 'The anology (sic) was used of the debate in the Labour Party over 'Black Sections', the introduction of which some would agree is an admission of failure since the ultimate goal should be for non-discrimination to be so all-embracing that nobody notices colour at all' (BPS to section proposers, October 1985, circulated to supporters).

In other countries, too, the name of the organization has been taken to indicate its position on the 'separatist' issue. In 1958, in the USA, the International Council of Women Psychologists voted to remove the word 'Women' from its title in a bid to become a division of the American Psychological Association. This was after Harry Harlow, then President of the APA, had said that 'a group that is 90 percent women is a women's group' – indicating quite clearly to (at least) one feminist psychologist of the time that 'the APA is a men's group' (Walsh, 1985). Here, too, the change of name did not produce the desired effect. The Australian proposers deliberately chose Women and Psychology to de-emphasize separatist suggestions (Gault, personal communication, undated, *c.* 1987): and this is also the title of choice in Canada, where the struggle has been perhaps the least heated of the countries surveyed, as far as one can tell.

Is it 'political'?

The change of name of the BPS section also led to 'speculation' as to whether the intentions of the proposers were to establish an organization 'which could in any way be construed as a quasi-political pressure group concerned with feminist causes' (BPS to section proposers, October 1985, circulated to supporters). The absolute proscription of activities (even remotely) regarded as 'political' – which is also a very strong theme running through accounts received from Australia and the USA – appears to be underpinned by (at least) two factors. The first is the false polarization of 'science' (as objective and value-neutral) and 'politics' (as subjective and partisan), which is a legacy of the continued dominance of the positivist mode of enquiry in psychology. The second, ironically, is the broader political climate pertaining at the time the proposal is considered. There is plenty of evidence for both of these assertions.

Thus, in the UK, the section proposers were told:

some of the things you have in mind for the Section are sufficiently loaded politically for the whole proposal to fail. I am sure that by rephrasing the difficulties can be overcome, as long as you also share the conceptual distinction between the scientific duty (sic) of the psychology of womanhood . . . and a feminist pressure group seeking to promote causes on the basis of moral conviction alone. (BPS to section proposers, July 1985)

It is also the case that the 1985 section proposal came at a time when, in common with the increasing professionalization of the discipline, the British Psychological Society was seeking Chartered status for appropriately qualified psychologists – and was therefore extremely conscious of its external image. The proposers were told, for example, that 'the Society has to maintain a neutral and evenhanded position on social issues on which individual Society Members will hold conflicting political views . . . The neutrality of the Society in the eyes of government might be compromised if . . . campaigning groups were allowed within the Society' (BPS to section proposers, July 1985).

Such arguments surface in almost identical form in Australia, as in the text of the following letter, which was published in the *Bulletin of the Australian Psychological Society*: 'if "psychological knowledge" is not objective, we may then become like any other Community group. What is our distinction if the professional body is identifiably partisan and is not maintaining integrity through objectivity? . . . if we are seen by the public and governments as partisan, as supporting particular points of view, our credibility is lost' (Little, 1985). The APS was a branch of the BPS until 1965 (Turtle and Orr, 1988).

In the USA, these issues were rehearsed much earlier with the formation of the Society for the Psychological Study of Social Issues (SPSSI) in 1936 (Mednick, 1984). By the time the Psychology of Women Division (Division 35) of the American Psychological Association was established, the women were able to demonstrate their political astuteness by emphasizing the scientific role of the division, and limiting their stated activist intentions to 'the intensely political purpose of knowledge' (Elizabeth Douvan, the first President of Division 35, quoted in Mednick, 1978). Indeed, Martha Mednick has confirmed that this was seen as 'the only way a division would have been supported at the time' (Mednick, personal communication, June 1988).

Undoubtedly this view of events in the States is too simple (I hope to be able to elaborate it in the future): for example, I have recently been told (Russo, personal communication, August 1988) that another reason for the APA women's use of 'scientific' rhetoric was to explain their apparent desertion of their activist roots in the Association for Women in Psychology (AWP). This had been (and still is) an overtly 'political' organization, whose four-year campaign provided the necessary pressure first for the founding of the APA Committee on Women in Psychology and then for Division 35 (Walsh, 1985).

In summary although the 1985 rejection of the Psychology of Women section by the BPS Council came as a shock at the time, it now appears relatively unsurprising: the arguments used (that it cuts across the subject-matter of other sections; that it is 'discriminatory'; and that it is 'quasi-political') had been well-rehearsed both in the 'advice' and comments given to the UK proposers, and in a number of other countries in similar circumstances. But what happened next in the UK 'saga'?

Back to the tale

Hard on the heels of the Council rejection in October came the Cardiff conference – which is described in some detail by Jan. I would just characterize it as a day of unparalleled stimulation and excitement, which took us from a 'low' to a 'high' – and seemed to promise great things for the future. Mathilde and Jan prepared a questionnaire for the delegates: and subsequent analysis of the responses revealed that 93 percent of those completing it ($n = 104$) were in favour of a new BPS section (Ta'eed, 1986).

The conference was followed by a well-attended meeting in London in January 1986. This produced a strong consensus as to the need for some sort of organization, but there was a lengthy debate over whether to continue to campaign for representation within the BPS or to set up and independent organization outside the Society. The main benefits of the BPS 'option' – apart from the academic/professional 'recognition' which we all felt was long overdue – were seen to be finance, office support, and a structure within which to operate. Others saw the latter (and BPS ideologies) as unacceptably constraining, arguing that an independent organization would allow much greater innovation, direct political action, and the possibility of women-only membership: which some saw as a prerequisite for the production of new knowledges about gender (Hollway, 1986).

The decision was eventually taken to found an independent organization called Women in Psychology (and open only to women), as it was agreed that this would best meet the needs of women at the time (particularly for a support network), and that it would not preclude a resubmission of the BPS section proposal at a later date. It was argued that should such a resubmission prove successful, the two organizations could operate in parallel as 'academic' and 'activist' wings, as with APA Division 35 and AWP in the States (although, of course, the relationship between the two is more complex than that: see, for example, Mednick, 1978; Walsh, 1985).

Women in Psychology quickly recruited over 200 members; a computerized mailing list was set up; local groups began to meet, particularly in London and the north-west; the first issue of a newsletter was compiled; and a planning group – co-ordinated by Sheila Rossan – was formed for a conference the following year. (The conference was held, very successfully, at Brunel University, west London, in July 1987.) However, by the end of 1986 we were talking about a possible BPS section again. Several of us felt very strongly that there should be a forum for our work within the national psychological organization, and that the refusal to admit one was ensuring the continued marginalization of women within psychology. In addition, Women in Psychology, while functioning very effectively at a local level, was experiencing the problems of administrative continuity (common to all small, independent organizations) in its national operation, and its long-term future appeared uncertain.

Thus, in January 1987, seven of us formed a steering group, which began to meet regularly in London, in order to prepare a resubmission of the case. By now we had all learnt a great deal about the procedures and practices of the BPS as an extremely patriarchal, bureaucratic institution, and we set about putting this knowledge into practice in a very deliberate way.

We completely rewrote the proposal, using successful section proposals as a model of academic respectability. We aimed to demonstrate a massive level of support, not only by obtaining signatures from individual BPS members (as is required in establishing a new section), but by seeking letters of support, both from other BPS sections and divisions, and as widely as possible outside the Society, e.g. from similar organizations in other countries and in cognate disciplines, and from 'big name' individuals within the field. Probably most important, though, we now understood something of how the BPS operates: the key people to influence, and how to go about it. Thus we set about lobbying (although we were warned that this could be seen as 'political'!) – as far as possible either from within committees or in supposedly 'informal' contexts, such as at conferences.

The Scientific Affairs Board supported the proposal at its meeting in April 1987, and it went to the Council in May (with 262 signatures of support). I was present (as the Social Section representative) to hear it warmly supported by the Chair of SAB (Tony Gale) and be accepted unanimously, as far as I could tell: the agenda item was over so quickly. It was almost an anticlimax – albeit one for which we were very grateful. The rest of the formal procedure was straightforward: over 300 people expressed an 'intention to join' (the largest ever for a BPS section), and the General Meeting – held at the 1987 London conference in December – voted in favour of the proposal (with only a couple of abstentions). We had got our section at last!

In one sense this is, as it appears, a 'happy ending' to the tale – but in other important senses the proceedings were not happy, nor have they ended. For example, it is traditional to accompany the formation of a new BPS section with a conference symposium (both to inaugurate its academic activities and to ensure a good turn-out at the General Meeting). Jane Ussher convened a symposium on feminist approaches to clinical practice – but this was rejected by the BPS Standing Conference Committee as 'too political'. The future of the section seems certain to be marked by continuing struggle.

Is the game worth the candle?

It is in the light of this that I would like, finally, to raise the question of whether the gains of obtaining representation, and continuing to operate within, a national psychological society are worthwhile for the feminist academic or practitioner. Many would say that we have 'sold out' to the establishment by coming this far; and that we will achieve nothing for women, or for the development of psychology, by continuing to play academic power games by the rules of the establishment. Further, some will say that within the constraints of psychology as it is presently constructed (both institutionally and theoretically) feminist objectives of an 'emancipatory psychology' cannot even begin to be met (Hollway, 1989).

It is a very difficult issue – and probably unresolvable. While being aware of the gains we have made (for example, there is now a guaranteed platform for women's work, via the Psychology of Women Section symposium, at every BPS conference), we are also cognizant of the limitations to achievement posed by the framework within which we are operating. Disciplinary change is bound to be slow, and major advances dependent on structural, as well as ideological, change.

We are aware, too, of the dangers of co-option by the system: this is difficult to resist when rewards accrue from conformity – and when we ourselves have been socialized to value such rewards. Our small success tastes of power – and, as some of us would readily admit, power is seductive. However, such success affords only limited satisfaction in the longer term: the development of skills in playing the academic game is little consolation when one wants to change the rules, or play a different game – one that is for women.

We cannot help but recognize the compromises we have made to date, and the way in which we have ourselves become (at least to some extent) a new 'elite': most women do not share even the little power we have, and we have now become the 'gate-keepers' who exclude them.

Some of us are acutely uncomfortable with this, and are trying both to develop more egalitarian and empowering modes of operation, and to ensure that the Section meets the needs of as many women as possible. However, it is equally important both that other kinds of organization are developed within academic and professional psychology, and that women who are outside the institutional structure of psychology continue to provide a vociferous critique of our activities. In order to achieve a psychology which is genuinely 'for women', work must continue on many diverse fronts.

References

Basow, S.A. (1987) Current issues in the psychology of women in the US. *British Psychological Society, Social Psychology Section Newsletter.* No.17, Spring, 23–31. (Special issue on women in psychology.)

British Psychological Society, Professional Affairs Board (1978) *Report of Working Party on the Sex Discrimination Act.* May. Leicester: BPS.

British Psychological Society (1988a) *The Register of Chartered Psychologists* (leaflet). Leicester: BPS.

British Psychological Society (1988b) *The Royal Charter, The Statutes, The Rules.* January. Leicester: BPS.

Chetwynd, J. and Hartnett, O. (1978) *The Sex Role System: Psychological and Sociological Perspectives.* London: Routledge and Kegan Paul.

Greenglass, E.R. (1973) Women: a new psychological view. *The Ontario Psychologist* 5 (2), 7–15.

Hartnett, O., Boden, G. and Fuller, M. (1979) *Sex-Role Stereotyping.* London: Tavistock.

Hollway, W. (1986) Why a women-only organisation? *Women in Psychology Newsletter* No.1, 16–18.

Hollway, W. (1989) *Subjectivity and Method in Psychology: Gender, Meaning and Science.* London: Sage Publications. (Gender and Psychology Series.)

Kahn, A.S. and Jean, P.J. (1983) Integration and elimination or separation and redefinition: the future of the psychology of women. *Signs: Journal of Women in Culture and Society* 8 (4), 659–71.

Little, R.B. (1985) Letter published in the *Bulletin of the Australian Psychological Society*, November, p.25.

Mednick, M.T.S. (1978) Now we are four: what should we be when we grow up? *Psychology of Women Quarterly* 3 (2), 123–38.

Mednick, M.T.S. (1984) SPSSI, advocacy for social change, and the future: a historical look. *Journal of Social Issues*, 40 (3), 159–77.

Spender, D. (1978) Women's studies: notes on the organisation of women's studies. *Women's Studies International Quarterly* 1 (3), 255–75.

Ta'eed, L. (1986) Women in psychology conference, Cardiff 1985. Unpublished paper. (Shortened version appears in *Women in Psychology Newsletter* No.1, 7–15.)

Turtle, A.M. and Orr, M. (1988) *The Psyching of Oz* (leaflet to accompany photographic exhibition on the history of psychology in Australia). Presented by the Archives Committee of the Australian Psychological Society at the 24th International Congress of Psychology, Sydney, Australia, August/September.

Walsh, M.R. (1985) Academic professional women organizing for change: the struggle in psychology. *Journal of Social Issues*, 41 (4), 17–28.

Wilkinson, S.J. (ed.) (1986) *Feminist Social Psychology: Developing Theory and Practice*. Milton Keynes: Open University Press.

II

Jan Burns

Early origins of a feminist psychologist

The idea that I would perhaps eventually regard myself as a feminist psychologist would undoubtedly have shocked me during my undergraduate days. However, that one could adopt such a position came as a great salvation during my later days, and was possibly the major factor that maintained me within psychology.

The transition from undergraduate to postgraduate is not an easy one, especially when starting a PhD. I look back on it now as a wonderful opportunity to indulge one's curiosity, but now, of course, I am a person altered by that very experience. However, what did come as a surprise to me was the additional pressure put upon me as a lone female, doing something vaguely 'social' in a department of applied science. I learnt that many of the males I was working with regarded social psychology as similar to the domestic chores women perform in the kitchen. There was some acknowledgement that such work has to be done (mostly to keep women amused), but it is not of the same value as the 'hard science' that men go out and do. It is coloured by all those silly variables that you can't control out, and is therefore meaningless. The split between what was regarded as hard science (i.e. real proper science) and soft science (often qualitative) was clear. Even the terminology of hard and soft betrays the emotion.

Not only was my position devalued, but I was also required to defend it at any point, whenever my male colleagues demanded. It was their 'sport' to try and engage me in the argument that 'women and social psychology are only fit for each other', as one of the senior lecturers so succinctly put it.

At the same time as these personal experiences occurred, I began to feel uneasy about the type of research in which I was involved. The aims, methods, and reasons for such research stood in great discord with my growing feminist awareness and commitment. Most of the people from whom I acquired my information were middle-aged housewives who were being employed – on low wages with no status or career structure – as 'carers' in group homes for people with mental handicaps. They were being employed to use their skills as homebuilders and carers, with no acknowledgement that these were indeed valuable and highly necessary skills.

Most of the research in the area had concentrated on very

quantitative factors, which were then taken as indices of 'quality'. It seemed to me that a whole area that is so pertinent to women, and women's place in society, was being ignored. The assumption seemed to be that these women could transfer their skills of home-making on to the handicapped individuals. However, in terms of research, these skills and the position of these women held such little value that they were never directly examined. Nevertheless, such illumination comes only with hindsight, and for the sake of academic legitimacy I did adopt, to a limited extent, the quantitative methods that had been used in prior research.

Not only did this approach feel counter-intuitive to me, but I also had to square it with the women with whom I worked. Fundamentally I felt they were the real experts, and they could tell me what I really needed to look at and how to design my study. My problem would be how to put this knowledge into practice. However, in reality I was seen as the expert, the researcher who was coming in with a lot of skills, and if the sorts of things that I wanted to know seemed strange to them, well, there must be a good reason behind it. What a hoax! The research system works against this type of collaborative approach.

To solve such dilemmas I ended up playing the science game – collecting data, number crunching, etc., but also carrying on a parallel study where I could indulge my intuitions in the collection of qualitative descriptive data, and be a receiver of the information that the participants wanted to give me. This made the whole task of a PhD much harder and I wonder how many women have been forced out of psychology or left with uncompleted PhDs because of these issues.

I hope by this introduction to have highlighted how, as a woman, and a feminist, I found my motives and interests in psychology uncomfortably compromised right at the outset of my career. It is perhaps unsurprising that such personal experiences proved to be the catalyst provoking a search for an alternative framework of psychology to the one in which I was already involved. In the same way as Sue Wilkinson has 'told the story' of the fight for the establishment of a Psychology of Women Section within the British Psychological Society (BPS), I want to tell a story of women organizing within psychology, but from a slightly more personal slant. My focus is upon the personal issues and decisions that arose out of the organizational changes which have occurred in psychology for women over recent years. I have wanted to place these personal experiences within the chronology of the development of a career in psychology, as I'm sure such experiences echo those of many other women still in, or those who have opted out of, psychology in Britain.

My emergence from the 'closet' as a feminist psychologist came when I went to the postgraduate conference sponsored by the British

Psychological Society in 1985. At a subsequent meeting of interested women psychologists Mathilde Idema and I took on the task of organizing the first Women in Psychology conference in Cardiff, in 1985.

The first Women in Psychology conference

As mentioned in the previous contribution, there had been one other conference associated with women in psychology, on the theme of Sexual Stereotyping. However, it was felt that there needed to be an event aimed more broadly at any women in psychology, be they researchers, teachers, students, or 'subjects' (i.e. those upon whom psychological research is performed) of psychology. We wanted to replicate on a larger scale the importance of the support we post-graduates had experienced by just sharing our experiences, as well as to heighten the profile of women in psychology, and give some platform to the large variety of psychological work that was of interest to women.

In retrospect I shudder at the naivety with which we took on the task of organizing the conference; however, I also think that it was partly our innocence that carried us through. This task landed in our laps not because we had good access to resources, which these days I would immediately turn my mind to if any suggestion of staging a conference was suggested, but because we both happened to be in the same city.

Each of our psychology departments, and the Welsh Branch of the BPS, kindly allocated some finances to sponsor the event, but on the basis that it was open to men too. The rest was up to us. As postgraduates we used what resources we had, which meant we typed every letter sent, and filled unforgettable piles of envelopes. However, the response we got was enormous and gratifying; women offered us help in all sorts of ways, from waiving the fees usually attached to booking rooms, to designing and printing the advertising material cheaply.

Compromises had to be made along the way, from running the conference in the slightly unorthodox but friendly way that we wanted, with the ease of handling large numbers of people and ensuring that everybody got a fair deal. Many women had expressed their dis-satisfaction at the traditional format of 'giving papers': standing up and speaking to an audience for half an hour with possibly a chance to ask a few questions at the end. Women not only feel daunted by this type of performance, but they also recognize the limitations of such an unreciprocal approach. Thus it was decided to mix the types of presentations being given, and accept that incumbent upon this would be difficult decisions over timetabling. Such decisions highlighted in a particularly painful way for Mathilde and me just where our feminist principles lay. In a conference, the first of its kind and (we hoped) one which would set a precedent for others to follow, just what does one do when faced with the decision that with only one slot left open a choice has to be made between a well-known academic's paper and an unknown student's paper.

However, the day went well, with over 250 participants (of whom three were men), a selection of the papers being published in a copy of *Equal Opportunities International*, and Dale Spender giving a very interesting talk in the evening on 'If women were in charge of psychology...' The conference confirmed our opinion that there was a body of keen and restless women already working out there in psychology, and there could be nothing but advantage gained from working towards some forum where these needs could be expressed. Such feelings were directed into action with the renewed endeavour to establish a section within the BPS – a story already told by Sue Wilkinson.

So far I have kept to the order of events as they took place on the road to putting women firmly within the psychological establishment by obtaining a Psychology of Women section within the BPS. However, these events did not happen in isolation, nor were they clear progressive steps. Controversy surrounded and still surrounds many of these developments. I have felt personally compromised by taking part in various decisions, and frequently torn between organizational ease and political opinion. Therefore, I want to continue this contribution by discussing some of these issues in a little more detail.

Susan Basow, who opened the first Women in Psychology conference in Cardiff, in 1985, as a visiting speaker from the States, highlighted a number of issues that have plagued the Division of the Psychology of Women, and the Association for Women in Psychology in the USA. We have certainly had to face these issues here in Britain and continue to do so. However, as most readers will recognize, these issues are not exclusive to women in psychology, but pervade all the areas where women have felt a need to unite. I'm now going to address three which I regard as the most important dilemmas currently facing women in psychology, and in some ways echo the questions just asked by Sue Wilkinson, adding to her analysis with a more personal perspective.

Separation versus integration

This has become such a familiar issue within any sort of women's initiative that to raise it once again is to endanger precipitating great yawns. Therefore I shall treat it only briefly, by just dwelling upon where exactly this issue is pertinent in the development of a psychology of women.

First, for those who are arguing from the position that a psychology of women crosses all boundaries and should be seen to pervade all research, the separation of a specific psychology of women from mainstream psychology, is to ghettoize the topic when it should rather be generalized. The comprehensiveness of such a movement as the psychology of women is made clear by Helen Weinreich:

> It would seem clear that the women's movement in its broadest sense is a dangerous truth that cannot be ignored, not only because the issues it raises for psychology concern half the human race, but because so many aspects of it as a phenomenon challenge the basic assumptions of positivistic psychology. (Weinreich, 1977, p. 640)

The argument would then follow that such isolation of a particular research area would lead to a devaluation of that area, especially considering the heritage of low value and low status that women's work frequently carries with it. Thus, within the ghetto of the psychology of women, some very fine work may be carried out, but to what end when the majority, i.e. mainstream psychology, is not forced to confront, examine or even adapt to the issues raised by the psychology of women's experience?

On the other side of the argument, does integration lead to a sliding scale of compromise after compromise eventually leading to a complete dilution of feminist principles and methods? As an example of this Susan Basow tells the tale of the International Council of Women Psychologists which was set up in the States in 1941. The aim of this organization was to promote the work of women psychologists in the war effort, and encourage women to participate in psychology as a profession. However, the organizers were at pains to point out that the group should not be 'militant-suffragist in tone' (Russo and O'Connell, 1980), and many members were uncomfortable at belonging to a single-sex professional association, fearing isolation and the devaluation of their work. In 1948 the group petitioned to become a division of the APA, but this was governed not viable as the group excluded men. Thus, they voted to allow men to join their ranks, and eliminate the word women from their title. The dangers are clear, as Basow points out: 'The first period in which women psychologists organized to help themselves professionally ended with women psychologists compromising their organization out of existence.'

I find this very close to my experience as one of the co-founders of Women in Psychology (WIPS) and the Psychology of Women Section (POWS). To some extent I chose to follow the second route of integration, and found myself in the painful situation of compromise. However, I also have the experience of the establishment of WIPS and years of battling with little structure, few resources and small access with which to communicate to a wide psychological audience. There is no answer to such an issue, except perhaps *action* in both directions. The real dilemma comes with the question of priorities, which may in the end rest upon the personal issues, commitments and tactical strategies of the individual.

Is there a psychology of women separate from other psychologies?

For me there is only one clear answer to this question, 'Yes, there is a psychology of women which is separate and distinct from other areas of psychology'. Arguments against this stance seem to take two forms. First, that to establish a psychology of women as a distinct area is inherently sexist, and will lead only to greater discrimination. This might be the case if those involved were unaware of sexual discrimination or had no idea of feminist theory. However, as one cannot really look at the psychology of women in the absence of our biological, cultural and social context, it would seem somewhat incomprehensible not to take on board the particular experiences of women and their often-disadvantaged position within that context.

A second argument might be that one cannot have a psychology of women that is not in comparison to men, and as such the focus should be on gender or sex bias rather than women alone. My response to that is that women do have experiences that are specific to being women, such as those associated with their reproductive nature. This is not to say that psychology has completely ignored the biological distinctiveness of women. Psychological aspects of female physiology are frequently examined, but usually in comparison to the prototype male. There is much evidence to suggest that the consequences of such an approach can be negative. For example, changes in the reproductive cycle, such as pregnancy, may be seen as a 'compromised state of health' (i.e. men do not get pregnant so this condition deviates from the norm and should be considered 'not healthy') and thus in need of medical attention.

Indeed, on the other side of the coin I feel there is a psychology of men that is worth pursuing on its own merit. However, the psychology of women has something extra with which to contend – as Nancy Henley stated in 1985 – *a psychology against women*. Naomi Weisstein (1970, p. 268) was one of the first to point out clearly where women stood in relation to psychology: 'Psychology has nothing to say about what women are really like, what they need and what they want, essentially because psychology does not know.'

Thus, early psychology was primarily performed by men on men, and women were either ignored, or only looked at in comparison to men – men being the norm. The result is the perpetuation of pseudo-scientific data which is not relevant to women. Karen Horney clearly summarizes the effect of women's position with regard to (men's) psychology:

> Like all science and all valuations, the psychology of women has hitherto been considered only from the point of view of men. It is inevitable that man's position of advantage should cause objective validity to be attributed to his subjective, affective relations to the woman, and according to Delius the psychology of women hitherto actually represents a deposit of the desires and disappointments of men. (Horney, 1974, p. 7)

A further argument from a feminist position would take pains to point out that there is no necessary homogeneity of women's experiences, since we are divided by the differential positions and power relationships of 'race', class and sexuality. According to this argument, the separate organization of women in psychology does not arise totally from essential differences in women's experiences or positions, but is tactically appropriate to counter the male hegemony of the discipline.

Thus, it is perhaps only when women began to question concepts and theories at variance with their own experience that we started to see the birth of a true psychology of women, a prerequisite being the legitimization of female experience. Hence, much endeavour at the start had to be invested in redressing the balance and gaining acceptance of women's critiques of psychology. Since then we have moved a long way, and as Parlee (1975) in her review article describes, there are now a number of types of research that are gaining acceptance from the rise of a psychology of women, such as critiques of traditional work, empirical research from a feminist perspective, theoretical contributions to psychology and theoretical contributions to problem-centered research. Surely the psychology of women could not have made such progress were it bound to making comparisons with men's experiences every step of the way?

Should POWS be a feminist organization?

Alternatively this question could be posed as 'Should politics have any place within the psychology of women?' As one who firmly believes that 'the personal is political', as the saying goes, and that one of the main aims of psychology of women should be to legitimize the personal within psychology, I am somewhat biased in my debate of such an issue. I think it is valid to transform the issue from one of feminism to politics because I believe the two go hand-in-hand, and it is hard to conceive of a feminist who would not regard her feminism as having some political content. So far in Britain we have had to cleanse out any hint of 'feminist doings' from the Psychology of Women Section, because the BPS takes no part in politics. This raises the larger issue of what an organization like this is doing washing its hands of political involvement.

The American Psychological Association has a history of political activity that is absent within the British Psychological Society. The American division of the Psychology of Women have commented on such subjects as rape, abortion and pornography. Although the British POWS is as yet in its infancy, it is hard to envisage, given the current climate, that such issues as rape, abortion and pornography will be brought to the forefront of psychology in anything but a dry, academic, empirical context, if that. Any political interpretation or intervention would definitely be left aside, even when these issues have such obvious political sequelae.

As an example, it is interesting to note the complete absence of comment from the British psychological community during 1987–88 when two government bills were being passed through Parliament that had important psychological consequences for women in this country. The first was the Abortion bill seeking to reduce the time limit for an abortion to take place from 28 weeks to 18 weeks. Great emphasis was given to the medical aspects of this debate, but the psychological factors for the mother were totally ignored. This is certainly not because there isn't any available research (see Broome, 1984, for a review). Thankfully the bill was not passed.

Also within that year we saw the instigation of Clause 28 of the Local Authority bill, which wanted to prevent the 'promotion of homosexuality', and guard against the 'acceptability of homosexuality as a *pretended* family relationship'. Such a bill had very serious implications for the homosexual community, and particularly lesbian mothers, as it appeared to be a further step in placing homosexuality firmly in the public view as unacceptable, amoral, unhealthy and possibly even punishable. Once again the British psychological community failed to stand up and point out the illogical thinking behind this clause, and the possible serious psychological ramifications of its implementation. One simple, informed comment could have been to rectify the faulty thinking that homosexuality can be 'caught' by children reading a very occasional book in which it features. Unfortunately, this bill did not face the same demise as the Alton bill. Although there has been no explicit attempt so far to enforce it, it remains lurking in the background as a factor for conservatism and self-censorship. It is perhaps unsurprising to learn that at this time the BPS were in the final stages of seeing psychology in Britain become a Chartered profession approved by Parliament.

At a level closer to home is the debate about whether the psychology of women should be seen as feminist. I believe that it is impossible to conceive of a psychology of women without some feminist intent, or it would surely be 'man's psychology of women'. It is clear that part of the wish to have a psychology of women is to redress the balance and recognize that women's experience has so far been absent in psychology. As I agree with Helen Callaway that feminism entails '. . . a strong critique of male-centred models of reality and the research that has validated traditional bodies of knowledge' (1981, p. 460), then it is clear that one of the main starting points of a psychology of women must be acknowledged as feminist. Thus, I regard the debate as really asking 'Can there be a psychology of women that is not feminist?' But what is so dreadful about being feminist anyway? Why may feminism not darken the BPS's door? The answer is again because it is 'political'. While I would not want to refute this, I do take issue with the claim that psychology is 'apolitical'. Feminism has been singled out as a particularly disruptive influence, sceptics would perhaps say, *because* it criticizes male-centred models of reality, and those in power who define the boundaries between what is and is not 'political' happen to be men. But I also believe the word 'feminism' carries with it the legacy of 'Women's Lib', and is seen only as pressure groups to do with equal rights and opportunities, so that the theoretical stance is either misunderstood or ignored.

And finally, feminist psychology

I have come to regard feminist psychology as part of the new paradigm movement which is taking place within the social sciences. This movement emphasizes alternatives to orthodox approaches, and is influenced by humanistic psychology, phenomenology, ethnomethodology, 'applied' behavioural science, existentialism and Marxism (Reason and Rowan, 1981). If this is not political I don't know what is! Yet feminism remains singled out as a disruptive force within mainstream psychology that needs to be excluded. Reason and Rowan (1981) make some interesting and I believe very accurate remarks in the foreword to their superb book *Human Inquiry: A Sourcebook of New Paradigm Research*:

> We are just beginning to see the relationships between feminist scholarship and new paradigm research, and just beginning to learn about the wealth of research of new paradigm character that has been carried out by women.

Again, we didn't look hard enough. And this is rather curious, because throughout this book are references to new paradigm research being a move away from 'male' towards a 'female' approach to inquiry.

So there seems to be a real danger that in new paradigm research men will take a 'female' way of looking at the world, and turn it into another 'male' way of seeing it. (p. xxiii)

I think this danger is a very real one, and may already be happening. We ourselves as feminist psychologists may even be contributing to it by not recognizing the importance of putting feminism firmly on the map of mainstream psychology. To get work heard, papers published, it may be tempting to drop the word feminism from the title and go in under the cloak of new paradigm research. I believe this must be resisted at all costs, for those reasons Peter Reason and John Rowan specify so clearly.

Furthermore, as new paradigm research becomes more acceptable women must fight for the acknowledgement that feminist psychology deserves in this development. As Reason and Rowan point out, many women have been doing new paradigm research for a long time with little recognition and credibility. Only now that it has been given a different name and taken under the more credible umbrella of new paradigm research has it become acceptable. Thus, feminist psychology should be recognized as not only participating in, but as being one of the leading influences of this changing paradigm within the social sciences.

As for the future of feminist psychology, I think we will have a very exciting time ahead. We have to overcome the political hurdle of acceptability within traditional psychology, which specifically means encouraging the BPS not to veto their involvement with anything with the word 'feminism' in the title, and to accept it as a valid approach with much potential for the advancement of the discipline. We now have an avenue to do this through the Psychology of Women Section. Wittingly or unwittingly the door has been opened for women in psychology and it is inevitable that feminism will also pass through that door. However, as gains in acceptability are made I see a feminist approach pervading all aspects of psychology, not just that related to women. This may result in a splitting apart of old divisions and frameworks, and the re-vision Helen Callaway writes about that brings about an 'imaginative sighting of possibilities' (1981, p. 457). Whatever the case, women will no longer be passive recipients of pseudo-psychological facts about their own experience, nor be lay or peripheral figures in the discipline of psychology.

References

Broome, A. (1984) Termination of pregnancy. In A. Broome and L. Wallace (eds). *Psychological and Gynaecological Problems.* London: Tavistock.

Callaway, H. (1981) Women's perspectives: research revisited. In P. Reason and J. Rowan (eds), *Human Inquiry: A Sourcebook of New Paradigm Research.* Chichester: John Wiley.

Henley, N. (1985) Psychology and gender. *Signs: Journal of Women in Culture and Society* 11 (1), 101–19.

Horney, K. (1974) The flight from womanhood. In J.B. Miller (ed.), *Psychoanalysis and Women.* Harmondsworth: Penguin.

Parlee, M.B. (1975) Psychology: review essay. *Signs* 1 (1), 119–38

Reason, P. and Rowan. J. (1981) *Human Inquiry: A Sourcebook of New Paradigm Research.* Chichester: John Wiley.

Russo, N.F. and O'Connell, A.N. (1980) Models from our past: psychology's foremothers. *Psychology of Women Quarterly* 3, 123–38.

Weinreich, H. (1977) What future for the female subject? some implications for the women's movement for psychological research. *Human Relations* 30 (6), 535–43.

Weisstein, N. (1970) 'Kinde, Kuche, Kirche' as scientific law: psychology constructs the female. In R. Morgan (ed.), *Sisterhood is Powerful: An Anthology of Writings from the Women's Liberation Movement.* New York: Random House, pp. 228–44.

10

Steps towards silence: women in educational psychology

> Against the faith men had in the institution they and not women had shaped, women upheld some other principles of selfhood in which being surpassed doing. Long ago men had noted something unruly in this. Women simply enclosed the space which men longed to penetrate. The men's hostility was aroused. (McEwan, 1987)

In this chapter we are going to examine our practice as educational psychologists within the local education authority where we have worked for the last ten years. During this period there have been many changes in the philosophy and practice of the Educational Psychology Service, some due to national or local pressures and some coming from within. We decided to make our contribution anonymously for a number of reasons. First, we are pleased to have worked for an authority that allowed the time and opportunity for personal development and would not wish to prejudice future initiatives. Second, we feel that we and other women who identified with us may suffer personally and/or professionally as a result of our comments. Lastly, we feel that this chapter itself may be highly censored by local education authority officers. This does not mean however, that we feel free to deviate from what we perceive as the truth.

First of all, we want to state that there are many positive aspects of being women working in educational psychology. Women develop a role which includes meeting the emotional needs of others both at home and in the workplace (Eichenbaum and Orbach, 1982). They acquire skills such as listening, empathy and warmth which form a central part of the professional expertise of the 'caring professional'. Working as educational psychologists we have been able to draw on our own personal strengths and to use them in a wide range of circumstances including those which are very emotionally demanding. The job fulfils popular expectations of the kind of work women should do. There is no conflict regarding role expectations as experienced by other women professionals as, for example, women engineers. Our work brings us into contact with many women both within school pastoral systems and in other caring professions. Our shared personal skills and experience provide a basis for working together on individual and wider problems.

The very strengths that we have identified cause difficulties. These strengths have become less and less recognized as an important part of our work and they can also be exploited in a workplace. We will discuss these aspects further on in this chapter.

Working as an educational psychologist

The experience of working as an educational psychologist within a County Psychological Service must be seen in the context of the local education authority (LEA) philosophy and practice. The interaction between them is increasing and all services are asked to be professionally and financially accountable. In our particular service this has meant a change of focus from individual responsibility to more control regarding methods of working and time spent on various activities. This is particularly relevant when considering equal opportunities. Although there is some token acceptance of this issue it is our experience that the local education authority and Educational Psychology Service within it have realized nor put into practice the full implications of such a policy and in fact, have given it low priority.

In terms of 'equal opportunities' the LEA has recently produced *Notes of Guidance on Good Employment Practice* which focuses on non-discriminatory practice in recruitment. This is to be welcomed, but we are still awaiting a clear framework providing guidelines for professional practice. There are two main areas of concern: there are no specific suggestions to schools of issues to be addressed and there is apparently no monitoring or evaluation of good and bad practice.

There has been a recent appointment of an inspector with the responsibility for equal opportunities and this is to be welcomed. Equal opportunities, however, form only part of her job description which also includes responsibilities for a number of areas of the curriculum, in particular personal and social education. An even more recent appointment is that of an advisory teacher for equal opportunities in the Technical and Vocational Education Initiative to work under the inspector. Her job is provided under the umbrella of TVEI but it is to be hoped that her role will spread more widely.

There has been very little in-service training on equal opportunities in the county although there are plans to improve this within the next few years. The County Inspector has included modules on equal opportunities within a general course on personal and social education but this may be because the present authors submitted a grant-related in-service training (GRIST) proposal entitled *Sexism in Schools*. The proposal was, in fact, rejected by the primary and secondary senior inspectors but has been included in a modified form. The title has been changed to *Equal Opportunities* because it was thought that members of the education committee would dislike the use of the word sexism.

Even having got to this stage it was debatable whether the course would be included but an administrative slip-up in the production of the GRIST booklet for 1988–89 ensured its incorporation. The lack of a strong equal opportunities policy means that in-service training in this area is separated from mainstream curriculum development. Equal opportunities is not seen as a baseline on which all other in-service training is built.

This has implications for our work with schools. Given the lack of in-service training on equal opportunities we find a limited awareness in schools of issues to do with sexism. It is an extremely rare experience for us to meet a teacher who appreciates the influence of the structure and curriculum of the school on the ways in which boys and girls learn and develop. Indeed, we sometimes meet enormous resistance, for example staff unable to see the connection between what they see to be a trivial matter such as separation of boys and girls for curriculum activities and the teachers' expectations of pupil behaviour.

Although pastoral staff in secondary schools are often women, headteachers of both primary and secondary schools, together with heads of departments, tend to be male. This situation is not helped by the fact that the vast majority of the inspectorate who make senior appointments are also male. In consulting with them we find them generally less likely to recognize the importance of anti-sexist policies.

One of the main areas of development within the LEA following the 1981 Education Act is that of 'special needs'. The act assumes that up to 20 percent of pupils will have special educational needs at some point in their school career. This indicates that the LEA, through the school, should be responsible for the identification and assessment of these pupils and for the provision to meet their needs. Educational psychologists have a statutory duty under the Act to assess a smaller group of children who have significant difficulties but increasingly our work with the schools has required us to help them to meet their responsibilities.

The Special Needs Service within our LEA remains focused on the primary-age child who is failing within the language area of the curriculum and this means most of the resources are directed towards meeting boys' needs at an early age. The Special Needs Service which supports the children in the mainstream school seems to be following the example of the special schools which have a primarily male population. Our role as advisers to schools and in assessments means, sadly, that we must own a large part of the responsibility for directing resources towards boys rather than girls.

The Educational Psychology Service (EPS) has seen major changes in its structure and philosophy over the last ten years which are reflected in its changing role. Although the 1981 Act heralded a statutory involvement with individual cases it also promoted the development of more generalized consultancy work. Our own EPS has been directed by its hierarchy, which is male-dominated, to respond at both levels in such a way that the individual educational psychologist (EP) is distanced from the emotional content of the cases presented. For example, for individual clients this means that the EP is encouraged to use a strongly behaviourist approach to change behaviour and not be involved in individual counselling or personal exploration. We have been asked to focus on an advisory/consultancy role which can be seen as a way of removing oneself to some extent from direct emotional contact with the problem under discussion. American-style business techniques such as personal management, prioritization, etc., have been promoted as a way in which to resolve professional conflicts. These steps may be necessary under the pressure of an increased workload but the effect has been to devalue the skills built on the strengths women tend to have. The emphasis is on action rather than reflection and on the instrumental rather than the expressive.

The 1988 Education Reform Act heightens these issues. This Act, which was designed to increase parental choice and power lays down the basis for a national curriculum and performance indicators for children's achievement at various stages in their school career. It is intended to allow parents to make more meaningful comparisons between schools so that they can choose between them. It also gives much greater powers to school governors, including financial management, and thus the LEA's control over schools will be diminished. Unfortunately they will only be able to control 7 percent of the schools' budget which means that some services will have to be privatized. The government has also made allowance for schools to take a further step towards independence from the LEAs, by 'opting out', with the agreement of parents, and receiving their monies directly from the Department of Education and Science (DES).

The implications for EPs are far-reaching and complex. The Act reinforces the concept of a client-based service which means that individual work, for which we have a statutory responsibility, will become the main focus for the service. The priorities of the service will be recognized as more in line with the work of the main grade EPs and the work of the male seniors will have to be re-evaluated. The legal focus of the work having been shifted even further to the main grade EPs, the viability of a top-heavy hierarchy will be highly questionable.

Concern remains, however, about the impact on our professional work, particularly as it is unclear how special educational needs will be met within the context of a national curriculum and standardized testing. We could find ourselves being used by schools to facilitate a procedure whereby children are excluded from the national curriculum in order to ensure that the school's test results are impressive. This would be contrary to the philosophy of integration. The equal opportunities issues including those of race, are unclear, but given the history of segregation in our school system, it is likely that a similar, situation might arise regarding exclusion from the national curriculum. The situation would be exacerbated should the financial constraints on the LEA require the EPS to be privatized, increasing the moral dilemma of fulfilling the requirements of our employer or upholding the rights of the child.

The impact on individual schools of the increase in parental choice of schools could lead to the creation of 'bin' schools with low standards of attainment, fewer teaching resources and low morale. It would be very difficult for LEAs to help these schools because of the financial constraints and the rigid formula distribution of the schools' budget. If these schools are also required to 'buy' LEA services, including those of the EPS, it is hard to see how the needs of the children are going to be effectively met. Ensuring equal opportunities in such a school is likely to be seen as something of a luxury.

Although the focus on casework has reaffirmed the importance of the main grade EPs' work, the emphasis on statutory work brings with it a means of accountability by which it is possible to monitor and control our work. While this may have some advantages, it is likely to lead to a much narrower role definition and could preclude counselling and therapy and our more general advisory role including INSET, and therefore our work in promoting equal opportunities.

The workplace

We would now like to describe in detail our more personal experiences as women working for an LEA.

Within the structure of the Educational Psychology Service, over two-thirds of the EPs in our LEA are women, and yet the management team is entirely male. The way the work is shared is that the basic grade EPs do the bulk of the school and statutory work and within the last couple of years the Area Seniors have been given reduced schools loads of between 14 and 24 percent to those of the basic grade EPs. This has enabled them to spend the rest of their time on management and administrative duties, leaving women carrying most of the work for which the service is recognized by the County Education Officer. This hierarchy sits uneasily in a service of equally qualified professionals and is particularly alien to our own egalitarian values and those of many other women in the service. It has raised considerable dilemmas for women who want the system to be different and have to decide whether to join it and seek promotion in order to try and make changes, or to remain without power but apart from a hierarchy whose operation holds very few attractions. The dilemma for women has been highlighted over the last three years by the sharp increase of 61 percent in the entire team of senior EPs.

Although there have been four women senior EPs in the period under discussion, one left six years ago and the other three all have positions which place them at a tangent to the bulk of the work in the county. They have not been asked to join the management team and are thus outside the male hierarchy.

The EPS has for many services supported itself by a wholly female group of clerical assistants and secretaries. Although the pay is low the service has managed to attract high calibre women who have performed their duties extremely well and enabled the service to be run on minimal funding. While they provide considerable professional and personal support for the EPs working in the service, it is difficult for female EPs to tap into this without reservations. We feel that we should provide support in turn.

Particular issues arise for part-time women EPs in the service. One EP recently returned from maternity leave and discussed with the County EP the possibility of a job-share. She was flatly refused. The County EP has since expressed the view that women in the service should fight for equality within the home and not expect concessions at work because, for example, their jobs are secondary to their husbands. When the EP requested advice from the union office of the Association of Educational Psychologists (AEP) she was not referred to the Equal Opportunities Commission (EOC) which could have advised her on research on job-sharing, case precedent, etc, but was told she should not expect to be treated any differently from a man. Since then she has spoken to a Deputy Education Officer who has given a much more positive response. This may be partly the result of union pressure on the subject of job-sharing.

In this context, a significant development was the creation of a national Women Psychologists' Group. At an EPS residential conference in November 1978 three women EPs discovered common interest and concerns centring around feminism, particularly as it applied to schools and psychology. The idea of forming a Women Psychologists' Group was born and a proposal was subsequently put to the County EP. At that time, when different areas of work were being explored, a study group focusing on feminist issues was accepted and allowed to meet on a regular basis throughout the year. The ethos of that time embraced the examination of personal issues and their effects on our professional work and the establishment of the group was seen to fit within that framework.

The group began to meet in early 1979, marking a period we now think of as the good years. For the first two years the group examined relevant literature and used this as a stimulus for consciousness-raising. This stage of the group's life ended with a residential conference called 'Female/Male: A Psychological Perspective'. There had been some early hostility and rejection of the idea of such a course and there was debate within the group about the extent to which it should challenge individual EPs' roles within their own families. In view of the early hostility and anxiety it was decided to organize a 'safe' course relying heavily on external contributors to establish the academic credibility of 'sexism' as a subject. The conference focused on the psychology of sex differences, parenting roles, sexism in schools and feminist therapy, but allowed little opportunity for self-examination. Although well received at the time its academic orientation allowed it to be easily assimilated without changing people in a way that suggested further work. Indeed it led to a feeling that issues of sexism had been tackled and resolved within the EPS.

One of the valuable contributions of the Women Psychologists' Group that was recognized at that time was that it gave women strength and support to speak out and air their views within the larger group. This effect continued for some time but the recent influx of seniors seems to have unbalanced the relative willingness of men and women EPs to speak.

Following the conference the group increasingly functioned as a support and self-help therapy group for its members. The self-help therapy book *In Our Own Hands* written by Sheila Ernst and Lucy Goodison, was used to guide us through some painful personal exploration (1981). We found this very helpful in our work. It allowed us to be supported away from our casework and the colleagues we met on a daily basis. Through sharing our personal experiences we were able to see how these affected our professional judgement. The change and function to a support group had not necessarily been sanctioned by the County Educational Psychologist Inspectorate and it was never clear whether it would have gained their approval.

The beginning of the end occurred in 1983 when there was a major reorganization of the EPS. This caused a great deal of anxiety and anger because of the way in which individual EPs were not consulted about changes which fundamentally affected their work. The function of the Women Psychologists' Group was changed yet again and it became a forum for managing the stress which had been created. This was positive and necessary in one sense but was unfortunate in that the valuable personal exploration was set to one side. The group seemed to become identified as a source of the general dissatisfaction with the reorganization and we began to become nervous about the continued existence of the group and our own career prospects and security.

Following reorganization, demands began to be made that all working groups report back on issues discussed and action taken to the County EP. This raised a number of problems for a group struggling to return to personal support. It was difficult to report back and we found ourselves adopting a defensive posture. This led to a period of negotiation about the group's arrangements which ended with a meeting between the group and the Chief Inspector, who would not agree to the continued existence of a single-sex group. The impression he gave by his words and style, including calling us 'ladies', and announcing that he was not sexist, was that he was not aware of either the general issues concerning sexism within the county nor the value of a personal support group to the EPS. He terminated the group within working time.

The effect of the official disbanding of the women's group was traumatic and silenced the discussion of feminist issues for some years. The County EP recently said 'we all believe girls should be equal', comparing this with issues of racism and classism which he clearly saw as more important. He also seemed to think a pious belief in equality is enough to ensure that it happens, at least as far as gender is concerned. As far as the service is concerned, the reorganisation, including the reduced workload of the seniors, has distanced the County EP from the stresses and strains and from the need for personal support. Because he has surrounded himself with other males he has very limited contact with the women in the service and their particular responsibilities and needs. When questioned about personal support he has directed the individual EP to the area teams which are expected to meet all our needs, professional and personal. As these teams form the base of the hierarchical structure of the EPS and are orientated towards decision making this is not really possible. The idea that one relationship can meet all one's needs seems to reflect a male perspective. In reality, the teams do not, on the whole, provide a forum for personal support except insofar as the women EPs tend to be drawn into supporting the men. The support given ranges from making the coffee and doing the washing up to providing an audience or a sympathetic ear.

On reflection, it seems that the Women Psychologists' Group not only provoked some hostility because it seemed to give support to women members within the service, but it also provoked envy from men who wanted the same degree of support. The idea of a Men's Group was suggested at the residential conference on sexism but there were only two takers and the group never got off the ground. Sadly, even within the caring profession, men seem unable to offer each other support. At present the male management team meetings have been described by participants as the very opposite of supportive.

The future

We face many difficulties in challenging the system. Almost a third of the women EPs working for the service are part-time and their influence is diminished by other pressures on them and the difficulty for them in participating fully in discussion. The career structure is controlled by men and, as already indicated, it is difficult for women to make the decision whether or not to climb within it. The current emphasis on strong management lines created problems for EPs who have no designs on power itself to achieve recognition.

We would like to see the following developments in the LEA and EPS. First, a further clarification of an equal opportunities policy including clear objectives and guidelines for schools and county services. Second, we consider that an equal opportunities approach should be the basis for in-service training in the county. And within the Educational Psychology Service, we would want to envisage a less hierarchical and more democratic structure with recognition, possibly by career grading, of experience and personal strengths. This should also be accompanied by a recognition and acceptance that face-to-face involvement is the foundation of our work and a valuing of the skills needed for this.

References

Eichenbaum, L. and Orbach, S. (1982) *Outside In, Inside out*. Harmondsworth: Penguin.
Ernst, S. and Goodison, L. (1981) *In Our Own Hands*. London: The Women's Press.
McEwan, I. (1987) *The Child in Time*. London: Jonathan Cape.

Postscript

The writing of this chapter has, in itself, started off a process of change within the county. Writing the chapter has exorcised the past and clarified our thoughts, thus allowing the discussion of feminist issues to be put back on the agenda. As the chapter has been written anonymously, the authors feel that it would be only fair to feed back some of our thoughts to our Principal. This was partly achieved through the medium of a survey, the results of which revealed that most of the EPs in the county saw the male domination of the management as a problem. Coincidentally, at the request of members of the service, a working party was set up to look at working conditions in general and the problem of the lack of women at management level was seen as a priority to be tackled. Strategies are currently being considered.

The Equal Opportunities course, mentioned earlier, has started and seems to be tapping great enthusiasm among the participants. The course is acting as a catalyst, bringing together otherwise isolated individuals to form a support group and provide the basis for a network throughout the county. A Secondary Inspector has expressed great interest in forming an equal opportunities interest group.

11

Women in the shadows: women, feminism and clinical psychology

Christine Adcock and Karen Newbigging

We decided to call this chapter by this name because we felt strongly that the women that we meet in our working lives have been largely misplaced in both the chronicling of the history of feminism and of psychology. Women, *as women*, have had no place of their own in psychology. Only latterly has some scant attention been paid to the particular concerns of women who have mental health problems with an emphasis on the patriarchal nature of the construction of psychology. We have yet to find an article which looks at the arena of women who have an intellectual disability. In our view, feminism is not exempt from the charge of ignoring these groups of women. While some of psychology has been forced to a take account of women who have mental distress, where has feminism addressed issues raised by women that have profound or less severe learning difficulties? In this chapter we want to present our understanding of how we came to recognize these omissions, how we came to question the conceptual world that was offered to us as a reality through the experiences of the women we met and worked with. We will describe how we tried to create a tenable rapprochement between what we saw, our training and our understanding of women's experiences.

As we discussed and wrote this chapter the issues seemed to get more complex as a direct result of our trying to manage the conflicts, and in trying to bridge the divide between our different areas of work with women with learning difficulties and women with mental health problems. Before we embarked on writing this we had felt that we faced similar issues in our work because we talked about the same problems. When we came to writing, the picture became more complex because of the different needs of the women we work with. We tried to figure out whether the crucial issue was being a woman or having either a learning difficulty or mental health problem. Through our discussion we came to realize the disabling effect of being devalued on two spheres – as a women, and as having a learning difficulty or mental health problem.

We began to feel increasingly uncomfortable with the models offered by clinical psychology during our training. The dissatisfaction we felt began as discomfort: the model presented failed to fit both our lives and the lives of people around us. As a scientific model its claims to be neutral, value-free and thus beyond reproach were difficult for us to swallow since it clearly did not present any convincing critical evaluation of the world we inhabited. Later we arrived at the conviction that the model was decontextualized and floated free from the constraints and forces which shape our everyday experiences. We had yet to grasp a coherent intellectual and political framework into which clinical psychology may finally fit and offer something. While clinical psychology was purporting to be *the* framework into which all else fitted, it lacked credibility. Understanding our own experience and that of other women in a capitalist society helped us to focus on and acknowledge what, when training, had appeared as an emotional disquiet. Everything in our training told us that this disquiet was unscientific, therefore wrong, therefore devalued. This we now see as the very processes by which science, as an instrument of patriarchy and capitalism, treats and dismisses women's experiences.

Our experiences as 'practising psychologists' testify to this perspective. The experience of people who have a learning disability or a mental health problem exemplifies the processes of devaluation. Within this, the experience of women appears as an oppression multiplied. In this chapter we discuss some of the steps we took towards understanding how women with a learning disability or a mental health problem are viewed and treated by this society, and how we, as women with professional status and power, can interact with their experience – an interaction which is so structured as to make the meeting of our two worlds extremely difficult.

Clinical psychology relies on an individualistic interpretation of the world. It assumes that difficulties people experience are due to an intra-psychic process which mediates the world through individual experience. Although acknowledging the 'forces of society', it asserts that these are not within its control and thus not open to enquiry by psychologists. These 'intervening processes', when dysfunctional, can be seen as distorting the experience of individuals and as a result people experience distress. Enter clinical psychology. If your level of analysis is individualistic, the natural response to distress is to try and 'fix' this dysfunctional process. The logic is flawless if confined to areas where distress is seen as a direct result of misperception of the real world. However, it increasingly seemed to us that misperceptions of this nature were rarely as simple as this and although psychology could (sometimes) alter this, it could also clearly further cause distress by failing to see the forces by which such misperceptions were set up, experienced and interpreted. The result of this focus thus views the distressed individual as in some sense faulty, and thus culpable. This sense of fault is easily equated with blame and increases feelings of inadequacy and guilt in most of us. If we then acknowledge why it suits society (while avoiding a functionalist analysis) to perpetuate such feelings, we come nearer, we believe, to understanding why psychology is structured as it is, and how minorities (racial and intellectual) and women get the worst possible deal from this.

Clinical psychology, in its assumption of the scientific, mirrors the society in which it operates, both in its basic philosophical values and in terms of the professionalism that forms part of its practice. Simply, the argument is somewhat as follows: clinical psychology is like medicine, medicine is scientific, science is a restricted code, therefore you need specialists to operate and understand this code. Also, if clinical psychology is scientific then it is deemed 'true' and this 'truth' is more acceptable, more valued, and more reliable within this world than the complexities and value systems underpinning political stances, or the experiences of people whose access to the truth is limited (due to inferiority? lack of understanding?). Clinical psychology is hence empowered to judge the experiences of such individuals, but is exempt from criticism. If the system reflects a capitalist and patriarchal society, then it is clear that women, particularly those not part of the work economy, are likely to be the losers. Unfortunately, the 'clients' of clinical psychology tend to be just these 'losers'. The only psychological frameworks of explanation available to account for women's positions either depict women as inherently 'faulty', or as 'victims' – linking into ubiquitous but rarely recognized stereotypes. For alternatives you just have to look for a wider understanding of the processes operating here.

Although we do not advocate that clinical psychology should be jettisoned as a result of this re-evaluation, we consider that it must be contextualized. We need to critically appraise which bits 'work' and are useful, which people it is used with/upon, in which circumstances, and by whom it is operated. While psychology is constructed to concur with a society whose norms are white, male and middle class, the evidence that shows this is disallowed through the monopoly on credibility exerted by 'scientific endeavour'. Since much of the material which counters this view comes from 'soft' sources which include women's reality, it is accorded no strength to criticize. Psychology thus becomes impervious to any body of knowledge that is critical unless that knowledge adheres to the 'science rules', which in turn function to support prevailing power relations.

The area of concern for psychologists is located around the individual. This focus ignores more macro, 'sociological' factors, and often leads us to mistake effects for causes. There are numerous examples of practice where such a mistake has refocused professional activity inappropriately. Psychology has given us a particular model of the person, and the system of referral to a clinical psychologist maintains (in very practical senses) both the model and the clinical psychologists, who through the model are persuaded that they are addressing central problems. In this situation women's experiences are rendered more complex because their level of disability becomes transformed and psychiatrized in order for *us* to understand it and feel confident that our level of skills can ameliorate it. What was pain and confusion for these women we transform into a behaviour problem which calls for a professional to set up a programme. And we do this even when we know that some of these women have a disability which limits their linguistic/conceptual ability! We nevertheless identify the problem as *their* problem, which *we* can fix.

As trained psychologists we were confronted with a conflict between an understanding of class and gender, and how services should respond to women who are totally or partially dependent on them. In particular, we grappled with the attempts to define the reality of women with reference to an individualistic, scientific, *correct* model of clinical psychology. It is only with hindsight that we can dignify what we were feeling with a critical theoretical framework. During training, scant attention had been paid to the reality of women's lives and there was no discussion of the psychological implications of motherhood, miscarriage, unemployment, poverty, menstruation, racial or sexual harassment or abuse, let alone a wider discussion of women's roles and society's expectations of women in a multicultural world. Further, the connection between the presentation of symptoms and gender was not made, nor the differential use and accessibility of health and social services to women, black and working-class people revealed.

These sins of omission are not psychology's alone but do reflect psychology's pursuit of science and its attempt to be 'gender-free'. In recent years, though after the time of our training, gender has been introduced into psychology and we welcome the changes this brings. But it almost goes without saying that putting gender on psychology's agenda is different from the political perspective feminism offers. By this we mean that feminism's project goes far beyond 'adding women in' to psychology, but rather envisages the transformation of existing power inequalities, which will no doubt have its reflection in the unsettling of current disciplinary boundaries.

However, the distorted content of training is only part of the story. Becoming a clinical psychologist also involved a process of pro-fessionalization upon which one of us unwittingly embarked, while the other left the profession as a way of coping with the discomfort. There are many strands to this process of professionalization. It starts with the limited entry to the profession (women are well represented in clinical psychology at the lower end of the pay scales). The language and theory is complex and relatively inaccessible – how we struggled with antecedents, contingencies and projective identification! The methods of intervention (note the language!) were sometimes highly intrusive or controlling in terms of someone's life, or if minimally intrusive seemed to assume an importance, to the psychologist that is, disproportionate with reality. The implicit rules about clinical relationships were different than for other relationships and reinforced the power differential between clinical pychologists and the people with whom they work. Finally, in its struggle for coherence, clinical psychology rejects or devalues the experiences of those who threaten the integrity of its theory and practice. All human services, and psychiatry in particular, fall foul of this approach, so that women are at risk of being described as 'defensive', 'manipulative', 'attention-seeking' – and 'non-co-operative' if we can't help. So one of us stuck with the profession and its contradictions, and the other began to work with a fairly radical health education unit around issues of mental health and handicap. It was partly the community development framework applied there, as well as support from women in the voluntary sector, which enabled her to understand the tensions between psychology and the world she experienced. During this time we began (with the help of many friends working in this area) to comprehend both the process and the degree of devaluation people with learning disabilities and mental health problems are subject to, the dehumanization and the resulting damage. But while this helped to put boundaries around our disquiet, the whole debate was, and remains to a large extent, class and gender-free.

It needed a fuller understanding of the issues around class and gender politics to finally make it clear, for example, that people with learning difficulties are so severely devalued when their disability is profound that they are actually seen as *gender-free*. This allows people to act towards women as if they were neutral and neutered. If the level of disability is less extreme we visit on women the oppression of an 'intellectualist' society as well as all the force of a sexist one. It sometimes appears as if services are set up to make it as difficult as possible for women who already have a learning difficulty to understand the rules of the world.

The ideas and practice born from people's experience that gain social legitimation reflect processes of selection which work in favour of the more powerful and against the least powerful. We have been particularly critical of clinical psychology in not taking the experience of women into account. Feminism, an ideology which purports to be women-centred, may so far have only taken the experiences of some, more powerful, women into account. Women with severe learning difficulties do not figure in the debates around women's issues, and although there has been some substantive effort and work on women and mental health, it is nevertheless open to the charge of not adequately reflecting the experience of all sorts of women, working class, black, those living in institutions and older women with severe mental health problems, such as Alzheimer's disease.

This chapter does not aim to be definitive but seeks rather to raise some of the questions which have arisen from our disillusionment with clinical psychology and our struggle with feminism to include all women in the picture. Also we must raise the question of how much the process of socialization, pay and status of clinical psychologists militates against real change, and the limitations of an individually focused response within a capitalist framework. We have to find ways of enabling each woman to have more positive experiences while being sensitive to the context in which her disability, class, race and gender place her. We have to find ways of valuing the importance of ordinary life events for women and rejecting the reduction of women's experience to symptoms, problems, or behaviour. Professionally we have to reject the 'throughput model' applauded by the medical model which encourages clinical psychologists to mirror their medical colleagues and see, treat and discharge people within a predetermined time-span. Getting to know someone and understanding her needs takes time, and any work towards change needs to be followed through into her life situation, and to be properly supported by people in her own networks as well as by whichever professional is appropriate. The current climate in the Health Service militated against this style of work which we see as the only way to effect change. The services we work in have always been (accurately) labelled as the 'Cinderella services' and the current politics of the service allows little room for developmental work: under pressure from progressive cutbacks and looming privatization, the emphasis of managers and hence workers is on 'spreading the jam more thinly'.

Women in north Manchester

At the time of writing, both of us have worked in north Manchester for a number of years as clinical psychologists. North Manchester is an inner-city area with a predominantly working-class population. In some parts of north Manchester people who were born and bred in the area still live there and most will tell you of the decline that has taken place over the last twenty years. In other areas ambitious but ill-conceived rehousing projects have decimated social and community life. People from different ethnic origins have settled in north Manchester: Asian, Jewish, Afro-Caribbean and Chinese people. The demographic characteristics paint a demoralizing but familiar picture of high unemployment, overcrowding, households without bathrooms, high infant mortality and poor health. Despite this the services and local resources available are in some areas minimal, and there is a noticeable lack of leisure facilities and public transport. The majority of health services are located in the large Victorian general hospital in the north, and more recently purpose-built health centres throughout the district. The majority of clinical psychologists are based at two hospitals but both of us work from houses based in the community. Christine works primarily with women with severe learning difficulties while Karen works mainly, although not exclusively, with women with mental health problems. The most important difference between our work is that by and large the women Karen works with already have a life in the community, whereas women with learning difficulties often rely on service providers for both their presence and participation in that community.

These women, as well as contending with the power differential imposed by gender, may face further disadvantage as a result of their ethnic origin, class, disability or sexual orientation. In addition, their relationship with health or social services often serves to enhance this. Both of us have been influenced by PASS (Programme Analysis of Service Systems) and normalization theory which had fostered an understanding of the damage services can do to service recipients, although this approach has only recently begun to acknowledge gender issues. The starting point for normalization is an understanding of the ways people who are different have been negatively stereo-typed, and the wounds which these people have experienced as a consequence. The stereotypes, ideas and images of people who are different usually imply that these people are less than truly human – as menaces, objects of pity, trivial, burdens of charity, sick: 'holy innocents' or eternal children, for instance. So far we have taken psychology to task for its construction of women as deviant or infantile. This is reflected in our everyday experience when we hear women described as 'neurotic', 'bitch', or 'sugar' and 'baby'. Normalization powerfully describes the cycle of deviance which results from this kind of labelling. Labelling leads to lowered expectations (and of course lowered self-esteem), which leads to the opportunities available being restricted, which in turn reinforces the low expectations and therefore justifies the label. Our own experience as women may help us to empathize with other devalued groups of people. However, the women we work with experience the process of devaluation not only as women but as a consequence of being labelled as different in another way, usually by virtue of having a learning difficulty or a mental health problem (particularly if they have spent some time in a psychiatric hospital). We suggested earlier that the oppression these women face is multiple, as a result of the compounding of gender norms with the stigma associated with other devalued groups. We are now going to expand on the issues that are specific to the different groups of women we work with.

In the next section we want to talk about the experiences that many women we know face. We want to do this in a way that gives a real taste of women's lives. We will use stories which represent the reality of their existence. To do this we have either negotiated with the women to gain permission, or we have used a montage of common experiences. (In both cases we have obviously changed the names of the women concerned.)

Christine's experience

In the next part I want to explore and offer my understanding of the experience of women with learning difficulties as mediated through a sexist and 'intellectualist' society. I must reiterate that it feels as if many women I work with are seen as gender-free because of the basic belief, both generally and within services, that people with severe learning difficulties are less than human and thus not subject to the same pressures as you and me. Here a clear distinction must be made which parallels the level of disability a woman has. Some of the women I meet and work with have a very severe learning disability and often a physical disabiltiy as well. The level of disability is such that many women have limited language and conceptual ability. Because of this I assume certain things as I have limited access into their own understanding. However, it is difficult for me to ascertain what self-concept the women have, what their understanding is of their history, their gender, their feelings. Many are almost *total* service recipients. By this I mean that they are dependent on family (often mother only) and service providers to offer food, clothes, experiences, and sometimes to enable women to eat that food, put those clothes, on or go to the toilet. In partnership with the mother (although services often act as an oppressor for the mother by withholding or offering support, demanding changes), we structure women's days and evenings, we decide what and when they should experience, learn, choose. We explain our understanding of their world. Often, the only way we know that women disagree with our interpretation of their lives is by the way they behave. It is difficult for me to communicate the immensity of the void we have to bridge when a women's only control over her life is to be 'difficult', to hurt herself or others, to throw things, because our understanding of her life may not even shadow hers.

Such a description will echo other women's experiences if we look at issues of powerlessness and control generally. The gender specificity for women with severe learning difficulties is shown in the way the control they exert is often seen in terms of withdrawal and depression, whereas many men in similar stituations are aggressive and destructive. While this is the general picture, however, my own experience of the women I know and work with is that they are expressing what I take to be their powerlessness and dissatisfaction by very outward expressions of aggressiveness in a way I can only admire. Is this because such women are shaped by factors other than gender? Is it that my projection of her as a sister is misplaced?

Psychology certainly teaches me so. Within clinical psychology we were trained to apply behaviour modification which assumes that behaviour has antecedents and consequences that can be recorded, from which a description (often taken as an explanation) can be developed. Within this analysis there is clearly no room for gender-induced powerlessness: bad behaviour is set up and maintained by these antecedents and consequences alone. As I have no way of conceptually 'checking out' these levels of analysis with the women because of their limited language, I have to make a value-based decision that views the women as similar to myself while not denying their disability. Oh, for the safety of science! For many of these women attitudes and structures which value intelligence are the greatest oppressors, while gender issues seem to run second. But gender issues are integral to our existing understanding of a person's social existence. For women with a learning difficulty, therefore, we must acknowledge the centrality of gender to our notions of a person's humanity. Indeed, the denial of women's gender is perhaps the greatest oppression of all. Within this framework, as we enable people to develop in a gender-specific way (as normalization theory would suggest), it is important that issues of sexism are firmly addressed. I feel quite muddled about this and maybe an illustration would clarify what I mean.

Catherine is 26 and has a very severe intellectual impairment. Throughout her life she has been 'managed' by a loving mother and not so loving services because she can be extremely difficult to be with in many ways. Her difficulties have defined her and her mother's life, and the service response to them. Any parts of growing up as a woman were ignored or seen as potential management issues and thus dealt with by 'fixing' or minimizing. So Catherine was given a hysterectomy when very young: there were legitimate fears of her personal danger of abuse (while not going out at all except to segregated places, sexual abuse from staff and men with learning difficulties was a reality in some of the places in which she spent time). Our ability to give her control in terms of informed decision-making, opportunity and support for caring for a baby, etc, were non-existent. Her rights as a person were not much considered and her rights as a woman were not even on the agenda. Against this were balanced her mother's needs: as a woman who supplies the main support to Catherine, who could not cope (in imagination or reality) with the consequences of Catherine having a sexual life, or with the concept of her wanting/'deserving' one. What decision should/could have been made?

Similarly, Catherine acts more aggressively when about to have a period, so we manage her periods. Pre-menstrual tension has become the bugbear of women in these services. It is used to explain everything, it prevents us having to attempt to understand women more. It is the alternative, 'right-on' medical model at work which allows us to locate all Catherine's bad behaviour around it and means we can avoid looking at why Catherine may be angry regardless of her hormonal state.

What are we telling Catherine about herself as we deliver all these well-meaning services? What does she understand about her own sexuality when she is dressed downstairs regardless of the sex of the onlookers? When male staff help her to the toilet? What does she understand as she lines up for the standard 'pudding-basin' haircut at the adult training centre? How does it affect her when her role model in her mother is of a carer, and she is a totally cared-for dependant, when the cultural analogue around her is of marriage and babies?

These are difficult questions that we may not be able to answer. But what about the ones that I was faced with next? If we take on board these gender issues and accept our responsibility, what can we actually do to address them? Do we perm Catherine's hair, offer her make-up, help her choose clothes? How do we connect with the problem that for most women, self-esteem and sexist forms are inextricably bound together? I think these are difficult but essential questions. Are we enabling Catherine to find more ways of being oppressed? Are we making it more likely that she will be abused while ducking the issue of giving her the control?

I have to ask these questions as a professional but in some sense I can only answer as a woman and then transform it into a professional response. I have to cope with a relationship with Catherine which is unbalanced and, to some extent, unreciprocated. I then have to make decisions as best I can, aknowledging the lack of parity, the hunches I play on, the extent and limits of projection. What I can no longer do is evade the issues by retreating into the security of professional psychology.

But here I am jumping ahead. Karen and I want to address some rapprochement in the final section. First I would like to share some other dilemmas women with learning difficulties face and challenge us with.

I have talked about Catherine who has very severe impairments. Jane also has a learning disability but is able, with support, to live in a flat of her own. Her disability is not so obvious, but affects her life as much as Catherine's. As with many people who are service recipients for much of their lives, Jane has few friends. Most of the people she has spent time with also have a learning disability and Jane has never wanted to be grouped with them on these grounds alone. Our patriarchal society has damaged and continues to damage Jane. What we have taught her is that having male company is more valued than having female company, and the way to get attention and talk to people is to flirt. So Jane eschews women's company and flirts with men, but because of the effect of her learning disability, and the construction of flirting as *normal* behaviour, Jane never learnt the boundaries around flirtation: what is permissible, what control she has, when she can pull out; and as a consequence she is abused sexually by a number of men.

Some years ago Jane had a child who, because of her disability, was taken away from her and for whom she mourns. She is often depressed and finds it difficult to comprehend why men hurt her and to know how to deal with her loneliness. We can 'teach' her the social rules, we can put her on a programme to learn to say 'no'; what we cannot do is to address the fundamental damage that has affected her so deeply and with which the services have colluded. Jane does not want to be with other women with learning disabilities, and women who have not been so labelled have their own needs and find Jane's deep desire to be the centre of things, talked about and with, very onerous. Although Jane has more verbal ability than Catherine, she is just as unhappy and possibly has even less understanding of why she feels so unhappy. Jane has never been viewed or viewed herself as gender-free in the way I was trying to indicate about Catherine, but she is trapped in traditional ways by that gender identification. Is this what we are asking Catherine to grow into? We know that people grow into the expectations they have of themselves and from others; when such sexist expectations are all that are available where can you go? If it has taken years of struggle for high status, white, middle-class professionals such as myself to begin to understand the parameters, where does that leave one of the most devalued groups of women I have ever met? Women who battle with distinct devaluing processes in their lives and have less aptitude than most to understand, rationalize or cope except by being increasingly 'difficult', and thus making it increasingly easy for professionals to lay the blame of the difficulty at the door of 'mental handicap' and continue to evade areas that we feel we cannot control.

Clinical psychology aids this evasion by narrowing the field of vision, and thus enquiry, to which it can interact with, and this closed circuit continues to fail to address substantive issues in women's lives.

Karen's experience

The ways in which mental health services undermine the autonomy and control women have in their lives has been graphically portrayed elsewhere (initially by Phyllis Chesler, 1972, and more recently by Judi Chamberlain, 1988). In order briefly to highlight this I wish to mention Anita: Anita is a Jamaican woman in her forties who is married and has two grown-up children. Her diagnosis of 'manic depression' has led to extensive contact with the medical profession, including periods of hospitalization. She feels her concerned family see her as 'mad', while her husband and male general practitioner form a formidable alliance. The psychiatric services enhance her powerlessness in this situation in a number of ways. They give her medication which makes her feel tired and her breasts start leaking: or they remove her from time to time to a psychiatric ward. Not only is the support available from traditional services not appropriate to her needs, it is not even supportive – so that her self-perception and sense of personal autonomy are continually eroded and her experience of depression perpetuated.

The issues stand out clearly – labelling, social expectations of inferiority, loss of valued roles, isolation and increased powerlessness. Although skilled, Anita has left employment, and her chances of employment in the future are overshadowed by her history of admission to psychiatric hospital. These are the kind of issues which I encounter daily, particularly in my working life. However, it is also the devaluation of women for the acceptable social role they play in nurturing family, relatives and neighbours, leaving little time for themselves, which undoubtedly leads to the familiar picture of exhaustion, anxiety and little sense of self-worth. Indeed, most of the women I encounter could be said to be over-coping, rather than failing to cope, but their experience of psychological distress is construed as failure rather than burn-out resulting from the demands of an exacting job. Rosie's situation provides a useful illustration.

Rosie is in her forties and has three children. She lives with the two younger children and a man whom she met eight years ago, Joe, who has a long history of contact with psychiatric services. He is often depressed but becomes verbally and physically explosive on occasion; not untypically, he threatens to kill himself if she leaves home. In addition Rosie not only minds her youngest grandchild but also pops in to keep an eye on an elderly neighbour. Rosie's own feelings of depression started following the death of her mother ten years ago, but it is not difficult to see the early origins of this in sexual abuse, and its continuation in her current situation where she lives on a knife-edge, desperately trying to keep the lid on the tension at home. Added to this picture are threats of violence from a neighbouring family, a low income and a council housing estate affected by inadequate refuse collection and housing repairs.

A complex picture, but it is clear what the price for this workload will be. Unlike the stressed executive, Rosie has no junior to delegate to (although daughters often fulfil this role) and social expectation, which concords with her own desire, will mean that Rosie will continue to experience exhaustion and depression. What role for the clinical psychologist? Helping Rosie to understand her situation in these terms, developing strategies for her to take time for herself and to reduce the burden of her responsibilities – how realistic is this when the alternatives are limited by the lack of resources; over-stretched childcare facilities; little time and expertise supporting women who live with men with mental health problems? This leaves her to rely on other women who may well be similarly stretched.

The final, but by no means least, theme which emerges is that of abuse: physical and/or sexual, experienced currently or in childhood. Clearly there is a role for counselling/personal support in order to limit the damage done to women who have been abused. Whether this is a role for clinical psychologists or for organized agencies like Rape Crisis/Taboo is open to debate. It raises the issue about the specialization of, and by implication limited access to, personal support. 'Clinical psychology', in linking psychology with the word clinical, one meaning of which is 'hospital-like' means that our experience is construed within a health/illness framework rather than a social one. In practice the emphasis is on pathology; people are referred for help with 'symptoms' indicating psychological distress which, as we have argued, have their origin in the social fabric. This would not be disputed by many clinical psychologists that I know, but the way in which the system is currently organized means that help is pre-determined so that access to support depends on the 'fit' between a woman's articulation of her distress and the doctor's assumptions, or on the clinical psychologist's view of what psychology can offer. This means that women with complex, less easily defined or poorly articulated difficulties may not get access to clincial psychology services. My experience of working in a community setting which encourages self-referrals suggests that there are many women with long-standing depression or physical ill-health related to psychosocial factors who would not be seen as candidates for the clinical psychologist.

It can be argued that the specialization of support further disempowers women. Take Ann for instance: Ann is in her forties but she looks much older, her appearance reflecting the physical abuse which she has endured through the course of her lifetime. She doesn't expect to live much longer and although she looks and talks about being ill, the doctors attribute her pain and discomfort to her psychological state. Ann has lost her children; they were taken into care because of her alleged incapacity to care for them. She is more or less homeless. She has few personal possessions or relationships, and spends quite a lot of her time wandering around.

Although it is possible to see how Ann's self-esteem can be developed, it has been difficult to do this together. Ann won't meet up regularly and usually drops in, at a time of crisis, asking for support. Ann challenges the ways in which services are traditionally organized: should we change what is offered to meet Ann's apparent need; or should we enable her to meet and get to know other women, who may or may not be more accessible, who could support her?

The fault with the model which we outlined earlier is the emphasis on the individual and the way in which the devaluation of the experience of oppression leads to the individual being perceived as deficient in some way. For some women, it may never be possible to effect change because of the extent to which their whole being and self-identity is tied up with this oppression. The need for the focus to be firmly on the political level stands out starkly.

Confusions and conclusions

The main tension for us, and it is by no means new, is that which is created by working within the system – which means that we inevitably end up compromised. We are both aware of using our 'professional role' when it would appear to serve the needs of a woman. This approach, however, can also be seen as furthering the interests of the individual woman at the expense of maintaining the larger patriarchal structures which systematically disadvantage her, and all women. As such it is a reformist tactic, and colludes in the perpetuation of gender, race and class inequalities, through its assertion of professional power. This contrasts with a more radical stance which confronts the system and disallows collusion. More specifically, this tension presents itself as facilitating access to a service provision opportunity for a woman, versus not colluding with the system that denies her that opportunity in the first place. These are very real dilemmas: for example, supporting a woman's application for rehousing on the basis of her mental ill-health, versus not doing so on the basis that to do so would label her and perpetuate the stereotyping which accompanies mental health problems and casts the woman as the victim of these.

We are concerned to find ways of relating to women as women rather than 'expert' and 'recipient' and to draw on our commonalities as women without denying the specific needs a woman might have or the differences between us. It does not make sense to deny access to the parts of our training that might support her. Rather it becomes important to work out what skills we have, and to strive for common agreement about what we and the women we work with are aiming for. By demystifying the process, the options available can be opened up for negotiation. Important elements of demystifying our skills include disentangling the language that further disempowers women, explaining what we are doing and by being clear about the areas of fallibility.

We have seen our role as empowering the women we work with and incorporating the elements of clinical psychology which support this. In practice this has meant not only working directly with women but often working in the background with other people such as staff, families, networks and self-help groups. Flexibility in the way that we work has been important, as has been getting to know women in a variety of situations with different people, if possible and appropriate. For example, women with mental health problems may traditionally be referred to a clinical psychologist by their general practitioner and then offered an appointment to meet the psychologist who may work with the woman on an individual basis or within a group often based in health centres, hospitals or maybe the woman's own home. In our work the opportunity to meet that woman in her home, on her own territory, in a mother and toddlers' group, as part of a women's group, etc, enriches and changes our understanding of her. Allied to this is our belief that women's networks are rooted in the community rather than around traditional structures, and hence can provide a more flexible and supportive environment.

The women we each work with face different difficulties, but both of us are involved in supporting skills development, such as assertiveness training, in the belief that this increases the opportunity for women to have more control. The issues this type of work raises concern the balance between valuing women's experience and playng a role in developing their experience. There is a potential problem in that a woman may be receiving very different messages from different parts of what is apparently the same system. This is often the case in mental health work: a woman distressed by her circumstances goes to her, often male, GP, who by the prescription of anti-depressants or anxiolytics conveys the message to her that she is ill. Some women get angry and find this unpalatable while for others it is a relief because the problem now has a name. The redefinition of a woman's experience in terms of life events, her situation, personal resources and relationships have implications for different actions on her behalf. All too often, though, the different messages contribute to the turmoil a woman is experiencing.

Another issue is raised by the different roles women play either as carers or as recipients of care. In this situation it may be that one woman is the focus at the expense of another, or that there are contradictory and conflicting interests involved: for example, mothers of women with severe learning difficulties, daughters of women with Alzheimer's disease. Ideally this area should be opened up for negotiation, although the women who are recipients of services in these examples may have difficulty communicating their needs, while competition thrives in a climate of inadequate and diminishing resources.

We have argued for shifting the focus from a purely individual level to consideration of the social and community levels. However, this does raise the issue of whether clinical psychologists have anything to offer, or whether we have just submitted an argument for expanding the numbers of community workers. We would conclude that there is a role for some of the skills psychology had given us in working with individuals but that these are less effective if decontextualized. Given the dilemmas inherent in working within the framework of the National Health Service, we have considered whether it is just too difficult to work within the system as it stands, and whether, like some of our sisters, we should pursue the opportunities outside – for example within women's therapy centres. Tempting as this is, the reality is that there are no real alternatives for the women we work with, and with their assumptions about language and intellectual ability, the inaccessibility of these alternatives is not just financial.

Although we do not have clear answers to these issues we do think that there are some opportunities to pursue which may lead us in the right direction. The consumer movement, in forging alliances between people with mental health problems or learning difficulties and grass-roots workers, appears to be a positive force in redressing the power balance. Supporting and enabling women, whatever their difficulties, to get together will continue to be an important part of our work, as will supporting skills development. With the advent of consumerism in the Health Service has come discussion about accountability, and although this debate often depoliticizes the issues, we think it important to find ways in which service providers are more directly accountable to people.

Finally, a comment about the climate within which we work. The NHS is under threat and opportunities to develop or work in more coherent ways is increasingly limited. There are performance pressures manifested as a preoccupation with data and quantifying what we do in terms of 'throughput' rather than content. This climate militates against the type of work we would advocate and means that those women with whom we work are even less likely to be seen.

References

Chamberlain, J. (1988) *On Our Own*. London: Mind.
Chesler, P. (1972) *Women and Madness*. New York: Avon Books.

Afterword

A book about feminism and psychological practices should end only by indicating dilemmas and directions, rather than offering tidy conclusions – for this would commit feminist psychology to a finite future, rather than enabling us to be open to the possibilities and issues arising from a changing context. The contributions in this book testify to the productiveness of psychology as well as the ambiguous and ambivalent ways this positions women who participate in its practices. There are now a number of pressing consequences of the current reorganization of education and professional structures that demand clear thinking on the part of feminists and progressives. Some of these are neither specific to feminists nor psychologists, but nevertheless still call for a response. This final section, then, is devoted to identifying some of these questions and indicating some possible courses of action.

Privatization (*clue*: Thatcher's panacea – *Guardian* crossword, 5 Jan. 89)

Across all areas of education and health, teaching and service provision is increasingly becoming subject to the market forces of industrial demand and sponsorship, rather than the needs of the 'consumers'; or rather, industry *is* the consumer. In terms of research, this means an increasing number of people will be chasing dwindling funds and have less freedom to determine what to do with them. As well as putting 'enterprise culture' in to our teaching, these changes mean that radicals have to reinterpret what they want to do imaginatively in terms that will make the securing of funds more likely. While this is not in itself new, making money dependent on industrial interests compromises subversive or critical work: we are positioned clearly as aiding patriarchy and capitalism – indeed the task for psychology is how to convince industry that it needs to harness psychological knowledge for its own ends. One of the most insidious outcomes of this is that we have to develop even more coded ways of talking about progressive work. The dangers of self-censorship are perhaps even greater than those of external constraints. Moreover, it is easy for our political analysis to become diverted: the strategies we develop to cope with these situations can slip into being formulated as principled positions, positions we would not otherwise want to adopt.

In clinical and educational psychology the dilemmas loom even larger. While health authority funding of clinical psychologists seems to be secure for the time being, the general direction of change makes the situation precarious and creates an atmosphere of retrenchment rather than promoting experimental or radical practice. Educational psychology has already been hit by legislative changes: while the Education Reform Act to some extent removes from psychologists their position as sole testers of children and hence demands a redefinition of their role, the changes in local government mean that local authorities have the power to delegate part of the funding of the service to schools. The scenario this presents is of educational psychological expertise effectively being commissioned by individual schools to deal with the problems presented by individual pupils. While it has always been a tricky issue to define who the 'client' of the educational psychologist is – child, parent, school, community or local authority – it is not difficult to see how an educational psychologist's autonomy is severely curtailed by these changes, and makes the 1970s reconstructionist calls for educational psychologists to act as change agents and child and community advocates very remote. These developments also have particular implications for feminists working to challenge racism and sexism.

The constraints with which women have to work as a result of privatization and local authority reorganizations are paralleled inside the institution of British psychology. The form this is currently taking is through debates over the 'future' of psychology and establishing psychology as a Chartered profession.

Chartering

The procedure whereby those seeking to use the title Chartered Psychologist have to be registered by the British Psychological Society is now well under way. This development has a number of important consequences.

Centralizing the organization of psychology Chartering overrides the various professional and academic psychological organizations already in existence which have provided a forum for the supervision of each area. Women's activity as psychologists often (deliberately) takes place outside patriarchal insititutions. Feminists, outside the newly formed Psychology of Women Section of the British Psychological Society, have or may want little to do with traditional male institutions.

Homogenizing the diversity of psychology The differences in approach, practice and audience will be collapsed together. No longer can being a psychologist cover an unspecified range of possibilities. The term Chartered Psychologist is being copyrighted and constrained to a specific meaning, generating some spurious uniformity for the variety of work we do in psychology. The default norms to which we will be invited to conform will be precisely those which as feminists we have tried to struggle against.

Confirming the efficacy of psychology   One of the main arguments advanced for the necessity of chartering is to protect the public against charlatans, and make psychological practice more accountable. Without denying the reality of the problems, the effect of this is to confirm the importance and effectiveness of psychology; since the abuse of psychology is harmful, by a curious sleight of hand its application becomes benign and desirable. Feminists have been all too aware that on balance most psychology is deeply destructive to women.

Confirming the facticity of psychology   Psychological knowledge is portrayed as neutral; the fault lies in its misapplication by individuals. The role of ideology in determining what research is and is not done, and which approaches are and are not adopted, and hence what interests structure that knowledge, is masked. What is also conveniently masked here is the way patriarchy revels in its status as a universal fact.

Legislating psychology   Chartering will serve to demarcate what is or is not considered 'proper' psychology. The BPS already governs the structure of undergraduate degrees through academic requirements set for eligibility for membership. This has now been heightened in that courses which seek to confer the Graduate Basis for Registration (the first step to becoming a Chartered Psychologist) must cover a specified syllabus. This is likely to be tightened up in the near future. Increasingly, chartering will bring all practising psychologists under the aegis of the BPS, and the resulting supervision of training and admission requirements can only be constraining. Although the criteria used to define psychology and scientific research in recent BPS documentation are broad, the definition and regulation by a party not specifically set up by each area to meet this purpose does not augur well. A small example of the problems ahead is indicated by how students taking joint or combined degrees may be penalized for their efforts to span disciplinary boundaries by becoming ineligible for membership and for Chartered status. This also has significant consequences for the complex and varied roles and services psychologists engage in and provide in education, health and social services, both for training and personnel. Developing feminist critiques in psychology have always had their roots outside 'proper' psychology, and the force of a Women's Movement inside the discipline rests on this political activity. Chartering increases the difficulties for feminists seeking to join forces across disciplinary boundaries, and reduces the opportunities for feminists to make 'legitimate' interventions within psychology.

The overall effect of chartering, then is to demarcate the boundaries of psychology. This means that those 'outside' are effectively disenfranchized, and the tightening up of disciplinary and institutional boundaries makes it more difficult for feminists working within psychology to have the space to analyse and comment on prevailing theories and practices in the course of doing what is deemed 'proper' psychology.

The Psychology of Women Section and women in psychology

In terms of the organization of women psychologists, the contribution in this book have identified the barriers and compromises involved in setting up a Psychology of Women Section within the British Psychological Society. However, current pressures make the choice of working within the system or not no longer relevant. With chartering either one is within the system or one has no right to say or do anything which impinges on its territory. The most hopeful scenario is one where the enforced presence of feminists within organized psychology creates more active and vigorous voices both inside and outside the section, which thus transcends the 'apolitical' remit with which it was initially instituted. A recent example of the promise of this position is the intervention made by the Psychology of Women Section through its response to deficiencies and omissions in its statement about the roles women and 'multi-ethnic society' play in *The Future of the Psychological Sciences* (BPS, 1988). The sense in which the section can be seen as the voice of women in psychology is of course constrained by the fact that it is not a women-only organization. It is also not very representative of women, since most women in psychology fail to see the relevance of the BPS – although chartering may change this. As various contributors indicate in their evaluation of the position of women in academia, and specifically the position of women in psychology, organizing within 'the system' requires correspondingly strong organization outside. Hence, an alternative would be to extend the parallel organization of Women in Psychology, the members of which might or might not be Chartered Psychologists, to provide an external forum for the development of strategies and ideas which can be applied elsewhere. Without these measures the debates could degenerate into a concern with 'equal opportunities' (usually no more than liberal sentiments exercised more on paper than in practice).

Section 28

The Local Government Act 1988 outlaws any local authority sponsorship of activities that could be interpreted as facilitating the 'promotion
of homosexuality'. By now it is clear that this only legally applies to
educational institutions under the control of local authorities, and
hence does not apply to university or polytechnic courses, or any other
training courses. Even though it now appears that the Act is unlikely to
apply to schools, the Act places particular pressures on those in
teaching. With the increasing promotion and popularity of psychology
as a subject taught in schools and colleges, (women) teachers will be
confronted with interpretations of the section designed to inhibit a
feminist perspective.

There can be no doubt that this Act constitutes a general attack on
the rights of lesbians and gay men. Although officially outside its
remit, there is a serious danger that issues relating to the experience,
recognition and value of lesbians and gay men will be excluded from
teaching and professional practice by self-censorship. We need to
ensure not only that this does not happen, but also to dissociate
ourselves publicly from its rationale and implications. This may mean
organizing within unions, departments and professional associations
to formulate policies and statements affirming opposition to Section
28, and it would mean the active implementation of an equal
opportunities programme incorporating discussion of these explicitly
into our teaching, training and practice. More than this, we might even
attempt to use some of the public prestige of psychology (risky though
this is) to counter the assumptions and implications of the Act,
although this would probably be proscribed by the BPS. So for
example we could indicate the ideological deployment of 'the family'
and its illusory nature to counter the insulting depiction of lesbian and
gay relationships as 'pretended families'. Or we could use our positions
as investigators of the domains of the intra-psychic and interpersonal
to highlight the processes that give rise to the production and
maintenance of 'homophobia'.

Feminist academics or academic feminists?

With the advent of women's studies, and the promotion of some
women to senior academic positions, the question of interests and
radical credentials necessarily arises. At what point is working within
the system selling out on our politics? There is a general sense in which
the project of education as self-development is at some point
necessarily in conflict with institutional needs. A number of contributions in this volume discuss this issue, and suggest that feminists

who rise to relatively powerful positions need to be accountable, both in their relations with their students and to the wider community of feminist activists. The arena of women's studies has itself some major dilemmas both to pose and to negotiate: is it reactionary for women to work in distinct disciplinary departments? Alternatively, does separating women's studies ghettoize and confine the impact of the radical educational developments? Does it support the existence of current structures by existing alongside them as if as another department? Positioned in these ways, how can it avoid reproducing some of the same inequalities?

The position of women in psychology has always been fraught with difficulties, and feminists have to address the complex theoretical and practical structures of the discipline. While the above collection of issues is neither exhaustive nor optimistic, it does at least highlight, as does the whole of this book, that psychology, as academia and technocracy, does not lie between the covers of books or within the obscurities of bureaucracy, but is also a living practice produced and reproduced by its participants. We must use our participation politically, sometimes as psychologists, always as feminists.

Reference

British Psychological Society (1988) *The Future of the Psychological Sciences: Horizons and Opportunities for British Psychology*. Report prepared for the Scientific Affairs Board by the working party on the Future of the Psychological Sciences. Leicester: BPS.

Index

abortion, 109, 159
abuse: physical, 185; sexual, 74, 117, 180–1, 182, 184
academics/academia 8, 16, 26, 55, 192, 194; feminist 16, 62, 68–9, 193–4; vs practitioners, 5, 7, 8, 11, 14; *see also* PhD; publishing
Access courses, 67
accessibility, 15, 17, 19, 37, 65, 175, 187
accountability, 15, 64–5, 69, 71, 74, 137, 164, 187, 191, 194
Adcock, C., 6, 11, 58, 139, 172–88
Aitkenhead, M., 123, 124, 131, 133
Alan Guttmacher Institute, 93, 102
Alton bill, 159
Alzheimer's disease, 177, 187
American Psychiatric Association, 120
American Psychological Association, 30, 144, 145, 159; *see also* Division 35; Lesbian and Gay Division
androgeny, 7
anonymity: of authors, 10; of 'clients', 11, 104
antipsychology, 76, 79–87, 121, 123; and feminism, 85–7; and institutions, 83–5; and psychology, 79–83; and social differences, 80; and teaching, 73, 81; as using power differences, 82–4
Arney, W. and Bergen, B., 95, 102
assertiveness training, 6, 186
Association of Educational Psychologists (AEP), 168; Guidelines on Sexism, 138
Association for Women in Psychology (AWP), 146, 147, 153
Australia, 146
Australian Psychological Society, 143

backlash, 38, 138, 169–70
Ball, B. and Bourner, T., 60
Basow, S.A., 143, 150, 155, 156
behaviour modification, 55, 109, 166, 175, 180
Bell, A.P., 120, 133
Bernard, J., 55, 60
Bhavnani, K.K., 5, 12, 16, 62–72, 90, 102
bias, *see* political bias
Billig, M., 7, 13
black advisory group, 94–5, 96, 101
black people: in education, 67; in educational psychology, 139; critiques of research, 90, 91; researchers, 94–5
Black Sections, Labour party, 145
Boston Lesbian Psychologies Collective, 121, 133
Bradley, J.V., 130, 134
Brah, A., 90, 102
Brannen, J., 97, 102
British Psychological Society (BPS), 3, 9, 13, 52, 53, 122, 128, 129, 131, 133, 139–41, 148, 150, 161, 190; Code of Conduct, 144; Professional Affairs Board, 141; *see also* chartering; Scientific Affairs Board
British Sociological Association, 64
Broome, A., 159, 162
Bruner, J. and Haste, H. 90, 102
Burman, E., 1–17, 73–5, 137–9, 189–94
Burns, J., 7, 10, 12, 36, 51, 59, 71, 122, 124, 134, 137, 142, 152–62
Bury, J., 93, 102
Butler, N., 93, 102

Callaway, H., 160, 161, 162
Canadian Psychological Association, 143–4
Carby, H., 68, 72, 90, 102
Cardea, C., 132, 134
carers, 152, 180–1, 187
Chamberlain, J., 183, 188
chartering, 3, 52, 141, 146, 160, 190–2
Chesler, P., 59, 60, 183, 187
Chetwynd, J. and Hartnett, O., 141, 150
Clause 28 (now Section 28), 131, 159, 193
clinical psychology, 42, 43, 56, 139 172–88, 190; and Aids, 58; and control, 180–1, 183; and experience, 173; and oppression, 185; and sexuality, 6, 181; as 'gender free', 56, 175, 176, 179; as progressive, 57–8, 186; as scientific practice, 55, 173–5; dominant models, 173–5, 184; medicalizing, 58, 177; pathologizing, 56–8; relationships, 58, 139, 176, 181, 186; training in, 139, 173
Clunis, M. and Green G.D. 121, 134
Collier, A., 104, 117
community work, 176, 187
compromise, 2, 8, 12, 14, 16, 28, 33, 42, 50, 58, 59, 65, 126, 133, 140, 149, 153–6, 185, 190
computer analysis, 35, 36, 39, 50
consumer movement, 187, 189
Coulson, M., 5, 12, 16, 62–72, 90, 102
countertransference, 74, 115–17
Crane, D., 52–60
Culley, M. and Portuges, C., 8, 12
Currie, D. and Kazi, H., 62, 72
cuts, 4, 38, 177

Davis, A., 68, 72, 90, 102
Davison, S.C., 120, 134
Decker, D., 120, 134
dehumanization, 176
de la Luz Reyes, M. and Halcon, J., 95, 102
Delaney, J. et al., 54, 60
dependence, 107, 110, 112
depression, 38, 74, 106, 108, 110–11, 180, 182–4
de-radicalization, dangers of, 65, 68–72, 132

differences, 190; as political strategy, 12, 70–2, 139, 158, 186; class, 70; in positions, 158, 177; *see also* gender; social differences; stereotypes
Dillon, J.T., 128, 134
Division 35, APA, 144, 146–7, 155
Division of Occupational Psychology, 141
Dowling, C., 76, 87

editorial pressure, 124–30
education, 193; as racially structured, 67, 69; cuts, 4; gender hierarchies, 165; higher, 3, 4, 33; funding, 4, 189; psychology's role in, 191; *see also* psychology education
Education Reform Act (1988), 166–7, 190
educational psychology, 42, 43, 136–8, 163–71, 189–90; *see also* behaviour modification
ego identity, 122
'ego psychology', 76, 80
Eichenbaum, L. and Orbach, S., 163, 171
equal opportunities, 65, 85, 160, 164–7, 192, 193; in Educational Psychology Service, 162–71
Ernst, S. and Goodison, L., 169,171
Essed, P., 4, 13
experience vs theory, 7, 11–12, 82
experiential accounts, 8, 11, 33, 104
experimental psychology, 34, 41

families: ideology of, 6, 109, 193; research on, 16; *see also* Clause 28
Farnham, C., 65, 72
feminism: alternative discourse, 73; and black experience, 74, 90, 101–2; and learning disability, 177; and orthodoxy, 11, 71; and racism, 68, 90; as antipsychology, 73, 79–87; as demystifying, 12, 19, 75, 133, 186; as empowering, 73, 75, 186; as fragmented, 62–4; as lifestyle, 132; *see also* power relations; practice
feminist psychology, 52, 53, 54, 74, 76, 77–9, 80, 101, 122–3, 131, 132, 160–1, 189; *see also* lesbian psychology
feminist research, 15, 36, 89–91; and interviews, 97–101
feminist therapy, 58, 74, 104–14; resistance in, 115; vs orthodox psychotherapy, 104–5
Fisher, B., 78, 87
Fontaine, C., 122, 134
Fraser, N., 97, 102
Freedman, M., 120, 134
Freud, S., 106, 117, 118
Friday, N., 76, 87
Frye, M., 122, 134
Furnham, A., 49, 60

Gardiner, J., 80, 87
gay psychology, 122,
gender: difference, 77; identity, 110; subjectivity, 77, 81; *see also* sex role
gender hierarchies: in academic psychology, 18, 22–4; in clinical psychology, 188; in educational psychology services, 138, 167,
170; in schools, 163–4; *see also* management structures; work
genetic screening, 45
Gilbert, G.N., 128, 134
Gilroy, P., 90, 102
Gove, W.R., 108, 118
Greenglass, E.R., 144, 150
Griffin, C., 89, 90, 102
GRIST, 164–5
Gutek, B.A., 20, 24, 32
Guthrie, R., 92, 102

Hartnett, O. et al., 141, 150
Henley, N., 92, 102, 157, 162
Henley, N. and Pincus, F., 120, 134
Henriques, J. et al., 8, 13, 90, 91, 92, 103
heterosexism, 75, 122
higher education, *see* academics; education
Hobson, R.E., 116, 118
Hollway, W., 55, 60, 147, 149, 150
'homophobia', 114, 120, 132, 193
homosexuality, *see* Clause 28; heterosexism; lesbianism
Hopkins, J., 121, 134
Horney, K., 158, 162
Hull, G., 90, 103
Hunt, H., 58, 60

Idema, M., 141, 142, 153
identification, 110, 116, 139; *see also* countertransference; feminist therapy; transference
identity, 38
inequalities, 64, 175; *see also* equal opportunities
integration, 167; *see also* separatism
International Council of Psychology, 156
interviews, 36, 43, 50, 74, 89, 94, 121; and 'colour matching', 100; and feminist research, 97–101; and power relations, 94, 98, 100–1; and social class, 97

Jackson, C., 132, 134
Jefferson, T., 5, 10, 12, 15, 34, 40–6
Jenkins, A., 92, 103
job-sharing, 44, 168

Kagan, C., 4, 12, 13, 14, 18–32
Kahn, A.S. and Jean, P.J., 144, 150
Kanter, R.M., 24, 27, 32
Kaplan, C., 78, 87
Kemeny, J.G., 128, 134
King, T. and Fullard, W., 95, 103
Kitzinger, C., 5, 6, 9, 12, 55, 60, 74, 119–36
Koeske, R., 50, 60

Lawrence, E., 90, 103
Laws, S., 57, 60
learning disability, 19, 152, 172–83; assumptions in relationships, 179–80; stereotypes of, 178
Leon, B., 121, 135
Lesbian and Gay Division, APA, 123

lesbian psychology, 121, 122, 123, 131
lesbianism: and psychiatry, 119–20, 121; and
   psychology, 119–20; theories of, 126; *see
   also* heterosexism, 'homophobia'
Levidow, L., 132, 135
Lewis, S., 4, 12, 13, 18–32
Little, R.B., 146, 150
Loulan, J., 121, 135

McAdoo, H., 92, 103
McAuley, J., 24, 32
McEwan, I., 163, 171
Mahony, M.J., 125, 130, 135
Malan, A.H., 114, 118
management structures, 69, 138, 171, 180, 181
managers, women as, 24
Mann, B., 132, 135
Manstead, A.S.R., 130, 135
Marable, M., 90, 103
marginalization, 14, 24–6, 30, 42, 49, 52, 147
Marshall, J., 22, 32
Maslow, A.H., 105, 118
Masters, M.A. and Johnson, V.E., 120, 135
Masterton, J., 120, 135
Mednick, M.T.S., 146, 147, 150
men's groups, 138, 170
menstrual cycle, 48, 54, 35; premenstrual
   tension in, 193
mental health: and feminine role, 106–9, 111–
   14, 183; and social structure, 57, 58, 104–8,
   173, 176, 182–5; as pathologizing, 57
Merton, R.K., 130, 135
Meyer, J., 123, 135
Mills, C. Wright, 105, 118
Mitter, S., 62, 72
Moghaddam, F.M., 122, 135
Mohanty C. T., 68, 72
Moraga, C. and Anzaldua, M., 68, 72
Morawski, J.G., 124, 135
Morin, S.F., 120, 135

National Health Service (NHS) 58, 175, 177,
   178, 186, 188; *see also* cuts
Nelson, J.S. et al., 129, 135
'new times', 63, 69
New Zealand Psychological Society, 144
Newbigging, K., 6, 11, 58, 139, 172–88
Nicolson, P., 124, 135
normalization theory, 6, 178, 179
north Manchester, 177–8
Norwood, R., 76, 87

Oakley, A., 97, 103
objectivity, 50, 74, 109, 124, 128, 146; vs
   'journalism', 127; vs politics, *see* political
   bias
O'Brian, M. and McKee, L., 11, 13
O'Leary, V.E., 29, 32
oppression, 173, 176, 179–80
Orbach, S., 76, 87
Over, R., 130, 135

Parker, I., 4, 13

Parlee, M.B., 158, 162
Parmar, P., 90, 103
part-time work, 20, 38, 138, 168, 171; *see also*
   job-sharing
PASS, 178
Penelope, J., 132, 135
Penfold, S. and Walker, G., 57, 60
performance pressures, 26, 38, 44–5, 188
PhD, 2, 5, 18, 26, 34, 35, 45, 48–9, 55;
   completing, 19, 37, 49, 50, 153; experience
   doing, 35–7, 152
Phipps-Yonas, S., 95, 96, 103
Phoenix, A., 6, 73, 89–103
political bias, 31, 37, 53, 101, 125–8, 132, 143,
   145–9, 159–60, 173
political involvement, 2, 34, 75, 131, 205; *see
   also* practice
positivism, 47, 50, 51, 126, 145
power relations, 8, 11, 26, 28, 74, 82; in
   teaching, 83–5; in therapy, 116; *see also*
   feminist therapy
practice, 1, 7; feminist, 2, 8–9, 16, 17, 35, 59,
   122–3, 133, 191–2, 194; psychological, 19,
   32, 173, 190–1, 194; vs theory, 40, 65; *see
   also* experiential accounts
privatization, 167, 178, 189–90
professional development, 15, 22–4, 38–9, 55,
   168
professionalization, 3, 123, 175, 181, 185; *see
   also* chartering
psychiatry, 108–9, 119–20, 121, 176, 183
psychoanalysis: and gender, 111–15; and
   psychology, 76; interpretation, 74, 115; *see
   also* countertransference; transference
psychology: and social positions, 90–1;
   applied vs theoretical, 24–5; as
   empowering, 16, 19, 58, 60; as gendered, 4,
   8, 18, 28, 34, 40, 48, 50–2, 68; as institution,
   2–5, 130, 140, 190–2, 194; as normalizing,
   5–6, 7, 84; as pathologizing, 92, 178; as
   reflexive, 1, 22; as science, 33, 42, 45, 46,
   52, 70, 78, 79; teaching, 25, 35, 38, 44, 77;
   (under)graduate courses, 34–5, 41, 47–8,
   191
psychology education, 73, 76–9
Psychology of Women, 51, 54, 59, 77, 85, 137,
   143; as separate, 1, 57–8; course, 3, 30, 49,
   122; Section (POWS), 7, 51, 54, 64, 102,
   122, 123, 124, 133, 137, 140–61, 190, 192;
   see also separatism; 'sex differences'
psychotherapy, 109; *see also* feminist therapy
publishing, 9–10, 26, 36, 52–3, 74, 125–9, 161
put-down, 26

qualitative methods, 36, 38, 39, 75, 121, 152–3
questionnaires, 36, 43

racism, 114, 190; *see also* black people
Reason, P. and Rowan, J., 160, 161, 162
Reber, A., 89, 103
reflexivity, 7–9, 22, 58, 59, 72, 81
Reicher, S., 125, 131, 135
research, 42, 74, 191; assistants, 35, 37–8;

black critique, 90, 91; feminist, 15, 36, 89-91, 97-101; funding, 15, 37, 39, 91, 94, 189; 'gay/lesbian affirmative', 120; *see also* PhD rhetoric, scientific, 128, 129, 133, 146
Richards, M. and Light, P., 90, 103
Richardson, M., 68, 72, 76, 88,
Riley, D., 6, 13
Robinson, P., 53, 60
Rorty, R., 128, 135
Rose, N., 5, 6, 13
Rosser, S., 25, 32
Russo, N., 76, 77, 88
Russo, N. and O'Connell, A.N., 156, 162

Sang, B., 120, 135
Sarachild, K., 120, 135
Sayers, J., 54, 60
science, 45; and sexual politics, 43-4, 152; psychology as, 4, 6, 33, 36, 41, 173-5; scientific method, 33; vs feminism, 49- 51; vs politics, *see* political bias; *see also* objectivity; positivism; rhetoric; 'up the hill model'
Scientific Affairs Board (SAB), 122, 133, 135, 142, 144, 148
Scott-Jones, D. and Nelson-Le Gall, S., 92, 103
Seidman, E. and Rappaport, J., 91, 92, 95, 97, 103
self-censorship, 190, 193
separatism: in organization, 144-5, 155-7; in teaching, 84
Serre, C., 132, 135
'sex differences', 30-1, 35
Sex Discrimination Act, 21, 141
sex role, 37, 42, 122; 'in educational psychology, 163-4; in feminism, 132; *see also* gender hierarchies; identity; stereotypes
sexism, 10, 14, 27, 85, 104, 109, 157, 164, 169, 170, 178, 180, 190
sexuality, 6, 55
Sharpe, S., 5, 10, 12, 15, 33-9
Shively, M.G. et al., 121, 135
Shotter, J. and Logan, J., 130, 135
Showalter, E., 104, 118
Simms, M. and Smith, C., 93, 103
Simons, H.V., 129, 135
social differences, 78, 79, 80, 84, 90-1
social problems, 91-3; defining, 90-1; researching, 91-2
social psychology, 34, 38, 41, 44, 45, 53, 54, 83, 109, 125, 128, 152
Social Psychology Section, 144; conference, 141
social research, 74, 89-103
sociology, 62, 63
'special needs', 139, 165, 166-7
Spender, D., 24, 32, 144, 150, 155
SPSSI, 146
Squire, C., 4, 12, 55, 60, 71, 73, 76-88
Stack, C., 80, 88
Stainton Rogers, R. and Kitzinger, C., 128, 129, 135

Standing, L. and McKelvie, S., 130, 136
Stanley, L., 90, 103
Stanley, L. and Wise, S., 8, 13
stereotypes, 24, 75, 109, 114, 174, 178, 181, 186
Storr, A., 119, 136
Strega, L. and Jo, B., 132, 136
support, 2, 29-31, 51, 74, 138, 169-71, 176, 177, 181, 182, 183, 184; specialization of, 185
Szasz, T., 57, 61, 136

Ta'eed, L., 146, 150
Taylor, A. et al., 89, 103
Taylor, M., 11, 74, 104-18
'teenage motherhood', 93-6
therapy, *see* feminist therapy; psychotherapy
transference, 74, 113-15
Turtle, A. and Orr, M., 146, 150
TVEI, 164
Tysoe, M., 129, 135

Unger, R., 54, 59, 61
'up the hill model', 128
Urwin, C., 4, 13
Ussher, J., 12, 16, 47-61, 149

Walkerdine, V., 11, 13
Walsh, M., 76, 69, 80, 81, 82, 85, 86, 88, 145, 147, 150
Weedon, C., 90, 103
Weinreich, H., 156, 162
Weisstein, N., 157, 162
Wells, N., 93, 103
West, D.J., 119, 135
Wexler, P., 8, 13
Wilkinson, S., 7, 10, 12, 13, 51, 53, 55, 59, 61, 71, 89, 103, 122, 130, 131, 136, 137, 140-51, 155
Wolpe, J., 56, 61
Woolgar, S.W., 129, 135
Women in Psychology (WIPS) 51, 124, 133, 137, 147-8, 156-7
Women in Psychology conference, 142, 147, 148, 153-5
Women in Society, 42
women-centred, 54; knowledge, 67-8; ways of working, 59
Women Psychologists' Group, 168-71
women staff, 27-8
women's groups, 138
women's movement, 35, 62-4, 65, 73, 85, 87, 109, 131, 191
women's studies, 5, 15, 16, 42, 52, 62-72, 193-4; and political direction, 65-6; and racism, 16; and women's careers, 65; as challenging psychology, 63; assessment of, 44; teaching of, 67; women studying, 66-7; *see also* antipsychology
work: and feminist consciousness, 18, 31, 137; atmosphere in, 26-7; gendered stereotypes in, 24; research on, 20; vs family, 19-22; *see also* marginalization

Zimmerman, B., 122, 135